Lecture Notes of the Institute for Computer Sciences, Social Informatics and Telecommunications Engineering 300

More information about this series at http://www.springer.com/series/8197

Xiaowen Chu · Hongbo Jiang ·
Bo Li · Dan Wang · Wei Wang (Eds.)

Quality, Reliability, Security and Robustness in Heterogeneous Systems

15th EAI International Conference, QShine 2019
Shenzhen, China, November 22–23, 2019
Proceedings

 Springer

Editors
Xiaowen Chu
Hong Kong Baptist University
Hong Kong, China

Bo Li
The Hong Kong University of Science
and Technology
Hong Kong, China

Wei Wang
The Hong Kong University of Science
and Technology
Hong Kong, China

Hongbo Jiang
Hunan University
Hunan, China

Dan Wang
The Hong Kong Polytechnic University
Hong Kong, China

ISSN 1867-8211   ISSN 1867-822X   (electronic)
Lecture Notes of the Institute for Computer Sciences, Social Informatics
and Telecommunications Engineering
ISBN 978-3-030-38818-8   ISBN 978-3-030-38819-5   (eBook)
https://doi.org/10.1007/978-3-030-38819-5

This Springer imprint is published by the registered company Springer Nature Switzerland AG
The registered company address is: Gewerbestrasse 11, 6330 Cham, Switzerland

Preface

It is our great pleasure to present the proceedings of the 15th EAI International Conference on Heterogeneous Networking for Quality, Reliability, Security and Robustness (QShine 2019), hosted in Shenzhen, China, November 22–23, 2019.

Computer networking has been embracing increased heterogeneity since its inception, in terms of the range of the applications it has to support, the various communication technologies it can run on, and the hierarchical, hybrid, and heterogeneous techniques it has to rely on to meet the challenges from both the diverse application requirements and communication technologies. As the only conference focusing on heterogeneous networking, QShine was established as the primary venue for researchers and practitioners to disseminate, exchange, and discuss all recent advances related to heterogeneous networking, particularly for quality, experience, reliability, security, and robustness. While still a young conference, QShine has already established itself as the premiere forum, bringing together faculty members, researchers, engineers, postdocs, and students to shape the future of this area.

The QShine main-conference technical program consisted of 16 full papers. This year, QShine invited seven speakers to present their most cutting-edge research. The program was enriched by the QShine keynote speech by Baochun Li (Toronto). We are extremely grateful to the chairs and members of the Technical Program Committee for shaping such a top-quality program for this conference.

Sincere thanks go to all those involved in the organization of QShine 2019. First of all, we would like to thank the authors for providing the high-quality content of the program, the Steering Committee for their thoughtful guidance, the chairs and the members of the Technical Program Committee as well as the additional reviewers for selecting the program and providing valuable feedback to the authors, and the local organization team for contributing to the realization of this event.

Special thanks go to the Program Chairs (Xiaowen Chu and Hongbo Jiang), the Local Chairs (Yang Qin and Qixin Wang), the Web Chair (Shaohuai Shi), the Sponsor and Exhibits Chair (Kaiyong Zhao), the Publicity and Social Media Chair (Xiang Sun), the Workshop Chair (Chuan Wu), the Publication Chair (Wei Wang), and the Conference Manager (Kitti Szilagyiova).

Furthermore, special thanks go to EAI for their guidance and organizational support, and to our sponsors. Most importantly, we thank the speakers and attendees for appreciating the aforementioned efforts by participating in the conference.

We sincerely hope you find these proceedings informative and enjoyable, and that it will bring you new perspectives to your research in this emerging and exciting field.

November 2019

Xiaowen Chu
Hongbo Jiang
Bo Li
Dan Wang
Wei Wang

Organization

Steering Committee

Imrich Chlamtac   Bruno Kessler Professor, University of Trento, Italy

Organizing Committee

General Chair

Bo Li   The Hong Kong University of Science and Technology, Hong Kong, China

General Co-chair

Dan Wang   The Hong Kong Polytechnic University, Hong Kong, China

TPC Chair and Co-chair

Xiaowen Chu   Hong Kong Baptist University, Hong Kong, China
Hongbo Jiang   Hunan University, China

Sponsorship and Exhibit Chair

Kaiyong Zhao   Hong Kong Baptist University, Hong Kong, China

Local Chairs

Yang Qin   Harbin Institute of Technology (Shenzhen), China
Qixin Wang   The Hong Kong Polytechnic University, Hong Kong, China

Workshops Chair

Chuan Wu   The University of Hong Kong, Hong Kong, China

Publicity and Social Media Chair

Xiang Sun   University of New Mexico, USA

Publications Chair

Wei Wang   The Hong Kong University of Science and Technology, Hong Kong, China

Web Chair

Shaohuai Shi   Hong Kong Baptist University, Hong Kong, China

Conference Manager

Kitti Szilagyiova   EAI

Technical Program Committee

Yuan He	Tsinghua University, China
Yuedong Xu	Fudan University, China
Fangming Liu	Huazhong University of Science and Technology, China
Jinsong Han	Zhejiang University, China
Xiangyang Li	University of Science and Technology of China, China
Zongpeng Li	Wuhan University, China, and University of Calgary, Canada
Haipeng Dai	Nanjing University, China
Yang Qin	Harbin Institute of Technology (Shenzhen), China
Jihong Yu	Beijing Institute of Technology, China
Hai Liu	The Hang Seng University of Hong Kong, Hong Kong, China
Qixin Wang	The Hong Kong Polytechnic University, Hong Kong, China
Guoliang Xing	The Chinese University of Hong Kong, Hong Kong, China
Zhenjiang Li	City University of Hong Kong, Hong Kong, China
Joseph Ng	Hong Kong Baptist University, Hong Kong, China
Wei Wang	The Hong Kong University of Science and Technology, Hong Kong, China
Chuan Wu	The University of Hong Kong, Hong Kong, China
Haiyang Wang	University of Minnesota at Duluth, USA
Lin Wang	Vrije Universiteit Amsterdam, The Netherlands
Jiangchuan Liu	Simon Fraser University, Canada
Yu Wang	University of North Carolina at Charlotte, USA
Amir H. Gandomi	Stevens Institute of Technology, USA
Igor Bisio	University of Genoa, Italy
JaeSeung Song	Sejong University, South Korea
Olivia Choudhury	IBM Research, USA
Enrico Natalizio	University of Lorraine, France
Reza Malekian	Malmö University, Sweden
Chonggang Wang	InterDigital Communications, USA
Kui Wu	University of Victoria, Canada
Mo Li	Nanyang Technological University, Singapore
Zhipeng Cai	Georgia State University, USA
Edith Ngai	Uppsala University, Sweden
Sherali Zeadally	University of Kentucky, USA
Yifan Zhang	Binghamton University, USA
Fu Xiao	Nanjing University of Posts and Telecommunications, China
Huber Flores	University of Helsinki, Finland
Xiaojiang Chen	Northwestern University, China
Jun Luo	Nanyang Technological University, Singapore
Ju Ren	Central South University, China
Xiulong Liu	Simon Fraser University, Canada

Contents

Mobile Systems

Search Planning and Analysis for Mobile Targets with Robots

Shujin Ye$^{(\boxtimes)}$, Wai Kit Wong, and Hai Liu

Department of Computing, The Hang Seng University of Hong Kong,
Siu Lek Yuen, Hong Kong
{sye,wongwk,hliu}@hsu.edu.hk

Abstract. With robotics technologies advancing rapidly, there are many new robotics applications such as surveillance, mining tasks, search and rescue, and autonomous armies. In this work, we focus on use of robots for target searching. For example, a collection of Unmanned Aerial Vehicle (UAV) could be sent to search for survivor targets in disaster rescue missions. We assume that there are multiple targets. The moving speeds and directions of the targets are unknown. Our objective is to minimize the searching latency which is critical in search and rescue applications. Our basic idea is to partition the search area into grid cells and apply the divide-and-conquer approach. We propose two searching strategies, namely, the circuit strategy and the rebound strategy. The robots search the cells in a Hamiltonian circuit in the circuit strategy while they backtrack in the rebound strategy. We prove that the expected searching latency of the circuit strategy for a moving target is upper bounded by $\frac{3n^2-4n+3}{2n}$ where n is the number of grid cells of the search region. In case of a static or suerfast target, we derive the expected searching latency of the two strategies. Simulations are conducted and the results show that the circuit strategy outperforms the rebound strategy.

Keywords: Robot search · Mobile target · Search planning and analysis

1 Introduction

From small toasters to huge industrial machines, robots are already an indispensable part of our daily lives. Automatic robots such as Unmanned Aerial Vehicle (UAV) can now be bought in many shops and are easily affordable by individuals. Some UAVs can be bought at several hundreds US dollars. It is not surprise to see UAVs flying nowadays. Apart from aerial robots, there are also other kinds of robots such as unmanned vehicles (e.g., Google driverless cars), AUVs/UUVs (autonomous underwater vehicle/unmanned underwater vehicles), and unmanned ships. The robots carry sensors such as accelerometers, infrared detectors, microphones and cameras. They can be used in many applications

© ICST Institute for Computer Sciences, Social Informatics and Telecommunications Engineering 2020
Published by Springer Nature Switzerland AG 2020. All Rights Reserved
X. Chu et al. (Eds.): QShine 2019, LNICST 300, pp. 3–21, 2020.
https://doi.org/10.1007/978-3-030-38819-5_1

including surveillance, search and rescue, payload delivery and military missions [1,2].

In this paper, we focus on searching missions using robots [7,25]. Figure 1 shows an example of the searching mission, where several robots are deployed to search for multiple targets in an area. In July 2018, a 44-year-old paraglider was blown off course from Sunset Peak in Lantau South Country Park in Hong Kong[1]. The missing person was believed to have fallen into the nearby jungle or the sea. It is difficult and slow to deploy ground machines or human forces to search in the jungle or the sea. The Hong Kong police considered searching for the missing person using UAVs, which could be massively deployed to assist the search at land, sea, and air at low visibilities. There could be multiple targets to be rescued and they may move from time to time. For example, in the incident of MH370[2], there are over 200 people missing and they may move following the ocean current. Using a large number of robots to assist in the search can increase the chance of locating the targets in the huge search area and hence may save more lives.

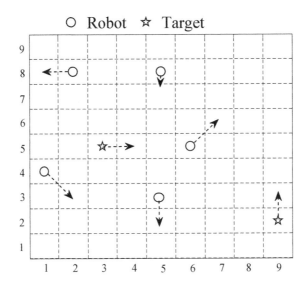

Fig. 1. Robots searching for mobile targets in the search area

Although searching for mobile targets using robots is common in practice, this topic has received little attention. To our best knowledge, we are the first to study and analyze the strategies of robot-based mobile target searching. We assume no information, such as speed and direction, about the target's movement

---

[1] https://www.hongkongfp.com/2018/07/27/hong-kong-paraglider-missing-since-sun day-found-dead-lantau-island/.

[2] https://www.usatoday.com/story/news/world/2014/03/07/malaysia-airlines-beijin g-flight-missing/6187779/.

is known. We use a divide and conquer approach to let the robots search in different areas. Each robot searches its assigned area in a pre-set path. There are two strategies: (1) Circuit strategy and (2) Rebound strategy. The search strategies are divided into two phases. In the first phase, both strategies detect every place in the map once to find the targets. However, as targets may move, the robots may miss the targets in the first phase. Then, in the second phase, the circuit strategy repeats the same path in the first phase until the robot runs out of energy. In the rebound strategy, a robot backtracks (i.e., going back along the path that it followed in the first phase) until its energy is depleted. Interestingly, as we have proven in this paper, the circuit strategy has a lower *searching latency* than the rebound strategy, i.e., the circuit strategy can find the targets in a shorter time. We have also analyzed the expected searching latency of our strategies. In specific, with n being the number of cells in the search area, we proved the following:

1. The expected searching latency of the circuit strategy is upper bounded by $\frac{3n^2-4n+3}{2n}$.
2. The expected searching latency of both strategies is $\frac{n+1}{2}$ when the target is static.
3. The expected searching latency of any strategy is n when the target is super-fast and can move to any location in the search area at any time.

The simulation results agree with our theoretical results and show that the circuit strategy has the lowest searching latency.

2   Related Works

Motion control of robots was modeled in [3–5,10,22,28] and has been applied in a number of applications, such as target searching [8,18,19] target tracking [16,23,24], formation of specific topologies and patterns [12,15,26], coverage area maximization [6,14,21,27], vehicle behavior description [11,13], and network connection maintenance [9,17,19]. We focus on the target searching literature as follows.

Several studies have examined searches for a single static target. Dimidov et al. [8] analyzed the efficiency of two classes of random walk search strategies, namely the correlated random walk and Lévy walk, for discovering a static target in either a bounded or open space. The search strategies were tested through simulations that used up to 30 real robots (Kilobots). During the experiment, communication between robots included sharing information about discovery of the target. Sakthivelmurugan et al. [20] introduced a number of searching strategies for the detection and retrieval of a static target, including the straight-line, parallel-line, divider, expanding square, and parallel sweep approaches. Experiments were conducted with up to four robots in an environment with known boundaries and showed that a parallel sweep with the divider approach was the most efficient strategy.

Searching for multiple targets was studied by Rango et al. [18]. They considered the mine detection problem using a modified ant colony algorithm. Given

Table 1. A summary of differences between our work and current literature

	Single/multiple targets	Static/mobile targets
This paper	Multiple targets	Both static and mobile targets
[19]	Single target	Static target
[8]	Single target	Static target
[18]	Multiple targets	Static targets

multiple mines that were randomly distributed in an unexplored area, the problem is to use robots to explore the area and detect all of the mines in the minimum time. During the searching process, the robots lay repelling anti-pheromones on the explored area. When a robot decides for its next next movement, it perceives pheromone information from their surroundings and travels to undetected regions with the least pheromone intensity. Once one or more robots discovered a mine, attractive pheromones were deposited to recruit other robots. After the required number of robots were attracted to the mine location, they worked cooperatively to disarm the mine.

Although the robot-based target searching has been studied, the previous works focused on the static target. To the best of our knowledge, this paper is the first one to consider mobile target searching using robots. In Table 1, we summarize the differences between our work and current literature.

3 Problem Definition and System Models

There are M targets (e.g., missing persons). They are located within a rectangular *search area* of size $w \times \ell$. They may move from time to time. The speed and direction of the targets are unknown and they can change at any time. Targets are assumed not to move outside the search area. There are N homogeneous robots (e.g., UAVs). Each robot is given a unique integer 1 to N as its ID. Each robot has a lifetime of L, representing the time it can spend to search for the target, e.g., before the battery is empty. Each robot has sensing ability so that it can detect a target within a small range. We define the *searching latency* of i-th target, denoted as T_i, as the time to locate the target since the start of the search. The problem is to design searching plans of the robots so that the chance for the robots to find all targets is maximized and the average searching time ($\frac{\sum_{i=1}^{M} T_i}{M}$) is minimized.

First, we discretize the problem as following. The sensing range of each robot is assumed to be a square[3] of length k so that the robot can detect the target if it is located in the square. We divide the search area into $w_c \times \ell_c$ cells where $w_c = \lceil \frac{w}{k} \rceil$ and $b = \lceil \frac{\ell}{k} \rceil$. We write (x, y) as the coordinate of each cell. $(1, 1)$ represents the bottom left corner while (w_c, ℓ_c) represents the upper right corner. Let $n = w_c \times \ell_c$ be the total number of cells of the search area. In our system,

---

[3] The actual sensing range could be a circle containing the square.

Table 2. Important notations.

Notation	Definition
w_c	Number of cells in width of the search area
ℓ_c	Number of cells in length of the search area
n	Total number of cells of the search area, $n = w_c \times \ell_c$
N	Number of robots
M	Number of targets
L	Lifetime of the robots
T_i	Searching latency of i-th target
t	The current timeslot

we consider that n is significantly larger than number of robots N as the search area in reality is normally very large. Time is also discretized (time-slotted). We define 1 unit of timeslot as the time taken by the robot to move from a cell to a neighboring cell (including diagonally) and perform the detection. In others words, after a robot has finished the detection at a cell, it can move in 8 directions and reach the next cell to perform the detection. Each robot performs the movement and detection for exactly 1 cell in 1 timeslot, i.e., the speed of the robot is 1 (cell per timeslot). A target is always located in one of the n cells of the search area. If a target and a robot are in the same cell at the same timeslot, the target is detected. The problem now becomes to design search paths of robots on the cells. Table 2 summarizes the major notations used in the paper.

4   Search Strategy of Robots

We use a two-phase search strategy as described below.

Phase 1: Explore all Cells Once. Without any information about the target's location, the first goal in the searching task is to check all the cells in the search area once. We use a divide and conquer approach to let the robots search in different regions at the same time. We take a side (width or length) of the search area, and divide it into N strips along this side, as shown in Fig. 2. Each robot is assigned a strip to search for targets and it visits every cell in the strip to find the targets. The side is selected in order to minimize the difference between the areas of the strips. Say for example, if w_c is divisible by N, we divide the search area along the width. Each strip is an equi-width rectangle of size $\frac{w_c}{N} \times \ell$. In general, say we divide the search area along the width and let $r = w_c \bmod N$. For robots with ID $\leq r$, each is assigned a strip of width $\lceil \frac{w_c}{N} \rceil$ and length ℓ_c. For robots with ID $> r$, each is assigned a strip of width $\lfloor \frac{w_c}{N} \rfloor$ and length ℓ_c. Each robot starts its search at the bottom left corner of its assigned strip at $t = 1$.

Phase 2: Re-visit Until All Targets are Found. If the targets are static, i.e., they do not move, it is guaranteed to find all targets in phase 1. Since the targets may move, the robots may miss some targets. The robots repeat the search until

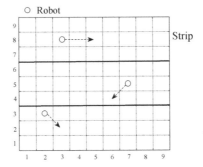

Fig. 2. Searching area is divided into two strips for two robots

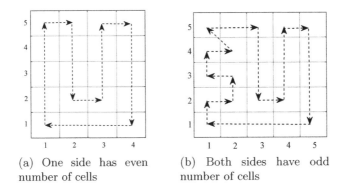

(a) One side has even number of cells

(b) Both sides have odd number of cells

Fig. 3. Search paths of the circuit strategy for different dimensions of the search area.

all targets are found. We consider the following two searching strategies for each robot.

Circuit Strategy. Each robot travels in a *Hamiltonian circuit* to visit all the cells in the assigned strip. After visiting all the cells once, the robot ends at the staring location. It repeats the circuit again and again until all targets are found. Hamiltonian circuit always exist when the width and length of the strip are over 1. Figure 3 illustrates the search paths of the circuit strategy.

Rebound Strategy. Each robot travels in a *Hamiltonian path*. After it visits all the cells once, it starts at the ending point and travels back the same Hamiltonian path in the opposite direction. It repeats the path back and forth until all targets are found. Hamiltonian path always exist. Figure 4 illustrates the search path of the rebound strategy.

5 Analysis on Searching Latency

We analyze the searching latency of the proposed searching strategies theoretically. We assume there is one robot only in the search area. It is trivial to extend

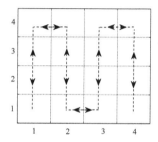

Fig. 4. Search path of the rebound strategy.

to the multi-robot case as each robot searches in a non-overlapping area. If the targets are all independent, the expected searching latency of any of them is the same. Our analysis focuses on the searching latency of j-th target, T_j. We divide the analysis into three parts:

Static Target. The target does not move but its location is unknown.
Superfast Target. We consider the target's speed v is over the size of the search map, i.e., $v \geq \max(w_c, \ell_c)$. The target can move from any cell to any cell between any two timeslots. In this case, the locations of the target at two consecutive timeslots are independent.
Mobile Target. The target may move and its speed v is smaller than the size of the search map, i.e., $v < \max(w_c, \ell_c)$.

5.1   Analysis on Static Target

As the robot searches in all cells, it is guaranteed to find the target. In Theorem 1, we show that both strategies have the same expected searching latency.

Theorem 1. *If the target is static, then the expected searching latency of a robot using either circuit strategy or rebound strategy is $E(T_j) = \frac{n+1}{2}$, where n is the number of cells of the search area.*

Proof. Since there are n cells, the target must be found at or before $t = n$. There is a probability of $\frac{1}{n}$ to find the target at $t = i$ for $i = 1$ to n. We have

$$E(T_j) = \sum_{i=1}^{n} \Pr(\text{Target found at } t = i) \cdot i$$

$$= \frac{1}{n} \sum_{i=1}^{n} i$$

$$= \frac{1}{n} \cdot \frac{n(n+1)}{2}$$

$$= \frac{n+1}{2}$$

$\square$

5.2 Analysis on Superfast Target

In Theorem 2, we show that any strategy has the same expected searching latency.

Theorem 2. *If the target is mobile with speed $\geq \max(w_c, \ell_c)$, then the expected searching latency of a robot using any strategy is $E(T_j) = n$, where n is the number of cells of the search area.*

Proof. The probability of the target appearing in any cell at any time $t = i$ is the same, i.e., $\Pr(\text{Robot meets target at } t = i) = \frac{1}{n}$. Note that the above probability is the same regardless of which strategy is used. The expected latency is

$$E(T_j) = \frac{1}{\Pr(\text{Robot meets target at } t = i)} = n$$

□

5.3 Analysis on Mobile Target

Every time a robot explores a cell and cannot find the target there, we can conclude that the target must be in one of the remaining cells. We model the target's movement as a probabilistic model where the target may stay at the same cell in the next timeslot with a probability p or may move to a neighboring cell with even probability. We can estimate the probability of finding the target at different cells using the following.

Let x be a cell in the search area and $\mathbb{N}_x$ be the set of reachable cells of x. Let $P_i^{(x)}$ be the probability of the target being located at cell x at $t = i$. Assume the robot does not explore x at $t = i + 1$. We have

$$P_{i+1}^{(x)} = P_i^{(x)} \times \Pr(\text{the target stays at } x) + \sum_{y \in \mathbb{N}_x} P_i^{(y)} \times \Pr(\text{the targets leaves } y)$$

$$\times \Pr(\text{the target moves to } x \mid \text{the targets leaves } y)$$

$$= p P_i^{(x)} + (1 - p) \sum_{y \in \mathbb{N}_x} \frac{P_i^{(y)}}{|\mathbb{N}_y|} \tag{1}$$

At $t = i + 1$, the robot explores one of the cells say z. Suppose the target is not found at z. Let $\widehat{P_{i+1}^{(x)}}$ be the probability of the target being located at cell x at $t = i + 1$ given that the target is not found at z. We have $\widehat{P_{i+1}^{(z)}} = 0$ and

$$\widehat{P_{i+1}^{(x)}} = \frac{P_{i+1}^{(x)}}{1 - P_{i+1}^{(z)}} \tag{2}$$

We use the special case where $w_c = \ell_c = 2$ to illustrate the idea, i.e., the search area has four cells in total. $|\mathbb{N}_x| = 3$ for all cells x. Suppose $p = 0.5$.

Figure 5 illustrates how the probabilities of finding the target at different cells change over time. Initially, at $t = 1$, each of the three unexplored cells has the same probability ($\frac{1}{3}$) to find the target. At $t = 2$, we calculate the probabilities according to Eqs. 1 and 2. $P_2^{(1,1)} = 0.5(\frac{1}{3}) + 0.5(\frac{\frac{1}{3}+\frac{1}{3}+0}{3}) = \frac{5}{18} = 0.278$. Similarly, $P_2^{(2,1)} = \frac{5}{18} = 0.278$. Since the robot explored (1, 1) and the target is not found, $\widehat{P_2^{(1,1)}} = 0$ (lower left cell). We have $\widehat{P_2^{(2,1)}} = \frac{\frac{5}{18}}{1-\frac{5}{18}} = \frac{5}{13} = 0.385$ (lower right cell).

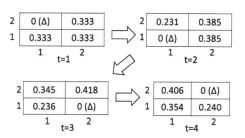

Fig. 5. Illustration of the probability of finding the target at different locations in a 2×2 search area from $t = 1$ to 4, given the target is not found. $p = 0.5$. Δ denotes the location explored by the robot at that timeslot.

Observe that *the probability to find the target is not even at all the cells*. A cell that is explored recently has the lowest probability to find the target. This probability increases as time goes until it is explored again. The same can be observed in the general case. From Eq. 1, $P_{i+1}^{(x)}$ is the smallest when the robot has explored x at $t = i$, i.e., $P_i^{(x)} = 0$. Assume $|N_x| = |N_y|$ for any cells x and y. The change in $P_i^{(x)}$, denoted as $\Delta P_i^{(x)}$, can be calculated as

$$\Delta P_i^{(x)} = P_{i+1}^{(x)} - P_i^{(x)} = (1 - p)(\overline{P_i^{(y)}} - P_i^{(x)}) \qquad (3)$$

where $\overline{P_i^{(y)}} = \frac{\sum_{y \in N_x} P_i^{(y)}}{|N_x|}$ denotes the average of $P_i^{(y)}$ for $y \in N_x$. When $P_i^{(x)}$ is small, $\Delta P_i^{(x)}$ is large. As $P_i^{(x)}$ gets larger, $\Delta P_i^{(x)}$ decreases, until $P_i^{(x)}$ approaches the average of $P_i^{(y)}$ of the neighboring cells.

Summary. To maximize the chance to find the target, it is preferred to explore the cells that are not explored for the longest time at each timeslot. In the first phase of the search, both the circuit strategy and the rebound strategy visit the unexplored cells once. This matches the principle above. At the beginning of the second phase, the circuit strategy and the rebound strategy restart the search at different routes. The circuit strategy explores the cells that have not been detected for a longer time. The rebound strategy, in contrast, visits the cells that are just visited not long ago. The circuit strategy is expected to have a better chance to find the target during this period. The rebound strategy leaves the cells around the starting point of the search path to be explored later. This increases the time gap between two detections on the same cell. However, as we have discussed in Eq. 3, the gain in the probability to find the target is marginal. Thus, we expect the circuit strategy to outperform rebound strategy.

Upper Bound of Expected Latency of the Circuit Strategy. The circuit strategy and the rebound strategy are simple and intuitive. They are similar in the sense that they travel through all the cells repeatedly to find the targets. However, as we have showed, circuit strategy has a smaller expected searching latency than rebound strategy. Circuit strategy is suggested in practice. In Theorem 3, we provide an upper bound of the expected searching latency of the circuit strategy.

Theorem 3. *The expected searching latency of the circuit strategy $E(T_j)$ is upper bounded by $\frac{3n^2-4n+3}{2n}$ searching a mobile target in a search area of n cells.*

Proof. The search path of the robot is static. Say, the path in Fig. 3(b) is used. Suppose now the target is at $(1,1)$ at $t = i$ and the robot is not here. We know that the robot cannot be at $(1,2)$ at $t = i+1$. The probability of being found at $t = i+1$ if the target moves to $(1, 2)$ is 0. We call this location the *blind spot*. The robot may appear in any of the remaining $n-1$ cells at $t = i+1$. Let C be the set of candidate locations that the target may move to at $t = i+1$. The target moves to any one of the locations in C with even probability. Let p be the probability of the target being found at $t = i+1$. If the blind spot is in C, we have $p = \sum_{i=1}^{|C|-1} \frac{1}{|C|} \cdot \frac{1}{n-1} = \frac{m-1}{m(n-1)}$. p is the smallest when $|C|$ is the smallest with the blind spot being one of the candidates in C. This happens when the target is moving at the speed of 1 cell per timeslot and is located at the corner, say $(1,1)$. There are only 3 candidate locations in this scenario: $(1,2)$ (blind spot), $(2,1)$, $(2,2)$. We denote the smallest of p, $p_{min} = \frac{2}{3(n-1)}$.

$E(T_j)$ is the largest (the upper bound) when the probability to find the target at any time is p_{min}. We denote it as $E_{max}(T_j)$. We calculate $E_{max}(T_j)$ as following.

Let E_i be the event of the target being found at $t = i$ and $\overline{S_i}$ be $\overline{E_1} \wedge \overline{E_2} \wedge \ldots \wedge \overline{E_i}$. At $t = 1$, the target is located at a random position. $\Pr(E_1) = \frac{1}{n}$. At $t = 2$, as we discussed above, $\Pr(E_i|S_{i-1}) = p_{min}$ for $i > 1$. We have $\Pr(\overline{S_i}) = \frac{n-1}{n} \cdot (1 - p_{min})^{i-1}$ for $i \geq 1$.

$$E_{max}(T_j) = \Pr(E_1) \cdot 1 + \sum_{i=2}^{\infty} \Pr(S_{i-1}) \cdot \Pr(E_i|S_{i-1}) \cdot i$$

$$= \frac{1}{n} + \sum_{i=2}^{\infty} \frac{n-1}{n} \cdot (\frac{3n-5}{3n-3})^{i-2} \cdot \frac{2}{3(n-1)} \cdot i$$

$$= \frac{1}{n} + \frac{2}{3n} \sum_{i=2}^{\infty} (\frac{3n-5}{3n-3})^{i-2} \cdot i$$

The term $X = \sum_{i=2}^{\infty} (\frac{3n-5}{3n-3})^{i-2} \cdot i$ is an arithmetico-geometric sequence. Let $q = \frac{3n-5}{3n-3}$ and so $1 - q = \frac{2}{3n-3}$. We have

$$X = \sum_{i=2}^{\infty} q^{i-2} i \tag{4}$$

and

$$qX = \sum_{i=2}^{\infty} q^{i-1} i = \sum_{i=3}^{\infty} q^{i-2}(i-1) \tag{5}$$

By subtracting Eq. 5 from Eq. 4, we have

$$X - qX = \sum_{i=2}^{\infty} q^{i-2} i - \sum_{i=3}^{\infty} q^{i-2}(i-1)$$

$$(1-q)X = q^{2-2}(2) + \sum_{i=3}^{\infty} q^{i-2} i - q^{i-2}(i-1)$$

$$(1-q)X = 2 + \sum_{i=3}^{\infty} q^{i-2}$$

$$(1-q)X = 2 + \frac{q}{1-q}$$

$$\frac{2}{3n-3}X = 2 + \frac{(\frac{3n-5}{3n-3})}{\frac{2}{3n-3}}$$

$$X = \frac{3(3n^2 - 4n + 1)}{4}$$

Substitute X into $E_{max}(T_j)$, we have

$$E_{max}(T_j) = \frac{1}{n} + \frac{2}{3n} \cdot \frac{3(3n^2 - 4n + 1)}{4}$$

$$= \frac{3n^2 - 4n + 3}{2n}$$

$\square$

6   Simulation

In this section, we present our simulation study to evaluate our search strategies: 'circuit' and 'rebound'. The purposes of the simulation are: (i) to verify our theoretical results; and (ii) to evaluate the performance of different strategies in practice. A 'random' strategy [8] is implemented as the baseline method for comparisons. In the random strategy, each robot randomly goes to a neighboring cell and detects the target. All simulations are performed on a computer with i5 3.4 GHz CPU and 8 GB memory. The experimental platform is Matlab R2018b. All results are averaged over 10000 independently simulation executions.

6.1 Simulation Setup

We consider a 2D search area with size 40×40. The search area is divided into cells, each with size 1×1, i.e., there are 160 cells in total. There are three types of the targets as discussed in Sect. 5: (i) static target; (ii) mobile target; and (iii) superfast target. For type (ii) mobile targets, each target is assumed to move randomly. At each timeslot, it goes to a random direction at a random speed bounded by v_{max}, a preset maximum speed. In our simulation, we tested v_{max} in $\{0.25, 0.5, 0.75, 1\}$.

We tested the strategies in two scenarios: (i) single target; and (ii) multiple targets. All strategies were evaluated using the following performance metrics:

1. Achievement ratio: the ratio of simulation runs that find all targets within robots' lifetime.
2. Average latency: the average searching latency to find all targets upon a successful search.

6.2 Simulation Results on Single Target Searching

We performed the simulation for searching a single target varying the number of robots from 4 to 10. Figures 6 and 7 show the achievement ratios and average latency of different strategies in our simulations.

We make the following observations from the simulation results:

1. The circuit strategy has the same performance as rebound strategy for static and superfast targets while the circuit strategy is slightly better than the rebound strategy for mobile targets in all speeds. The circuit strategy is the best among the three in all scenarios.
2. The random strategy is the worst in all scenarios. The gap is significantly large except for superfast target (in which any strategy has the same chance to find the target for superfast target, as discussed in Theorem 2).
3. As the number of robots increases, the achievement ratio of the three strategies increases and the average latency decreases.
4. When the number of robots is 10, the achievement ratio of the circuit strategy and the rebound strategy is very close to 1.

6.3 Simulation Results on Multiple Targets Searching

In this scenario, the number of robots is fixed to be 10. We performed the simulation for searching for 2 to 6 targets. The targets move independently.

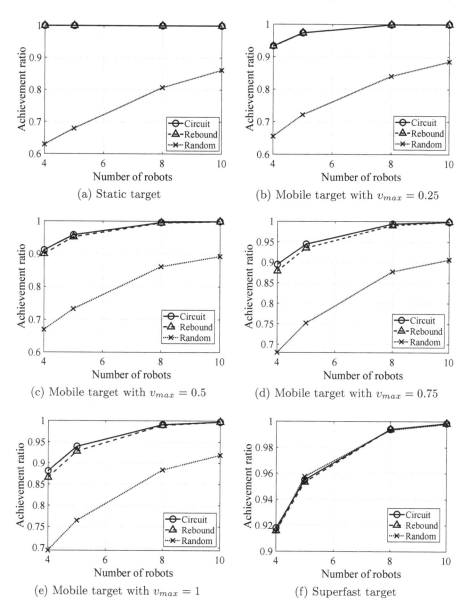

Fig. 6. Achievement ratio of different strategies varying number of robots.

Figures 8 and 9 show the achievement ratios and average latency of different strategies in our simulations.

We make the following observations from the simulation results:

1. Similar to single target searching, the circuit strategy is the best among the three strategies. The circuit strategy and the rebound strategy have almost

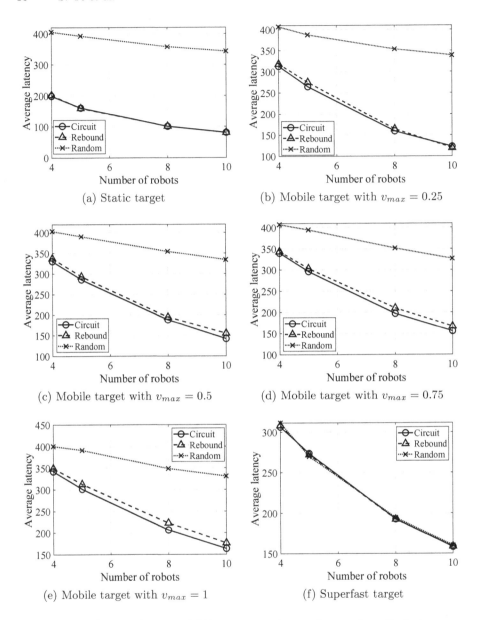

Fig. 7. Average latency of different strategies varying number of robots.

the same achievement ratio. Yet, the average latency of the circuit strategy is smaller than the rebound strategy for mobile targets (except for the case $v_{max} = 0.25$).

2. The average latency is not affected by number of targets. This is expected as the targets are independent.

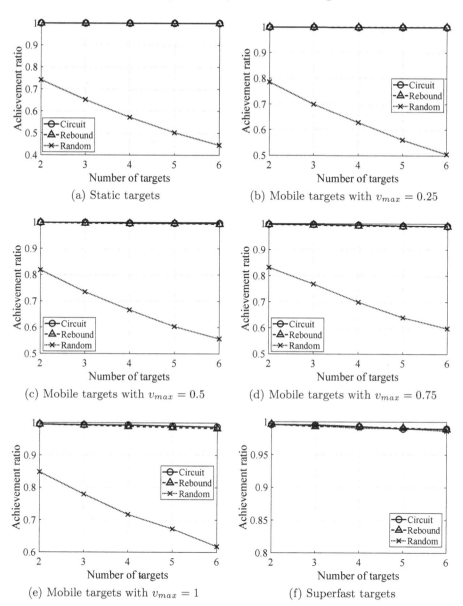

Fig. 8. Achievement ratio of different strategies varying number of targets.

3. The random strategy is significantly worse than the circuit strategy and the rebound strategy in terms of both achievement ratio and average latency, except for case of superfast targets.

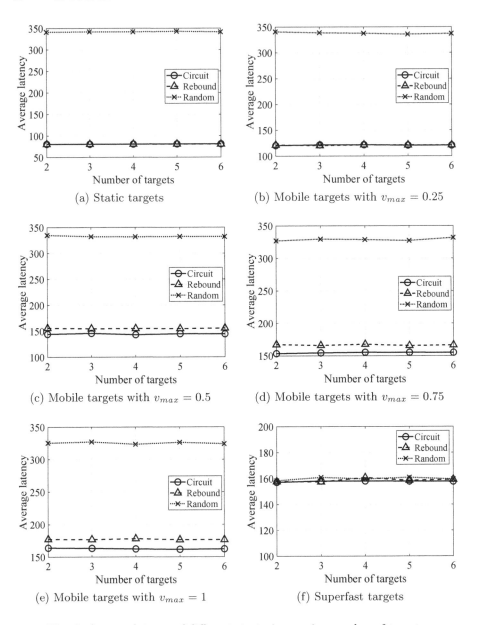

Fig. 9. Average latency of different strategies varying number of targets.

4. As the number of targets increases, the achievement ratio of the random strategy drops significantly. The achievement ratios of the circuit strategy and the rebound strategy remain steady.

6.4   Discussions

All simulation results agree with our theoretical analysis. The reuslts show that the circuit strategy is the best in terms of achievement ratio and average latency. The performance of the rebound strategy is close to the circuit strategy but never outperforms the circuit strategy. The circuit strategy is suggested in practice for searching. In contrast, the random strategy is the worst and its performance is significantly worse than the other two strategies. This highlight the importance of picking the right strategy for searching in a disaster rescue mission.

7   Conclusions and Future Work

In this paper, we study the problem of mobile target searching using robots. No information about the targets is known. We propose a divide-and-conquer approach to divide the search areas into strips and let each robot search in one strip. We study two searching strategies, namely circuit strategy and rebound strategy. We theoretically analyze the searching latency in the strategies under different scenarios and conclude that the circuit strategy is better. The results are verified with extensive simulations. In the future, we plan to extend the model to allow the robots to communicate with each other during the search. This allows a more intelligent search strategy at the cost of increased communication cost and reduced lifetime of robots.

Acknowledgements. This work is partially supported by the Faculty Development Scheme (Ref. No. UGC/FDS14/E03/17 and UGC/FDS14/E01/17), The Deep Learning Research & Application Centre, and The Big Data & Artificial Intelligence Group in The Hang Seng University of Hong Kong.

References

1. DARPA Announces "Gremlins" UAS Program (2015). http://www.unmanneds ystemstechnology.com/2015/09/darpa-announces-gremlins-uas-program/
2. Department of Defense Announces Successful Micro-Drone Demonstration, January 2017. https://www.defense.gov/News/News-Releases/News-Release-View/A rticle/1044811/department-of-defense-announces-successful-micro-drone-demonst ration/
3. Celikkanat, H., Sahin, E.: Steering self-organized robot flocks through externally guided individuals. Neural Comput. Appl. **19**(6), 849–865 (2010)
4. Couzin, I.D., Jens, K., Franks, N.R., Levin, S.A.: Effective leadership and decision-making in animal groups on the move. Nature **433**(7025), 513–6 (2005)
5. Cucker, F., Dong, J.G.: Avoiding collisions in flocks. IEEE Trans. Autom. Control **55**(5), 1238–1243 (2010)
6. Delight, M., Ramakrishnan, S., Zambrano, T., MacCready, T.: Developing robotic swarms for ocean surface mapping. In: 2016 IEEE International Conference on Robotics and Automation (ICRA), pp. 5309–5315, May 2016. https://doi.org/10.1109/ICRA.2016.7487742

7. Dell'Ariccia, G., Dell'Omo, G., Wolfer, D.P., Lipp, H.P.: Flock flying improves pigeons' homing: GPS track analysis of individual flyers versus small groups. Anim. Behav. **76**(4), 1165–1172 (2008)
8. Dimidov, C., Oriolo, G., Trianni, V.: Random walks in swarm robotics: an experiment with kilobots. In: Dorigo, M., et al. (eds.) ANTS 2016. LNCS, vol. 9882, pp. 185–196. Springer, Cham (2016). https://doi.org/10.1007/978-3-319-44427-7_16
9. Fang, H., Wei, Y., Chen, J., Xin, B.: Flocking of second-order multiagent systems with connectivity preservation based on algebraic connectivity estimation. IEEE Trans. Cybern. **47**(4), 1067–1077 (2017). https://doi.org/10.1109/TCYB.2016.2537307
10. Ferrante, E., Turgut, A.E., Stranieri, A., Pinciroli, C., Birattari, M., Dorigo, M.: A self-adaptive communication strategy for flocking in stationary and non-stationary environments. Nat. Comput. **13**(2), 225–245 (2014)
11. Fredette, D., Özguner, U.: Swarm-inspired modeling of a highway system with stability analysis. IEEE Trans. Intell. Transp. Syst. **18**(6), 1371–1379 (2017). https://doi.org/10.1109/TITS.2016.2619266
12. de Marina, H.G., Jayawardhana, B., Cao, M.: Distributed rotational and translational maneuvering of rigid formations and their applications. IEEE Trans. Robot. **32**(3), 684–697 (2016). https://doi.org/10.1109/TRO.2016.2559511
13. Han, T., Ge, S.S.: Styled-velocity flocking of autonomous vehicles: a systematic design. IEEE Trans. Autom. Control **60**(8), 2015–2030 (2015). https://doi.org/10.1109/TAC.2015.2400664
14. Liu, H., Chu, X., Leung, Y.W., Du, R.: Simple movement control algorithm for bi-connectivity in robotic sensor networks. IEEE J. Sel. Areas Commun. **28**(7), 994–1005 (2010)
15. Michael, R., Alejandro, C., Radhika, N.: Robotics. Programmable self-assembly in a thousand-robot swarm. Science **345**(6198), 795–9 (2014)
16. Olfati-Saber, R., Jalalkamali, P.: Coupled distributed estimation and control for mobile sensor networks. IEEE Trans. Autom. Control **57**(10), 2609–2614 (2012). https://doi.org/10.1109/TAC.2012.2190184
17. Qiang, W., Li, W., Cao, X., Meng, Y.: Distributed flocking with biconnected topology for multi-agent systems. In: International Conference on Human System Interactions (2016)
18. Rango, F.D., Palmieri, N., Yang, X., Marano, S.: Swarm robotics in wireless distributed protocol design for coordinating robots involved in cooperative tasks. Soft. Comput. **22**(13), 4251–4266 (2018)
19. Sabattini, L., Chopra, N., Secchi, C.: Decentralized connectivity maintenance for cooperative control of mobile robotic systems. Int. J. Robot. Res. **32**(12), 1411–1423 (2013)
20. Sakthivelmurugan, E., Senthilkumar, G., Prithiviraj, K., Devraj, K.T.: Foraging behavior analysis of swarm robotics system. In: MATEC Web of Conferences, vol. 144, p. 01013. EDP Sciences (2018)
21. Semnani, S.H., Basir, O.A.: Semi-flocking algorithm for motion control of mobile sensors in large-scale surveillance systems. IEEE Trans. Cybern. **45**(1), 129–137 (2015). https://doi.org/10.1109/TCYB.2014.2328659
22. Szwaykowska, K., Romero, L.M., Schwartz, I.B.: Collective motions of heterogeneous swarms. IEEE Trans. Autom. Sci. Eng. **12**(3), 810–818 (2015). https://doi.org/10.1109/TASE.2015.2403253

23. Vásárhelyi, G., et al.: Outdoor flocking and formation flight with autonomous aerial robots. In: 2014 IEEE/RSJ International Conference on Intelligent Robots and Systems, pp. 3866–3873, September 2014. https://doi.org/10.1109/IROS.2014.6943105
24. Virágh, C., et al.: Flocking algorithm for autonomous flying robots. Bioinspir. Biomimet. **9**(2), 025012 (2013)
25. Ward, A.J.W., Herbert-Read, J.E., Sumpter, D.J.T., Jens, K.: Fast and accurate decisions through collective vigilance in fish shoals. Proc. Natl. Acad. Sci. U.S.A. **108**(6), 2312–2315 (2011)
26. Zhang, H., Chen, Z., Fan, M.: Collaborative control of multivehicle systems in diverse motion patterns. IEEE Trans. Control Syst. Technol. **24**(4), 1488–1494 (2016). https://doi.org/10.1109/TCST.2015.2487864
27. Zhao, H., Wang, H., Wu, W., Wei, J.: Deployment algorithms for uav airborne networks toward on-demand coverage. IEEE J. Sel. Areas Commun. **36**(9), 2015–2031 (2018). https://doi.org/10.1109/JSAC.2018.2864376
28. Zhao, H., Liu, H., Leung, Y.W., Chu, X.: Self-adaptive collective motion of swarm robots. IEEE Trans. Autom. Sci. Eng. **15**(4), 1533–1545 (2018)

Stability of Positive Systems in WSN Gateway for IoT&IIoT

Jolanta Mizera-Pietraszko[(✉)] and Jolanta Tancula

Opole University, Opole, Poland
{jmizera, jtancula}@uni.opole.pl

Abstract. Modern sensor networks work on the basis of intelligent sensors and actuators, their connection is carried out using conventional or specifically dedicated networks. The efficiency and smooth transmission of such a network is of great importance for the accuracy of measurements, sensor energy savings, or transmission speed. Ethernet in many networks is typically based on the TCP/IP protocol suite. Regardless of whether or not the network transmission is wired or wireless, it should always be reliable. TCP ensures transmission reliability through retransmissions, congestion control and flow control. But TPC is different in networks based on the UDP protocol. The most important here is the transmission speed achieved by shortening the header or the lack of an acknowledgment mechanism. Assuming the network is an automatic control system, it has interconnected elements that interact with each other to perform some specific tasks such as speed control, reliability and security of transmission, just the attributes that define stability being one of the fundamental features of control systems. Such a system returns to equilibrium after being unbalanced. There are many definitions of stability, e.g. Laplace or Lupanov. To check the stability of the sensor network connected to the Internet, different stability criteria should be used. We are going to analyze the stability of a computer network as a dynamic linear system, described by the equations known in the literature. In this paper, we propose the method of testing stability for positive systems using the Metzlner matrix in sensor networks such as IoT or IIoT. We will carry out tests in a place where wide area networks connect to sensor networks, that is in gates.

Keywords: Wireless sensor networks · Network system stability · Industrial IoT · Metzler matrix · Software testing methodology

1 Introduction

The work concerns an important topic which is the stability of computer networks as dynamic systems. Stable network operation allows the construction of efficient, fast and optimally working networks. Stability testing methods are known from the automation literature. The authors propose the use of these methods in computer science, and in particular, in computer networks. The use of sensor networks not only in IoT, but also in industry 4.0 (IIoT) is constantly growing and the research on their reliability should be continued. The proposed method may contribute to improving quality of such networks.

© ICST Institute for Computer Sciences, Social Informatics and Telecommunications Engineering 2020
Published by Springer Nature Switzerland AG 2020. All Rights Reserved
X. Chu et al. (Eds.): QShine 2019, LNICST 300, pp. 22–37, 2020.
https://doi.org/10.1007/978-3-030-38819-5_2

Networks that rely on the RED algorithm using AQM and packet queuing in routers and its variants do not always give good results. Hence, the methods for testing the stability of such networks is studied. They allow us to compare how the network stability conditions and its parameters will change depending on the method used.

Thus, stability of dynamic systems is an important concept associated with automation. Comparing the computer network to a dynamic system will allow analyzing its stability. Defining stability boundaries will give us the opportunity to design a more efficient and fault-tolerant network. Such studies can be applied to sensor networks. The use of sensor networks not only in IoT, but also in industry 4.0 (IIoT) is constantly growing and research into the reliability of such systems should be improved. One of the methods described in this article is testing the stability of positive systems. Therefore, motivation of this research work is to improve network parameters significantly, i.e. to improve its reliability and overall performance.

LoraWAN network research has been presented in [12–14]. They mainly concern the improvement of network scalability. Works on time synchronization, which plays an increasingly important role in information systems, are described in [15, 16]. However, the research carried out in this article concerns the improvement of network parameters in IoT and industrial IoT networks. They focus on network parameters such as: capacity, number of session and propagation time (capacity, number of sessions or propagation time). The analysis of positive systems will allow to improve the performance and scalability of wireless sensor networks.

When compared to conventional networks, wireless sensor networks (WSN) are arranged much more densely, their topology changes dynamically, additionally they have more limitations like memory or energy resources. Also, WSN creates a distributed measurement network to be applicable to measure air humidity and soil, monitoring traffic, tectonic movement, or avalanches. Other application areas include industry, medicine or the army. Sensors communicate with each other in real time and keep on sending data. The sensor topology is rather unpredictable. As a principle, sensors are divided into groups (clusters). This is a hierarchical network topology. All the measured data is sent to the main nodes and then to the overriding (parent) nodes. The parent nodes play the crucial role in a network gateway. Sometimes the sensors don't see the parent node and the data is sent in steps from one sensor to another always towards the parent node (see Fig. 1).

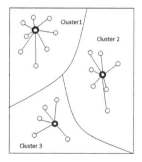

Fig. 1. Clustering and master sensors of WSN

2 LPWAN Networks

Development of IT technologies has a huge impact on smart cities. One of the most important aspects of this development is connectivity or wireless communication. Standards implementing IoT tasks for smart cities are WiFi, BLE, Zigbee, Thread or LoRaWan.

LPWAN (Low Power, Wide Area Network) is a new category of universal networks with a similar structure to that one used in mobile network. It mostly has a star topology and uses BTS (Base Transceiver Station) as a communication center for network cells. In some standards like Zigbee, it has a mesh topology for whose the central point is a coordinator.

LPWAN enables long distance communication at low bit rates and low power consumption. These networks work based on protocols that have better parameters in terms of resistance to interference and signal loss, at the expense of inferior bandwidth. They work on frequencies belonging to the unlicensed ISM band, which minimizes the costs of their use.

3 WSN Communication

A network layer model is adopted for WSN just like in conventional networks. In addition to the physical layers, data link, network, transport layer and application layer, there are also 4 planes such as energy management plane, displacement plane and two task management planes. All the planes cooperate with each other so that the sensors can share their resources, save energy or route the data [11]. Such a scheme determines efficiency of the network (see Fig. 2).

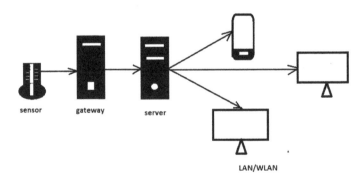

Fig. 2. Communication between WSN and WLA

In this paper, we focus on the transport layer. It serves as a combination of application layer and network layer whose major task is to control the mechanism of traffic congestion. All these tasks are performed by the TCP protocol, however for the sensor networks, they have some variations.

Network traffic moves from the child nodes to the parent node. Reverse traffic channel is used to manage the whole network. Acknowledgment mechanism for the data transfer is not required here for the reasons of network energy savings. However, the mechanism move from the parent node to the user or to the global Internet needs to be supervised for reliability purpose.

4   WSN Gateway

A device connecting the WAN network with the sensor network is a gateway operating in the Ethernet standard (see Fig. 3). The gateway may be a typical sensor, but having much larger RAM and a faster processor, then it is supplied by the power line. Alternatively, the gateway can be a router, as so called a routing network device or a coordinator, just as for example, in the Zigbee standard. WAN Gateway is a data collecting point which transfers them to the Internet. It mainly deals with the data conversion to packets by forwarding them. Packets are then sent to the network servers using conventional TCP/IP based networks.

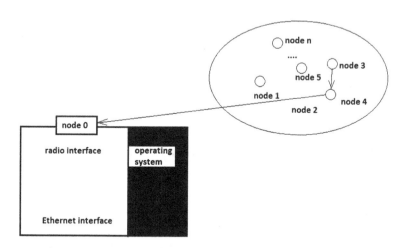

Fig. 3. WSN and WLAN Gateway scheme

5 Industrial Network Standards

Industrial networks, and in particular Industrial IoT (IIoT) networks, are becoming nowadays an inherent element of industrial infrastructure. Efficient data management enables to optimize production processes, whereas standardization of networking supports this objective.

5.1 ZigBee Standard

One of the standards created for the purpose of the radio communication in WSN, which does not need very high bandwidth, is the ZigBee standard with the numerous nodes. Usually, it has one of the following topologies: a star, tree, or a mesh topology. ZigBee model is layered, quite similarly to the TCP/IP model. This model is defined as the standard (protocol) of IEEE 802.15.4 [9]. It defines all the layers, out of which the two lowest layers are named: the physical PHY (PHYsical) and the MAC layer (Medium Access Control Layer).

The MAC layer is responsible for access to radio channels using the CSMA-CA (Carrier Sense Multiple Access - Collision Avoidance) mechanism. This layer may also process the transmission of signal beacons, provide synchronization and reliable transmission mechanism.

Radio transmission works on two frequency ranges: 868 MHz (one channel - Europe standard) and 2.4 GHz (16 channels - the whole world).

Access to the network is carried out in two ways:

– beaconing - transmission during operation of devices in a continuous mode,
– non-beaconing - transmission during operation of devices in periodic or random mode.

Two types of nodes have been defined in the IEEE 802.15.4 protocol:

• the node with reduced functionality RFD
• the node with full functionality FFD.

The node that manages the network (coordinator) is the type of FFD [8].

5.2 ZigBee Gateway

Wired connections in industrial automation networks are known as not a very good solution because they are not applicable in industrial companies located on large areas or in places where the temperature is high. Whereas, wireless networks may have adverse effects in the form of interference or signal reflection, automatic routing techniques are aimed to prevent them.

Standard Zigbee enables not only to build new industrial networks, but also to connect new to existing ones. Such network integration is possible thanks to modems and gateways. Ethernet gateways can convert data from Zigbee to TCP/IP and vice versa.

6 IoT Network Standards

We define two major IoT network standards such as LoRaWAN and Sigfox.

6.1 LoRaWAN Standard

The LoRa (Long Range) standard is a wide narrow band long-range network that has been optimized for the lowest possible energy consumption. It provides two-way, simultaneous data transmission. Information exchange takes place via a common medium in both directions. LoRaWAN is the standard for network communication M2M (Machine-to-Machine) and IoT. Also, it can be either an alternative or complement solution to battery supply.

The LoRaWAN network new modulation technique is an asynchronous method of digital modulation based on direct sequence spread spectrum (DSSS). It enables user to choose the diffusion string and bandwidth in order to meet the requirements for the connection.

Regarding energy consumption, three classes of terminal equipment are defined in the LoRa standard [6]:

Class A - the most energy-efficient, downlink devices receive data after sending their own uplink. The data is sent in specific time intervals.
Class B - energy-saving class. Communication is divided into slots and synchronized with network signaling. The nodes in this class send more information than those of class A.
Class C - is the least energy-efficient, the nodes are set to smart watch [7].

6.2 LoRaWAN Gateway

Topology of this network is usually the star, whose gates transmit data between end devices and central servers (or cloud). Gates are connected to servers based on Ethernet or WiFi technology, and communication between the gates and terminal devices is carried out through the LoRaWAN modules. The LoRaWan gate diagram is shown in Fig. 4.

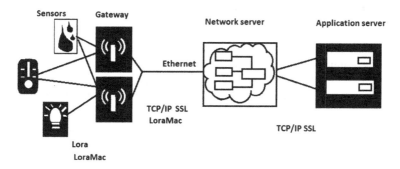

Fig. 4. Architecture of LoRaWAN Source [10]

6.3 Sigfox

Sigfox technology allows low power consumption while transferring a small amount of data. The device sends data up to 12 bytes long, while up to 8 bytes can be sent to the device. Data can be sent in the smart watch window after the device has finished the transmission. Smart watch and data receival by the terminal device is triggered by the action of transmitting data from the device to the base station.

6.4 Sigfox Gateway

Transmission acknowledgement mechanism can be implemented but it is not required. Transmission reliability is ensured by several base stations receiving the signal with simultaneous tripled repetition of the transmission by the terminal device. Transmissions are performed on randomly selected frequencies (frequency hopping). The network should be designed in such a way that the client is within a distance of at least three base stations. Sigfox works in the unlicensed ISM band. It needs a communication module working on 868 MHz with DBPSK (Differential Binary Phase-Shift Keying) modulation for the uplink channel and GFSK (Gaussian Frequency Shift Keying) for the downlink channel. Access gates and network applications that ensure the transfer of the network data guarantee the same quality of service.

7 Algorithm for Testing Network Stability

Computer networks have been operating based on standard network protocols for many years. For industrial networks or IoT, we do not have to create new solutions from scratch, it is enough to modify these solutions. We can then use them to improve the network bandwidth, save the end devices or to increase the speed of the connection.

We will apply asymptotic stability of positive systems to our research. Our activities concern creation of an algorithm that improves the network parameters based on traditional network protocols.

For the WLAN network, we have the Ethernet standard and the TCP or UDP transport layer protocol. The TCP protocol with overload control is described by the window size W and the average queue length in buffer q with the equations according to [3].

In order to perform the task, the steps listed should be followed:

Step 1 Transform equations describing the size of the window and the length of the queue to the form $x' = Ax$
Step 2 Determine if matrix A is the Metzlner matrix
Step 3 Prove that the system of equations is a positive system
Step 4 Investigate the asymptotic stability of the continuous positive system.

Such a system will allow for the analysis of the stability of real sensor networks as a way to improve the uplink speed and to establish stability boundaries that may contribute to better use of bandwidth or small delays. Network stability on the WLAN side will help reduce queues in buffers allowing consequently to reduce delays in the WSN network caused by a delay in queuing packets in the buffers or their loss caused by too long waiting for the reduction of the network delays.

Wireless sensor networks can accumulate packets in network device buffers, their overflow or queuing delays. Variety of queuing models enable to build a server wakeup model from the idle state as an efficient use of energy in servers.

8 Methodology for Testing Network Stability

There are many methods for testing stability of dynamic systems. They include analytical or graphical methods. Frequency methods (graphical) using the principle of an argument such as the Mikhailov's method (criterion or modified Mikhailov's criterion method) are the most popular methods for testing asymptotic stability at the set parameters of delay. To test such a system stability, the operator's transfer function (transition function) is calculated and the quasi-polynomial is determined. The distribution of quasi-polynomial zeros on the complex plane sets the stability boundaries.

As described in [2], one of them is the zero exclusion method, the uncertain parameter space method and so on. There are also methods for testing stability in which stability does not depend on the amount of the delay.

8.1 Testing Method for Delay-Independent Stability

In this method, on having derived a system of equations describing the network, a quasi-polynomial is determined, and the Hurwitz criterion is used to check the location of the polynomial roots. The designated zero lines of the quasi-polynomial are shown in the Fig. 5.

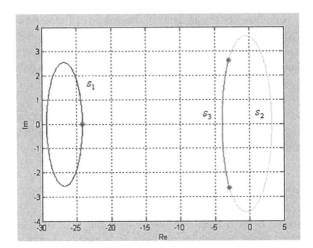

Fig. 5. The lines of the quasi-polynomial zeros

Figure 5 shows the closed curves which intersect the imaginary axis, that is they do not meet the criterion of stability. It means that the quasi-polynomial is not stable regardless of delays. So that in this case, it is necessary to change the network parameters to make the system stable [2].

8.2   Method of Space of Uncertain Parameters

In the method of space of uncertain parameters for testing the network system stability, it is necessary to determine the stability limits characterizing the operation of the computer network for the given parameters. This method is an extended variant of the classical method of division D, which allows for the appropriate selection of parameters so that the curves resulting from the substitution of the parameter values into the system equations do not exceed the limits set by the parameter deviations [2]. Because direct checking in multidimensional space is not easy, therefore in the case of polynomials it is possible to apply projection of stability boundaries on the plane of two selected uncertain parameters.

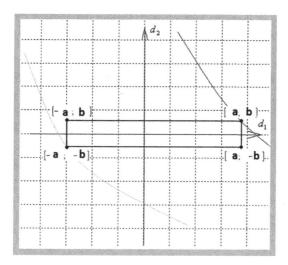

Fig. 6. The resulting rectangle created from the deviations of the values of uncertain parameters, sets the stability limits

Figure 6 shows a rectangle built up of the parameter deviations from their nominal values. To test stability, it is necessary to check whether or not the curves generated when changing the values of the quasi-polynomial parameters on the plane, intersect the rectangle. As the first value, we calculate the limit of complex zeros, that is we solve the system of equations of two variables, and then the limit of real zeros. Then the common part of both sets is determined, which gives the limit of stability of the entire system. We get a graph of three curves that intersect the rectangle formed from the parameter deviations or not. The values of those curves that intersect the rectangle are the values for which the system is stable (see Fig. 7).

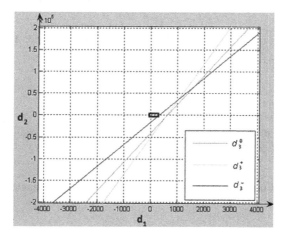

Fig. 7. Curve d_3^- intersects the deviation rectangle

Testing stability of dynamic systems by adopting the method of uncertain parameters and the method of delay independence are included in [4] and [5].

9   Stability of Positive Systems – Fundamental Assumptions

In order to conduct network analysis, we will introduce some fundamental theorems and definitions regarding positive systems. We will also present criteria for their stability [1].

Definition 1
Matrix $A = [a_{ij}] \in R^{nxn}$ is called Metzlner matrix if all its elements lying outside the main diagonal are non-negative, that is, $a_{ij} \geq 0$ for $i \neq j i, j = 1, 2, \ldots, n$

The positive continuous system is described by the equation

$$x' = Ax \, x(0) = x_0 \tag{1}$$

where A is a Metzler matrix.

The solution of Eq. (1) has the form

$$x(t) = e^{At} x_0 \tag{2}$$

Definition 2
A positive system (1) is called asymptotically stable if and only if Eq. (2) satisfies the following condition

$$\lim_{t \to \infty} x(t) = 0 \tag{3}$$

for each x.

Eigenvalues s_1, s_2, ..., s_n of matrix A are the roots of the equation $\det[Is - A] = 0$ whereas a set of these eigenvalues is called the spectrum of matrix A.

Theorem 1
The positive system (1) is asymptotically stable if and only if when the coefficients a_{ij} of the characteristic polynomial

$$w_A(s) = \det[Is - A] = s^n + a_{n-1}s^{n-1} + \ldots + a_1 s + a_0 \tag{4}$$

are positive ($a_{ij} > 0$) [1]

Quite often, the problem of positive system stability can be resolved by using the following sufficient condition of instability [1].

Definition 3
A positive system is unstable if at least one element on the main diagonal of matrix A is positive.

10   The Network Model

The gateway device is the intermediate device between the Ethernet network and the sensor network. Flow control mechanisms should be implemented in the gateway. They are not as restrictive as in conventional TCP. The packet flow window size does not have to be very large. In the sensor networks nowadays, data flow is fast enough because the data itself is relatively small. However, sometimes, the packets cannot be regained very quickly by the retransmission.

The window size is limited. It does not generate the appropriate number of duplicate acknowledgments pointing out to the packets outside the queue.

There exist some solutions which ensure reliable transport simply because the base station sends the entire window. The advantage of this approach is that there is no need to wait for confirmation of receipt of each packet.

Stability is a feature of dynamic systems. Computer network is an example of such a system. It can be described, like in [3], with differential equations. In TCP there is so-called Congestion Window. However, we need to modify this model to be applicable to the gates for sensor networks. Thus, if we assume that the base station (gateway) sends the whole window, then retransmissions will occur only after sending the entire window. Consequently, we should skip RTT time and replace it with propagation time. Following the feedback proposed in [3] the equations have a negative sign, which does not allow testing the system described by the equations for testing stability of positive systems. Yet, this feedback is not a must, as we will not regulate the transmission before the entire window is broadcast. Such that the equations should allow study the stability of positive systems.

According to the equations in the network model [3], we get equations

$$\delta W'(t) = -\frac{N}{R_0^2 C}(\delta W(t) + \delta W(t - R_0)) - \frac{1}{R_0^2 C}(\delta q(t) - \delta q(t - R_0))$$
$$-\frac{R_0 C^2}{2N^2}\delta p(t - R_0) \tag{5}$$

$$\delta q'(t) = \frac{N}{R_0}\delta W(t) - \frac{1}{R_0}\delta q(t) \tag{6}$$

where:

q -   is an average queue in the gateway,
R -   is propagation time,
C -   denoted throughput,
p -   is probability of the lost packet,
N -   is a number of packets.

We aim to obtain a positive continuous system from Eqs. (5) and (6)

$$f(t - t_0) = f(t) - f'(t)t_0 - \frac{1}{2}f''(t)t_0^2 + \ldots \tag{7}$$

$$f(t - t_0) = f(t - t_0)^2, f(t - t_0) = t^2 - 2(t - t_0)t_0 - \frac{1}{2}2t_0^2$$
$$= (t - t_0)^2 \tag{8}$$

Then we have

$$\delta W'(t) = -\frac{1}{R_0 C}\delta q(t) + \frac{1}{R_0^2 C}\delta q(t) - \frac{1}{R_0^2}\delta q'(t)R_0$$
$$-\frac{N}{R_0^2 C}\delta W(t) + \frac{N}{R_0^2 C}\delta W'(t)R_0 - \frac{1}{2}\frac{R_0 C^2}{N^2}\left(\delta p(t) - \delta'(t)R_0\right) \tag{9}$$

$$\delta q'(t) = \frac{N}{R_0}\delta W(t) - \frac{1}{R_0}\delta q(t) \tag{10}$$

For $\delta W(t) = x_1(t)$, $\delta q(t) = x_2(t)$ we obtain

$$\begin{pmatrix} 1 - \frac{N}{R_0 C} & \frac{1}{R_0 C} \\ 0 & 1 \end{pmatrix}\begin{pmatrix} x_1'(t) \\ x_2'(t) \end{pmatrix} = \begin{pmatrix} -2\frac{N}{R_0^2 C} & 0 \\ \frac{N}{R_0} & -\frac{1}{R_0} \end{pmatrix}\begin{pmatrix} x_1(t) \\ x_2(t) \end{pmatrix}$$
$$+ \begin{pmatrix} -\frac{1}{2}\frac{R_0 C^2}{N^2}\left(\delta p(t) - \delta p'(t)R_0\right) \\ 0 \end{pmatrix} \tag{11}$$

Now we compute inverse matrix

$$\begin{pmatrix} 1 - \frac{N}{R_0 C} & \frac{1}{R_0 C} \\ 0 & 1 \end{pmatrix}^{-1} = \begin{pmatrix} \frac{1}{1 - \frac{N}{R_0 C}} & -\frac{R_0 C}{1 - \frac{N}{R_0 C}} \\ 0 & 1 \end{pmatrix} \tag{12}$$

we multiply both sides of Eq. (11) by (12) and obtain

$$\begin{pmatrix} x_1'(t) \\ x_2'(t) \end{pmatrix} = \begin{pmatrix} -\frac{3N}{\left(1 - \frac{N}{R_0 C}\right)R_0^2 C} & \frac{1}{\left(1 - \frac{N}{R_0 C}\right)R_0^2 C} \\ \frac{N}{R_0} & -\frac{1}{R_0} \end{pmatrix}\begin{pmatrix} x_1(t) \\ x_2(t) \end{pmatrix}$$
$$+ \begin{pmatrix} -\frac{1}{2}\frac{R_0 C^2}{N - \frac{N^2}{R_0}}\left(\delta p(t) - \delta p'(t)R_0\right) \\ 0 \end{pmatrix} \tag{13}$$

$$\begin{pmatrix} x_1'(t) \\ x_2'(t) \end{pmatrix} = A \begin{pmatrix} x_1(t) \\ x_2(t) \end{pmatrix} + B \tag{14}$$

$$\lim_{t \to \infty} W(t) = 0 \tag{15}$$

We assume that the coefficients of Eq. (14) are positive, that is $B > 0$, and that the matrix A is a Metzlner matrix. As we can see, the window size decreases with the transmission time, thus we can say that we have constructed a positive system model

$$A = \begin{pmatrix} -\frac{3N}{\left(1-\frac{N}{R_0 C}\right) R_0^2 C} & \frac{1}{\left(1-\frac{N}{R_0 C}\right) R_0^2 C} \\ \frac{N}{R_0} & -\frac{1}{R_0} \end{pmatrix} \tag{16}$$

Matrix A meets Definition 1 and is a Metzlner matrix because all its elements lying outside the main diagonal are non-negative that is $a_{ij} \geq 0$.

11 Analysis of the Results

If we assume that the number of packets sent and received is a known number for a given gateway, the final result is affected by the propagation time of the given network and its capacity (throughput). In matrix A, the elements outside the main diagonal must be positive, that is

$$a_{21} = \left(1 - \frac{N}{R_0 C}\right) R_0^2 C \geq 0 \tag{17}$$

And

$$a_{12} = \frac{N}{R_0} \geq 0 \tag{18}$$

If the network traffic is smooth, then the inequality (18) is always satisfied, while in the inequality (17) the result depends on the first factor of the product, because the second factor is always positive. After transformation, we get inequality

$$\frac{R_0 C - N}{R_0 C} \geq 0 \tag{19}$$

Then we have

$$R_0 C \geq N \tag{20}$$

Assuming that propagation time is a fixed value, it looks like the link capacity exceeds the number of packets sent through the network of a given window size. Following Definition 3 it shows that the positive system is unstable if at least one element on the main diagonal of matrix A is positive. In our case this is not the case, therefore we can say that Eq. (14) describing the particular configuration of the WLAN network is a continuous positive system, which is an asymptotically stable system.

12 Conclusion and Future Work

Determining stability limits of dynamic systems will allow designing wireless or sensor networks as more efficient, faster and resistant to errors related to imperfections of transmission media. Application of the equations proposed in the paper to the IoT or IIoT networks will allow these technologies to be improved.

Our model proposed meets the new challenges from the perspective that it shows how to set the parameters for particular network to ensure its stability in order to achieve the performance quality required for the environment where it is planned to work.

For the future, computer network models with queuing algorithms will be analyzed even further. These studies will cover sensitivity of stability to changes in network parameters and how to improve the environment of the network to maintain its stability depending on other methods used and depending on the type of queuing.

The research will also address the networks based on the UDP protocol. We will create another mathematical model of the network and test it for stability under some specific environment requirements. We will try to analyze the UDP-based network and compare it to the TCP-based model. Then, we will propose some new solutions for the IoT and IIoT infrastructure.

References

1. Kaczorek, T.: Positive 1D and 2D Systems. Communication and Control Engineering, p. 273. Springer, Heidelberg (2002). https://doi.org/10.1007/978-1-4471-0221-2
2. Buslowicz, M.: Robust stability of positive continous-time linear systems with delays. Int. J. Math. Comput. Sci. **20**(4), 665–670 (2010)
3. Hollot, C.V., Misra, V., Towsley, D., Gong, W.B.: Analysis and design of controllers for AQM routers supporting TCP flows. IEEE Syst. Control Methods Commun. Netw. **49**(6), 945–959 (2002)
4. Klamka, J., Tancula, J..: Examination of robust stability of computer networks. In: 6-th Conference Performance Modelling and Evaluation of Heterogeneous Networks. Institute of Theoretical and Applied Informatics of the Polish Academy of Sciences, Zakopane (2012)
5. Mizera-Pietraszko J., Tancula J., Huk M.: Improving scalability of web applications based on stability of the network with the use of controller PI. In: CYBCONF, p. 520. IEEE Computer Society, Gdynia (2015)
6. Farrell, S.: Low-Power Wide Area Network (LPWAN) Overview. IETF, Rfc 8376, Dublin, Ireland (2018)
7. Cheong, P.S., Bergs, J., Hawinkel, Ch., Famaey, J.: Comparison of LoRaWAN classes and their power consumption. In: 2017 IEEE Symposium on Communications and Vehicular Technology (SCVT). IEEE Computer Society (2017)

8. Elkhodr, M., Shahrestani, S., Cheung, H.: Emerging wireless technologies in the Internet of things: a comparative study. IJWMN. Preprint ArXiv (2016) https://doi.org/10.5121/ijwmn.2016.8505

9. ZigBee specification: Zigbee Alliance, ZigBee Standards Organization, Document No. 053474r20, San Ramon, CA, p. 620 (2012)

10. LoRaWAN - What is it? A technical overview of LoRa and LoRaWAN. LoRa Alliance, Technical Marketing Group, p. 20 (2015)

11. Kochhar, A., Kaur, P., Singh, P., Sharma, S.: Protocols for wireless sensor networks: a survey. J. Telecommun. Inform. Technol. 1, 77–87 (2018)

12. Mikhaylov, K., Petaejaejaervi, J., Haenninen, T.: Analysis of capacity and scalability of the LoRa low power wide area network technology. In: Proceedings of the European Wireless 2016 22th European Wireless Conference, Oulu, Finland (2016)

13. Capuzzo, M., Magrin, D., Zanella, A.: Confirmed traffic in LoRaWAN: pitfalls and countermeasures. In: Proceedings of the 2018 17th Annual Mediterranean Ad Hoc Networking Workshop (Med-Hoc-Net), Capri, Italy (2018)

14. Slabicki, M., Premsankar, G., Di Francesco, M.: Adaptive configuration of lora networks for dense IoT deployments. In: Proceedings of the 16th IEEE/IFIP Network Operations and Management Symposium (NOMS 2018), Taipei, Taiwan (2018)

15. Reynders, B., Wang, Q., Tuset-Peiro, P., Vilajosana, X., Pollin, S.: Improving reliability and scalability of LoRaWANs through lightweight scheduling. IEEE Internet Things J. 5, 1830–1842 (2018)

16. Oh, Y., Lee, J., Kim, C.K.: TRILO: A Traffic indication-based downlink communication protocol for LoRaWAN. Wirel. Commun. Mob. Comput. 2018, 14 (2018). https://doi.org/10.1155/2018/6463097. Article ID 6463097

Utility-Aware Participant Selection with Budget Constraints for Mobile Crowd Sensing

Shanila Azhar[1], Shan Chang[1(✉)], Ye Liu[1], Yuting Tao[1],
Guohua Liu[1], and Donghong Sun[2]

[1] Computer Science and Technology, Donghua University, Shanghai, China
{415029,yeliu,taoyuting}@mail.dhu.edu.cn,
{changshan,ghliu}@dhu.edu.cn
[2] Institute for Network Sciences and Cyberspace, Tsinghua University,
Beijing, China
sundonghong@tsinghua.edu.cn

Abstract. Mobile Crowd Sensing is an emerging paradigm, which engages ordinary mobile device users to efficiently collect data and share sensed information using mobile applications. The data collection of participants consumes computing, storage and communication resources; thus, it is necessary to give rewards to users who contribute their private data for sensing tasks. Furthermore, since the budget of the sensing task is limited, the Service Provider (SP) needs to select a set of participants such that the total utility of their sensing data can be maximized, and their bid price for sensing data can be satisfied without exceeding the total budget. In this paper, firstly, we claim that the total data utility of a set of participants within a certain area should be calculated according to the data quality of each participant and the location coverage of the sensing data. Secondly, a participant selection scheme has been proposed, which determines a set of participants with maximum total data utility under the budget constraint, and shows that it is a Quadratic Integer Programming problem. Simulations have been conducted to solve the selection problem. The Simulation results demonstrate the effectiveness of the proposed scheme.

Keywords: Mobile Crowd Sensing · Utility · Budget · Data quality · Incentive

1 Introduction

In recent years, there is an enormous increase in the usage of handheld smart devices (i.e. smartphones, PDAs, tablets, smartwatches, and music headsets, etc.). According to Ericsson, the total number of worldwide smartphone subscriptions has reached 7.9 billion in Q2 2019, and it grows around 3% year on year [1]. In addition to the cellular communication standards (3G/4G), these mobile devices support numerous communication technologies Wi-Fi 802.11a/b/g/n, NFC and Bluetooth). They also come with high-performance processors and several compact size embedded sensors (e.g. camera, microphone, GPS, barometer, ambient light, gyroscope, accelerometer, magnetometer, and digital compass, etc.) to gather sensing data (e.g. traffic situation, temperature, and

X. Chu et al. (Eds.): QShine 2019, LNICST 300, pp. 38–49, 2020.
https://doi.org/10.1007/978-3-030-38819-5_3

noise level, etc.) from surrounding [2]. The advancement and pervasive usage of such mobile devices give an emergence of a new sensing paradigm called Mobile Crowd Sensing (MCS). MCS encourages ordinary users to collect sensing data from surroundings by simply using their smartphones, and to share that data for facilitating a large number of new applications; e.g. traffic management, monitoring [3], health monitoring [4], public safety [5], and even psychological survey questionnaires [6]. In typical MCS scenarios, after a server publishes a sensing task, the interested mobile users register for a sensing task, and then the server will select a set of users to join in the task according to a pre-determined selection scheme. The most commonly used metric for selecting participants is the data quality, which is however not enough. It is desired that those data are sensed over the whole target sensing area instead of from the same or neighboring locations, to avoid bias results. In this paper, we propose a novel participant selection scheme named Utility-aware participant selection (UPS), which considers the following key factors.

First, during the participation activities of users, mobile devices consume resources, i.e., battery, computing power, giving identity or location, etc. Many users may not probably like to contribute in the sensing activity due to the time and cost of resources utilized. Therefore, an incentive mechanism is essential to apprehend active and reliable MCS sensing and to encourage enough number of users to report their precise sensed data [7, 8], and thus guarantee high-quality sensed data. Considering that the server budget for a certain sensing task is limited, it desires a mechanism that maximizes the utility of sensing data under the constraint of a budget.

Second, the quality of data is an essential factor in MCS. Low-quality data might affect the performance of SP, resulting distrustful MCS system. We use the quality of data in measuring the utility of the MCS system. If a mobile device user holds high-quality data at a reasonable price, the user has more chances to be selected as a participant of a sensing task.

Third, since most sensing tasks are location-dependent, locations from where the sensing data is collected also need to be considered. Thus, it is important for SP to monitor and gather data from participants present at different locations in a grid to attain data reliability, as selecting the participants nearby each other or near the center of the grid can lead to an inefficient MCS system. Therefore, we also measure the distances between the users to maximize the location coverage when calculating the total data utility, as the farther the distance of participants from each other, the wider will be the area covered in a grid.

We define the total sensing data utility of a participant set, the value of which relates to both data quality of sensing data, and the distances between participants. If the participants in the set are far away from each other and hold high-quality data as well, then their total data utility should be high. We formulate the problem of selecting a participant set as maximizing the total utility under the constraint that the total data price required does not exceed the budget. The main contributions of this paper include:

- We consider the importance of quality and location coverage of sensing data of participants and introduce a new definition of data utility.

- We considered the data utility, data price of mobile device users, and budget of sensing tasks into account and propose a novel utility-aware participant selection scheme, to maximize the total data utility under the constraint of a budget. We prove that the selection problem can be formulated by a Quadratic Integer Programming (QIP) problem.
- We conduct simulations to show the efficacy of the proposed scheme. Simulation results depict that our scheme can achieve good performance in terms of the maximized data utility within the satisfactory budget cost.

The remainder of this paper is organized as: In Sect. 2 we discussed some related work. In Sect. 3, we present our proposed MCS system model. In Sect. 4 we give the problem formulation. In Sect. 5, we describe the performance evaluation and simulation setup and results. Finally, Sect. 6 concludes our work.

2 Related Work

Many of the participants' recruitment schemes in the MCS system have been investigated. The selection scheme plays an extensively important role in the success of any MCS system. The high density of smartphone users in an area, allows the MCS system to select a set of participants and result in better performance. To achieve high-quality data, a simple solution is to select as many participants as possible [9].

Numerous systems and experimental studies show the experimental study on the MCS coverage area and the general structure of participant recruitment [10]. *Chon et al.* [11] has performed an experimental study on the scaling and coverage properties and show likely results that MCS can provide relatively high coverage levels especially given area with large size. Besides, many theoretical studies on different sensing task allocation and participant selection problems have some tradeoffs of task completed, sensing cost, efficiency, and user incentive [12, 13].

Other researchers focused on the incentive mechanisms and auction methods for rewards and biding, respectively, to motivate and ensure the contribution of participants, also it encourages them to sense and send good quality data. Sun *et al.* [14] designed a reputation aware incentive mechanism to get the maximum weighted social welfare of the system and guarantee the individual rationality and truthfulness. Lee et al. [15] proposed an iterative reverse auction-based incentive mechanism, where mobile users sell their sensed data to the service provider with their demanded bid price. Chen et al. [16] used a double auction method in incentive mechanism for smartphone users as well as for sensing multiple tasks. Jaimes *et al.* [17] used the reverse auction method and considered the smartphone users covering location information to select the participants, and considered the budget limits of a service provider. Feng *et al.* [18] also used reverse auction in incentive mechanism design and considered the location information.

Most of the participants' recruitment schemes have the same purposes to develop a cost-effective selection scheme with high user density. These schemes require auction methods to assign or negotiate incentives with smartphone participants [19]. However,

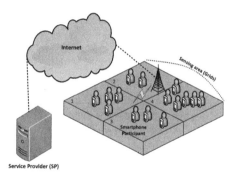

Fig. 1. MCS system.

until now the quality of utility and the sensing data from recruiting participants is still neglected. We considered these challenging parameters in our work.

3 System Model

We consider the MCS system as shown in Fig. 1. The service provider SP intends to collect the data in an area through the contribution of the set of mobile participants. SP announces the sensing task through mobile Apps. Mobile device users, who choose to conduct sensing task download and install these Apps and participate in the sensing process. The entire sensing area is divided into M grids denoted by set $G = \{g_1, g_2 \ldots, g_M\}$. In a grid $g_k(1 \leq k \leq M)$, the number of users interested to participate in the sensing task is n_k, and a mobile device user $P_i(1 \leq i \leq n_k)$ is associated with numerous attributes.

- Bid price b_i: which is the payment/reward that participant P_i hopes to receive from SP for conducting a sensing task.
- Data quality q_i: which reflects the accuracy and truthfulness of sensed data provided by P_i at a certain location. SP assigns sensing tasks to users based on their report of quality of data. The data quality affects the performance of MCS systems, low-quality data can degrade the efficiency of SP and the reliability of the MCS system.
- Location l_i: which is the precise location where P_i conducts sensing tasks.

We give Fig. 2 to illustrate our MCS model. It depicts the main activities performed during the entire sensing process. The MCS model comprises two major modules; Service provider (SP) and Mobile Participants (P_i). Following steps illustrate the step by step MCS sensing process labeled above in our sensing model (assuming all interested participants already have necessary Apps on their devices);

- The SP advertises a sensing task in a region and intends to recruit a set of participants within the region.
- Mobile device users interested in sensing tasks within the vicinity send a registration request to SP and announces SP about their locations, data qualities and bid price.

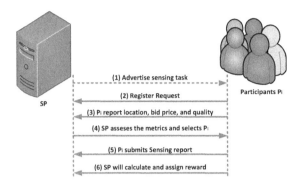

Fig. 2. System model for the MCS system.

- SP selects the subset of participants using a global algorithm satisfying the constraints of bid price and budget.
- Winning set of participants submits the sensing report.
- SP assesses the submitted data reports, and assign rewards to the participants.

4   Participant Selection

To guarantee high-quality MCS applications, the SP desires to collect sensing data with high utility. Since the budget of a sensing task is limited, it is impossible to recruit all participants who are interested in the task. Thus, the primary objective of SP is to attain maximum data utility within a limit of the total Budget. We also argue that the utility of data is not only related to the quality of sensing data but also the location where the data are sensed. Given a set of participants, it is desired that their data are high-quality and cover the overall area that needs to be monitored. Thus, we introduce a novel definition of the utility of data from a participant set.

Definition 1. The Utility of Data of a Participant Set W can be measured as:

$$U_W = \sum_{P_i \in W} q_i * \sum_{\substack{i \neq j \\ P_i, P_j \in W}} d_{ij}, \text{ where } d_{ij} = \left\| (l_i - l_j)^2 \right\| \tag{1}$$

In the definition, we consider q_i to represent the quality of data submitted by the participants and d_{ij} denotes the Euclidean distance between the participant P_i and P_j, because we intend to recruit those participants that have high-quality data and also we aim to select those participants that are not located in the same place. For instance, if two users with high data quality are selected, but both are near to the same location, it will not assure high-quality data from the entire grid. Instead, we want participants to be distributed all over the grid to maximize the distance between them and achieve data reports from locations at farther distances in a grid. We give the following example to better explain Data Utility:

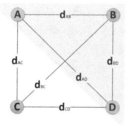

Fig. 3. Participants $\{A, B, C, D\}$ w.r.t their distances from each other.

Let's consider, SP decides to select participants A, B, and D as shown in Fig. 3. The Data Utility of the participant set $\{A, B, D\}$ achieved for this selection can be formulated by substituting it in Eq. (1) and expressed as;

$$U_{ABD} = q_A * (d_{AB} + d_{AD}) + q_B * (d_{BA} + d_{BD}) + q_D * (d_{DA} + d_{DB})$$
$$= d_{AB} * (q_A + q_B) + d_{BD} * (q_B + q_D) + d_{AD} * (q_A + q_D)$$

Thus, we formulate the participant selection problem as follows:

Definition 2. For a set of participants W (containing n participants), given the bid price b_i and data quality q_i of each participant P_i, and the constraints of budget C, the participant selection problem can be formulated as the following optimization problem;

$$W' = arg_{W' \in \Pi} max \sum_{P_i \in W'} U$$

$$\sum_{P_i \in W'} b_i < C$$

Where, W' is a winning set of participants to perform a sensing task, and Π is the possible set of participants to perform the sensing task.

We find that the above problem can be rewritten as a Quadratic Integer Programming (QIP) problem. The objective of the QIP is to find an n-dimensional vector x, that will

$$maximize \frac{1}{2} x^T H x$$

$$subject \ to \ Bx \leq C,$$

$$x \in \{0, 1\}$$

Each dimension of x is an indicator to show whether the corresponding participant in W is selected as a participant for the sensing task. If $x_i = 1$, it means that P_i is selected, otherwise, P_i is unselected. x^T denotes the vector transpose of x. H is an $n \times n$-dimensional symmetric matrix, in which $h_{i,j}$ (the element on the i-th row and j-th

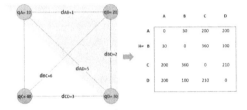

Fig. 4. The quality of each participant in W, and the distances among them, and the corresponding matrix H.

column) can be calculated by $h_{i,j} = d_{ij} * (q_i + q_j)$, i.e., the sum of data quality of participant P_i and P_j times the distance between them. A is an n-dimensional vector to represent the bid price of each participant, i.e., $B = [b_1, b_2, \ldots, b_n]$, and C is the total budget. Consider the above example again. The set of participants is $W = \{A, B, C, D\}$, the quality of each participant, and the distances between any two participants are shown in Fig. 4. Then, we have

$$
H = \begin{bmatrix}
0 & 30 & 200 & 200 \\
30 & 0 & 360 & 100 \\
200 & 360 & 0 & 210 \\
200 & 100 & 210 & 0
\end{bmatrix}
$$

Assume that SP selects $W' = \{A, B, D\}$, i.e., $x^T = [1 \quad 1 \quad 0 \quad 1]$, then we can compute

$$
U_{W'} = \frac{1}{2} x^T H x = \frac{1}{2}[(30 + 200) + (30 + 100) + (0) + (200 + 100)] = 330
$$

The budget C is 0.8, and $B = [0.1, 0.2, 0.3, 0.4]$, thus we can verify that

$$
Bx = [0.1 \quad 0.2 \quad 0.3 \quad 0.4] * \begin{bmatrix} 1 \\ 1 \\ 0 \\ 1 \end{bmatrix} = 0.6 < 0.8
$$

It means the total SP expenses do not exceed the budget, i.e., the budget constraint is satisfied.

It is known that the QIP problem is NP-hard [20], which means that the optimal set of winning participants and the maximum data utility cannot be solved in polynomial time. Thus, we adopt a branch and bound algorithm proposed by Körner [21], to find an approximate optimal solution.

5   Performance Evaluation

In this section, to evaluate the performance of our scheme, extensive simulations have been conducted in terms of the optimum data utility with the budget constraints of SP. First, we compare the UPS scheme with the random selection method to show the superiority of our QIP solution; later, we analyze the performance trend for the varying number of mobile device users and the varying number of grids, respectively.

5.1   Simulation Setup

We consider the MCS system in which the whole sensing area is a 10 km × 10 km square. This square was further divided into several square grids. In the area, we randomly generate 100 mobile device users, i.e., they are randomly located in grids, and the distances between them are measured. The data quality of a user and the bid price of data both are real values between 0 and 1, and the budget of a sensing task is set as a real value between 10 and 50. We generate bid price and quality of sensing data of each participant using uniform distribution. Table 1 summarizes the settings of parameters in our simulations.

Table 1. Simulation parameters

Simulation area (km)	10 × 10
Number of Grids	4 to 100
Total no. of randomly generated users	10 to 100
Total budget C	$10 < C < 50$
Data quality q_j	$0 < q_j < 1$
Bid price b_j	$0 < b_j < 1$

5.2   Performance Comparison

We compare the UPS scheme with the following random selection scheme.

- **Random Selection Scheme:** Initially, we randomly select one mobile user and check the claimed bid price, if the bid price is smaller than the budget; we again randomly select another user and add it into the target group of participants, and compute the total bid price to see if the total bid price is still smaller than budget. We do it several times until the total bid price is larger than the budget when the bid price exceeds the limit the selection procedure is ended.

For the UPS we randomly generated users and consider the bid price, location, and quality of sensing data submitted by each participant. We run the simulation 10 round times and calculate the total utility achieved by UPS and Random selection. Figure 5 shows the utility curve of both the schemes for 10 rounds. The x-axis and y-axis represent the number of rounds and the total utility, respectively. It can be seen that the

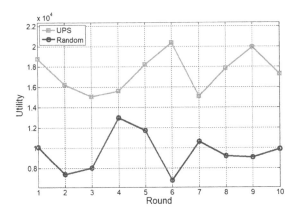

Fig. 5. Achieved utilities of UPS and random selection in 10 rounds.

UPS achieves much larger utility values in all rounds comparing with the random selection scheme.

5.3 Impact on Utility Due to Number of Participants

Figure 6 shows the impact of an increasing number of mobile users on the utility. In this set of simulations, we consider the effect of a larger number of users on the utility in association with the Budget range. The x-axis and y-axis represent the number of participants and the utility, respectively. Where the number of mobile users increases in an area from 10 to 100 at a step of 10. We determine the utility for various ranges of the budget value, from 10 to 50. For the small number of users under a given budget, most of the users can be selected into the target group. As the number of users increases, for a lower budget more and more participants exclude from the target grid (as Fig. 6 shows for B = 10). However, for the higher budget value, it can support many more

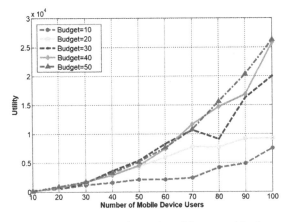

Fig. 6. Utilities vs. numbers of participants and budgets.

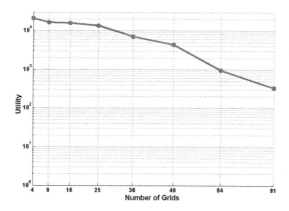

Fig. 7. Utilities vs. numbers of grids.

participants to be selected in the target group. We see at the value of budget 50, the utility increase significantly, even with 100 participants the majority of the users can still be selected into the group.

5.4 Impact on Utility Due to Number of Grids

In this set of simulations, we modify the number of grids in the simulation area. We divide the longitude and latitude directions of the area into 2 to 10 segments, respectively. Consequently, the corresponding numbers of grids increase as a squared factor from 2^2 to 10^2. We set the total budget in the whole area as 30, and evenly distribute the total budget to each grid. Figure 7 shows the impact of the numbers of grids on the utility. We can see that with an increase in the number of grids, the total utility of all grids decreases. It is because dividing the area into grids implies that each grid has its own local optimal set of participants. When we combine those sets into a whole participant set and calculate the total utility, the utility will be smaller than that of a global participant set obtained by solving a global QIP problem directly. Furthermore, more grids mean more participants might be excluded from participant sets, as more constraints of the budget should be satisfied. It should be noticed that a large grid means more users located in it. Thus, the computation complexity will be relatively high. To get a better trade-off between the computational complexity and the utility, a reasonable number of grids are 5^2.

6 Conclusion

Taking optimization of the data utility into consideration, a novel scheme for participant selection has been presented to collect the well-measured sensing data from the set of participants. The selection scheme significantly improved the participant recruitment process by assessing the data quality of the contributed data and their sensing location. Besides, the total budget of the MCS was stabilized by the bid price constraint. The evaluation of scheme performance was carried out by comparing the UPS scheme with a random selection scheme, determining the impact of the number of participants on the utility, and the impact of the grids on the utility. Furthermore, the presented results significantly validated the effectiveness of the proposed scheme in terms of utility, quality of data, and budget restraint.

In the end, this work opens some research directions for the future, we can customize it with other auction methods, or incentive mechanisms, etc. Also, the integration of reputation assignments in the MCS system can ensure and encourage a more refined selection of participants.

Acknowledgement. This work was supported in part by the National Natural Science Foundation of China (Grant No. 61972081, 61672151, 61772340, 61420106010), National Key Research and Development Project (Grant No. 2016QY12Z2103-2), Shanghai Rising-Star Program (Grant No.17QA1400100), National Key R&D Program of China (Grant No. 2018YFC1900700), Shanghai Municipal Natural Science Foundation (Grant No. 18ZR1401200), the Fundamental Research Funds for the Central Universities (Grant No. EG2018028), DHU Distinguished Young Professor Program and 2017 CCF-IFAA Research Fund.

References

1. Ericsson: Ericsson Mobility Report, pp. 1–3, August 2019
2. Lane, N.D., Miluzzo, E., Lu, H., Peebles, D., Choudhury, T., Campbell, A.T.: A survey of mobile phone sensing. IEEE Commun. Mag. **48**(9), 140–150 (2010)
3. Wang, X., et al.: A city-wide real-time traffic management system: enabling crowdsensing in social internet of vehicles. IEEE Commun. Mag. **56**(9), 19–25 (2018)
4. Kalogiros, L.A., Lagouvardos, K., Nikoletseas, S., Papadopoulos, N., Tzamalis, P.: Allergymap: a hybrid mHealth mobile crowdsensing system for allergic diseases epidemiology: a multidisciplinary case study. In: 2018 IEEE International Conference on Pervasive Computing and Communications Workshops (PerCom Workshops), pp. 597–602. IEEE, March 2018
5. Roitman, H., Mamou, J., Mehta, S., Satt, A., Subramaniam, L.V.: Harnessing the crowds for smart city sensing. In: Proceedings of the 1st International Workshop on Multimodal Crowd Sensing, pp. 17–18. ACM, November 2012
6. Schobel, J., Pryss, R., Reichert, M.: Using smart mobile devices for collecting structured data in clinical trials: results from a large-scale case study. In: 2015 IEEE 28th International Symposium on Computer-Based Medical Systems, pp. 13–18. IEEE, June, 2015
7. Yang, D., Xue, G., Fang, X., Tang, J.: Crowdsourcing to smartphones: incentive mechanism design for mobile phone sensing. In: Proceedings of the 18th Annual International Conference on Mobile Computing and Networking, pp. 173–184. ACM, August 2012
8. Jaimes, L., Vergara-Laurens, I., Labrador, M.A.: A location-based incentive mechanism for participatory sensing systems with budget constraints. In: Proceedings of the IEEE International Conference on Pervasive Computing and Communications (PerCom 2012), pp. 103–108, March 2012
9. Mendez, D., Labrador, M., Ramachandran, K.: Data interpolation for participatory sensing systems. Pervasive Mob. Comput. **9**(1), 132–148 (2013)
10. Reddy, S., Estrin, D., Srivastava, M.: Recruitment framework for participatory sensing data collections. In: Floréen, P., Krüger, A., Spasojevic, M. (eds.) Pervasive 2010. LNCS, vol. 6030, pp. 138–155. Springer, Heidelberg (2010). https://doi.org/10.1007/978-3-642-12654-3_9

11. Chon, Y., Lane, N.D., Kim, Y., Zhao, F., Cha, H.: Understanding the coverage and scalability of place-centric crowdsensing. In: Proceedings of the 2013 ACM International Joint Conference on Pervasive and Ubiquitous Computing, pp. 3–12. ACM, September 2013
12. Zhao, D., Ma, H., Liu, L.: Energy-efficient opportunistic coverage for people-centric urban sensing. Wirel. Netw. **20**(6), 1461–1476 (2014)
13. Xiong, H., Zhang, D., Wang, L., Chaouchi, H.: EMC 3: energy-efficient data transfer in mobile crowdsensing under full coverage constraint. IEEE Trans. Mob. Comput. **14**(7), 1355–1368 (2014)
14. Sun, J., Pei, Y., Hou, F., Ma, S.: Reputation-aware incentive mechanism for participatory sensing. IET Commun. **11**(13), 1985–1991 (2017)
15. Lee, J.S., Hoh, B.: Sell your experiences: a market mechanism based incentive for participatory sensing. In: 2010 IEEE International Conference on Pervasive Computing and Communications (PerCom), pp. 60–68. IEEE, March 2010
16. Chen, C., Wang, Y.: SPARC: strategy-proof double auction for mobile participatory sensing. In: 2013 International Conference on Cloud Computing and Big Data, pp. 133–140. IEEE, December 2013
17. Jaimes, L.G., Vergara-Laurens, I., Labrador, M.A.: A location-based incentive mechanism for participatory sensing systems with budget constraints. In: 2012 IEEE International Conference on Pervasive Computing and Communications, pp. 103–108. IEEE, March 2012
18. Feng, Z., Zhu, Y., Zhang, Q., Ni, L.M., Vasilakos, A.V.: TRAC: truthful auction for location-aware collaborative sensing in mobile crowdsourcing. In: IEEE INFOCOM 2014-IEEE Conference on Computer Communications, pp. 1231–1239. IEEE, April 2014
19. He, S., Shin, D.H., Zhang, J., Chen, J.: Toward optimal allocation of location dependent tasks in crowdsensing. In: IEEE INFOCOM 2014-IEEE Conference on Computer Communications, pp. 745–753. IEEE, April 2014
20. Billionnet, A., Elloumi, S., Plateau, M.C.: Quadratic 0–1 programming: tightening linear or quadratic convex reformulation by use of relaxations. RAIRO-Oper. Res. **42**(2), 103–121 (2008)
21. Körner, F.: Integer quadratic optimization. Eur. J. Oper. Res. **19**(2), 268–273 (1985)

Toward Optimal Resource Allocation for Task Offloading in Mobile Edge Computing

Wenzao Li[1,2(✉)], Yuwen Pan[1], Fangxing Wang[2], Lei Zhang[3], and Jiangchuan Liu[2]

[1] College of Communication Engineering,
Chengdu University of Information Technology, Chengdu, China
lwz@cuit.edu.cn, yuwenpan@163.com

[2] School of Computing Science, Simon Fraser University, Burnaby, Canada
{fangxinw,jcliu}@sfu.ca

[3] College of Computer Science and Software Engineering, Shenzhen University,
Shenzhen, China
leizhang@szu.edu.cn

Abstract. Task offloading emerges as a promising solution in Mobile Edge Computing (MEC) scenarios to not only incorporate more processing capability but also save energy. There however exists a key conflict between the heavy processing workloads of terminals and the limited wireless bandwidth, making it challenging to determine the computing placement at the terminals or the remote servers. In this paper, we aim to migrate the most suitable offloading tasks to fully obtain the benefits from the resourceful cloud. The problem in this task offloading scenario is modeled as an optimization problem. Therefore, a Genetic Algorithm is then proposed to achieve maximal user selection and the most valuable task offloading. Specifically, the cloud is pondered to provide computing services for as many edge wireless terminals as possible under the limited wireless channels. The base stations (BSs) serve as the edge for task coordination. The tasks are jointly considered to minimize the computing overhead and energy consumption, where the cost model of local devices is used as one of the optimization objectives in this wireless mobile selective schedule. We also establish the multi-devices task offloading scenario to further verify the efficiency of the proposed allocating schedule. Our extensive numerical experiments demonstrate that our allocating scheme can effectively take advantage of the cloud server and reduce the cost of end users.

Keywords: Mobile edge computing · Task offloading · Genetic algorithm · Computing overhead · Allocating schedule

1 Introduction

The recent success of Internet-of-Things (IoT) [11,12,17] facilitates an explosive increase of mobile devices as well as computing tasks. It is reported that more than 7 billion resource-limited devices are connected in the Internet of Things (IoT) in 2018 [1]. These interconnected devices further integrate as an intelligent information system and call for more smart applications [18]. Mobile devices are usually assigned with a variety of computing tasks for processing, while they mostly suffer from the constrained power supply and the limited processing capabilities [22]. Edge-cloud computing provides a promising opportunity by offloading the computing tasks of mobile devices to nearby servers to reduce the computation cost and save energy [14]. The limitation of shared wireless bandwidth however restricts the entire task offloading, only allowing a portion of tasks to move to the cloud servers [16]. The task offloading scheme can effectively reduce the computational burden for end devices. However, how to select an offloading task will affect the computing energy, the number of tasks, and bandwidth utilization. Generally, given the diverse optimization objectives, massive tasks and multiple constraints, such a resource allocation problem is quite complicated. To this end, we introduce a genetic algorithm that considers both the channel resource allocation and task cost to address this problem.

A 5G base station (BS) usually owns hundreds of ports, which can support to send and receive signals from many users at once on the same frequency [15]. The high density of users in the covered area of a BS will result in limited data processing given the limited wireless bandwidth. Then, we maximize the number of computation offloading tasks as well as tasks with a high cost in a period. We thus propose a genetic algorithm, named computation offloading with Genetic Algorithm (COGA), to solve the selected tasks of computation offloading in MEC. It can achieve superior task selection, computing cost, and energy efficiency during a period.

The contribution of this paper is summarized as follows. The paper models the computation offloading problem in the MEC scenario as an optimization problem. Energy consumption, computing latency and the number of tasks are jointly considered in our design purpose. Therefore, we propose a genetic algorithm COGA, which is based on a unified objective function to optimize multiple targets for concerned issues. We further propose Enhanced COGA, which considers the features of the computation offloading scenario to achieve smart offloading and energy saving. Numerical simulations demonstrate the superiority of our solution.

The rest of the paper is organized as follows. We present the computation offloading model in Sect. 2. Section 3 introduces the system model. Then, we propose a genetic algorithm introduced in Sect. 4. In Sect. 5, we present the numerical experiments and discuss the results to evaluate the performance. We finally discuss the related work in Sect. 6, and conclude paper in Sect. 7.

2   Proposed Computation Offloading System Model

The computation offloading is a complex problem, and the considered factors are inconsistent in different system models [5,13]. Given that those devices are all connected to a BS, carrying out the offloading strategy at a BS is a simple way

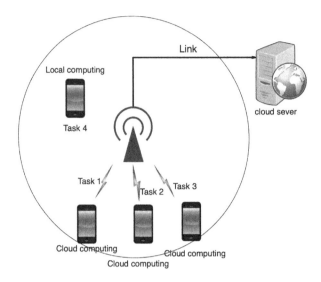

Fig. 1. The task offloading in multi-user MEC system

to reduce the terminal cost. We also consider the set $\mathcal{U} = \{u_1, u_2, ..., u_i, ..., u_{N_t}\}$ as the covered terminals by a BS. And these devices belong to a BS $\mathcal{B}$, which provides the wireless channel to the set $\mathcal{U}$. We assume that the set $\mathcal{U}$ will not be changed during the offloading period $\mathcal{T}$ and each device has one task offloading requirement. Generally, the number of devices and channel gain may be changed due to the mobility of users covered by the base station. Each device in the scenario owns more than one task for computation offloading and it will be further discussed in future works. Therefore, the task set $\mathcal{T}_{task} = \{L_1, L_2, ..., L_i, ..., L_{N_t}\}$, where $L_i \in u_i$. Each covered device only has one task in the model and the task of device is required to offload to the near cloud by centralized control of the BS. As shown in Fig. 1, the task offloading scenario has four important parts, the offloading tasks, the wireless channel, the local users and the remote cloud.

The communication mode, mobile device and cloud play as pivotal roles in the MEC. These models are introduced in detail as follows.

2.1 Communication Model

In the OFDMA communication system, the total bandwidth is partitioned into several sub-channels. The OFDMA-based cellular network can adopt the full-duplex (FD) ratio technology and FD based BS supports multiple half-duplex (HD) users [6]. The numerous subcarriers of each sub-channel can be assigned to a user in a centralized model. If the $g(i)$ represents the channel gain for mobile i, the channel bandwidth is B, and the transmission power is S_U. We unified use N_0 presents the average noise power, it is usually considered as Gaussian channel noise. Then, the maximum transmission bit rate C_U can be calculated by equation

$$C_U = B * log_2(1 + \frac{g_U S_U}{N_0}), \tag{1}$$

where the C_U represents the maximum data rate. It means the maximum data transfer rate can be provided to BS covered users. But it is restrained by some specific parameters of BS. In actual situations, the actual data transfer rate $C_S(U)$ is very below the theoretical value of C_U. Although there is data conflicting in the same spectrum, it can be improved by the physic layer channel access schedule such as CS-MUD and SCMA [2,7]. From the Eq. (1), the limited transfer data rate may not satisfy the ultra dense devices to offload to the cloud. For the reason of task processing efficiency, the more tasks benefited from the remote cloud, the better in MEC scenarios.

2.2 Mobile Device Computation Model in Task Computation Offloading

The energy consumption and computing time in local device are frequently discussed [5,20], we assume that device i has only one task $L_i \triangleq (da_i, f_i^l)$, the f_i^l denotes the CPU cycles of mobile devices per second. Then the local computing time can described as

$$t_i^l = \frac{d_i}{f_i^l}, \tag{2}$$

where the t_i^l can also be understood as execution time or the execution cost of a terminal user. Then, the energy consumption can be described as

$$e_i^l = \mathcal{J}_i d_i, \tag{3}$$

where the $\mathcal{J}_i$ denotes the coefficient consumed energy per CPU cycle. If we transform this problem as the energy consumed per bit of CPU processing, we can describe the energy consumption as

$$\eta_i^l = \frac{\mathcal{P}_i t_i}{\mathcal{D}_i}, \tag{4}$$

where the $\mathcal{P}_i$ represents the CPU power consumption. The t_i denotes the processing time of task L_i and the $\mathcal{D}_i$ represents the number of processing data for the task L_i. From the (3) and (4), the processed amount of data or the number of CPU cycles for the task are proportional to energy consumption. Note that the CPU keeps the computing frequency in the processing period and it is difficult to accurately calculate the energy consumption per cycle due to the complicated work model of a CPU. Hence, the $\mathcal{J}_i$ can be understood as a coefficient of energy computing. After we establish the computing time and energy consumption model with (2) and (3), then the task cost of local user u_i can be defined as

$$\mathcal{C}_i^l = \lambda_t t_i^l + \lambda_e e_i^l, \tag{5}$$

where the λ_t and λ_e denote the weight parameters, which influence the optimization target for the concerned network indicators. If the system cares about the energy consumption, then it can set $\lambda_t < \lambda_e$ and the $\lambda_t, \lambda_e \in [0,1]$. It is the common processing way in the weight method.

2.3   Cloud Computing Model

The remote cloud is to consider to have sufficiency computing ability, and the computing energy has no constraint due to the power supply. Some studies focus on the overall operation reaching a reasonable balanced state. For instance, the task offloading need to satisfy $C_i^l < C_i^c$, where the C_i^c denotes the task computing cost in the cloud [5]. Some other studies do not only consider the computing capability of the remote cloud but also considers the capacity of the wireless channel. As shown in Subsect. 2.1, the channel capacity is limited by C_U and there are $\mathcal{M}$ sub-channels. Their respective bandwidths make up the available bandwidth B. To get the benefits of the cloud servers through the limited bandwidth which is a challenging question.

3   Distributed Computation Offloading in a BS

The proposed computation offloading has been discussed in this section. As represented in the prior section, a sub-channel is severed to user i. Therefore, the channel capacity can reach the maximum data rate as follow:

$$C_{\bar{s}}(i) = \lambda_\gamma \bar{B} * log_2(1 + \frac{g_i S_i}{N_0}). \tag{6}$$

The $\bar{B}$ represents the bandwidth of a sub-channel and λ_γ can be understood as channel utilization. Then we can formulated the channel data rate C_U as $C_U \geq \sum_{m=1}^{n} L_m(m)C_{\bar{s}}(m)$, where m denotes the determined offloading tasks. So the resource allocation problem under the constraints on the channel data rate can be formulated as follows:

$$\mathcal{Z}_{\mathcal{B}_m, \mathcal{B}_c} = \begin{pmatrix} \max\limits_{\mathcal{B}_m} f(\mathcal{B}_m) \\ \max\limits_{\mathcal{B}_c} f(\mathcal{B}_c) \end{pmatrix} = \begin{pmatrix} \max\limits_{\mathcal{B}_m} \sum_{m=1}^{n} L_i(m) * C_{\bar{s}}(m) \\ \max\limits_{\mathcal{B}_c} \sum_{m=1}^{n} L_i(m) * C_i^l(i) \end{pmatrix}$$

$$s.t. \quad C_U \geq \sum_{m=1}^{n} L_m(m)C_{\bar{s}}(m) \tag{7}$$

$$L_i \leq N_t, i \in N_t, C_i \leq C_{\bar{s}}(i)$$

The Eq. (7) describes the demand for task offloading, the purpose of the scenario requires that maximum tasks need to offload to the cloud, but it should face the limited bandwidth. And the compute offloading still needs to consider the energy efficiency $\sum_{i=1}^{m} e_i^l$ and the compute time $t \sum_{i=1}^{m} t_i^l$. In the model, the cloud computing capabilities are considered to be sufficient. Both the energy cost and computing time require the maximum value to reduce the burden of end-users. Obviously, this is a multi-objective optimization problem. And unfortunately, it is extremely challenging to obtain an optimal solution.

Then we need to make the decision of computation offloading. It can be considered that, which tasks should be selected to offloading. Similarly, the selected tasks should have the maximum cost. This strategy will minimize the overall burden of the terminals.

4   Task Computation Offloading Decision Based on Genetic Algorithm

In this section, the proposed optimized problem is formulated as the Eq. (7), and the offloading schedule is designed with a heuristic search method. To solve this challenging problem, this genetic algorithm focuses on closing the optimal performance.

4.1   Initialization Model

First, a matrix In is given to express the decision of computation offloading. The number of rows in the matrix represents the number of offloading decision combinations.

$$In = \begin{bmatrix} \delta_{1,1} & \delta_{1,2} & \cdots & \delta_{1,N_t} \\ \delta_{2,1} & \delta_{2,2} & \cdots & \delta_{2,N_t} \\ \cdots & \cdots & \cdots & \cdots \\ \delta_{m,1} & \delta_{m,2} & \cdots & \delta_{m,N_t} \end{bmatrix}, \tag{8}$$

where the δ_{ij} means the task number j, the each matrix row represents the offloading task order form set $\mathcal{T}_{task}$. The matrix is established by random way at the beginning, each task index is unique and $\delta_{ij} \in [1, N_t]$. Besides, the initial matrix is executed in each period t_p. The size of the row is $n = N_t$, which denotes the number of pending offloading tasks in the BS. And the fitness function $\psi_f(\bar{N}_t, \mathcal{C}_i^l)$ need to be given according to the optimized object

$$\psi_f(\bar{N}_t, \mathcal{C}_i^l) = \lambda_{\bar{N}_t}^f M(\bar{N}_t) + \lambda_{\mathcal{C}}^f M(\mathcal{C}_i^l), \tag{9}$$

where the $\lambda_{\bar{N}_t}^f$ and $\lambda_{\mathcal{C}}^f$ denotes the coefficient separately. The function of $M()$ is a mapping function, which can solve the problem of adding non-similar physical dimensions. They are mapped in $[0, \delta]$, then it can be compared within a quantified range. And the $\bar{N}_t$ represents the determined offloading tasks, which are taken values from the matrix row $\delta_{i,...}$. Additional, the $\mathcal{C}_i^l$ means the cost value of determined offloading tasks, which is described as the Eq. (5).

4.2   The Selection Processing of COGA

After the COGA establishes the matrix with random values. Then, the COGA will consist of four phases of operation: roulette algorithm, elite retention strategy, cross operation, and mutation operation.

Roulette Algorithm (RA): In RA, there are three steps for matrix reorganization. First, the fitness value of matrix In should be calculated as the set $f^v(i = 1, 2, 3..., m)$. Second, the survival probability $p_r(r_i)$ is calculated by

$$p_r(r_i) = \frac{f^v(r_i)}{\sum_{j=1}^{m} f^v(r_j)}. \tag{10}$$

Third, $p_r(r_i)$ is used to establish the array, then the m times selecting operations will establish a new matrix In_r.

Elite Retention Strategy (ERS): The ERS just selected a maximum fitness value of a row in In_r, the *best* row is kept as the $m + 1$ row. Thus, a new matrix In_e is established.

Cross Operation (CO): COGA randomly selects two rows of In_e (except the $m + 1$ row) for *crossing operation*. And it generates an index p, and $p \in \{p \in N | 1 \leq p \leq N_t\}$, then the two rows will change the values before $\delta_{p,...}$ between the two rows with distance one or two position. In addition, a crossing probability P_c, which is introduced in [3], can be described as

$$P_c = \begin{cases} max(P_c) - \frac{max(P_c) - min(P_c)*(\alpha - \beta)}{\delta' - \beta}, & \alpha > \beta, \\ max(P_c) & , \alpha \leq \beta \end{cases} \tag{11}$$

where $max(P_c)$ denote the maximum cross probability, and the $min(P_c)$ means the minimum cross probability. α represents the maximum fitness value of the two selected rows (the two orders of offloading decisions). β denotes the average of calculated fitness value for the whole matrix, and the δ' denotes the maximum calculated fitness value for the matrix In_e. If a randomly variable seed $S_d < P_c$, after CO, the new matrix In_c is established. It should be noted here that the task index should be unique in each row after CO. It can be achieved by traversing the task index.

Mutation Operation (MO): After the CO, we can get the new matrix In_c. The COGA operates the MO for each row of matrix In_c. First of all, the mutation probability P_m can be described as [3]

$$P_m = \begin{cases} max(P_m) - \frac{max(P_m) - min(P_m)*(\alpha - \beta)}{\delta' - \beta}, & \alpha > \beta, \\ max(P_m) & , \alpha \leq \beta \end{cases} \tag{12}$$

The variables is similar to the Eq. (11). The $max(P_m)$ represents the maximum mutation probability and the $min(P_m$ represents the minimum mutation probability. The $max(P_c)$, $min(P_c)$ is set as 0.9% and 0.6%, respectively. At the same time, $max(P_m)$, $min(P_m$ is set as 0.9 percent and 0.6%, respectively. Each row of in_m will process the MO by the probability P_m. If a row is determined to be mutated, randomly swap the positions of the two index in the row. Such a MO iterates through the first m rows of the entire matrix In_c.

After the MO, the row with the lowest fitness value will be deleted. Then, the new matrix In_m becomes $m * N_t$. The COGA will iterate until the fitness value is stable.

In the computation offloading scenario, the number of tasks may be relatively high in a BS covered area. The searching process will be lengthy. Therefore, the CO stage is redesigned to strengthen the dramatic changes in each row. In the CO stage of COGA, the cross operation just runs at once and it is regardless of the number of initial tasks. Hence, the CO times $\phi(m)$ is designed as

$$\phi(m) = \frac{m}{\lambda_b + \lambda_g \delta}. \tag{13}$$

where the λ_b and the λ_g are constant coefficients, the value of $\phi(m)$ is positively related to m. The δ represents a random seed. Then, the more dramatic CO leads to less convergence consumption times.

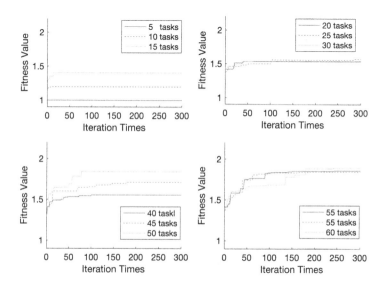

Fig. 2. Algorithm convergence under different task numbers

5   Simulation Results

We completed the proposed scenario and the COGA algorithm. Then, several simulation results are presented for evaluating the performance of the COGA strategy. In actual situations, mobile computing tasks vary in data size. The channel capacity of BS is also related to its own model. From the design principle of the algorithm, the size, number of tasks and the assumption of BS bandwidth do not affect the effectiveness of the proposed algorithm.

There are up to 60 mobile devices in a BS covered area, the channel gain is not considered in this scenario due to the principle of algorithm. The channel bandwidth $C_{\bar{U}} = 5\,\mathrm{MHz}$, the transmission power $S_i = 100\,\mathrm{mw}$ and the noise

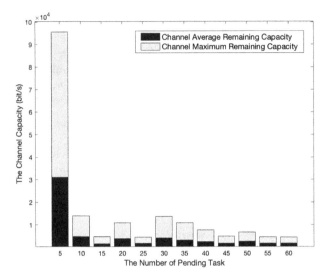

Fig. 3. The comparison of channel average remaining capacity and maximum remaining capacity

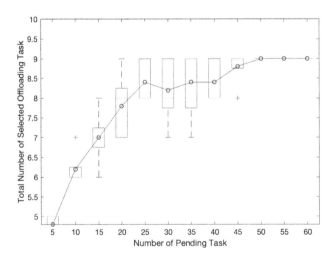

Fig. 4. The number of offloading task in different task density

$N_0 = -100\,\mathrm{dbm}$ [5]. In this scenario, each device owns a task for offloading computing requirements, the $\mathcal{J}_i = 8.9 * 10^{-12}\,\mathrm{J/cycle}$. The amount of offloading data size is randomly generated in the range of $(0.125 * 10^5, 0.175 * 10^5)\,\mathrm{bit/s}$. The coefficient λ_t and λ_e are set as 0.3, 0.7, separately. Since the task data is randomly generated, the COGA runs to select offloading tasks. To verify the validity of the method, each experiment is carried out five times. The performance should be tracked at four aspects in different task density: the convergence status, the remaining capacity of the channel, the offloading tasks and offloading cost of proposed GA algorithms.

To observe the convergence of the COGA, the fitness calculation process of twelve different number of task offloading scenarios are shown in Fig. 2. All of them can effective converge after a number of iterations. Besides, the more tasks have required the computation offloading, the more iterations are needed.

Figure 3 displays the average remaining capacity and maximum remaining capacity in different task density. When the limited channel capacity is calculated for 5 tasks, there is more capacity left due to the small data offloading requirements. From the results, the remaining capacity waves in a small range when the number of tasks increases. In the scene of intensive tasks, the remaining space is very small, therefore, it shows the effectiveness of residual capability control. If the channel capacity that can be used for task offloading is too small and the rate of all pending tasks are big sizes, then the remaining channel capacity will not change too much. We also give the results of the number of offloading tasks in different task density with the box figure.

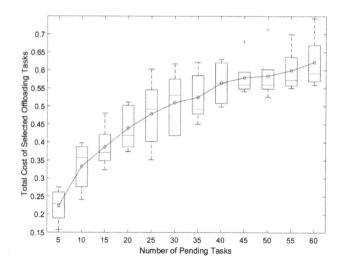

Fig. 5. The cost of offloading task in different task density

From the Fig. 4, the top horizontal line and the bottom horizontal line represents the maximum and minimum of 5 time's result, separately. The cycle denotes the average value, and the middle horizontal line means the medium number of tasks. The results are stable in the relatively intensive task scenes. It indicates that it near the best-optimized result in the current bandwidth situation. Similarly to the results in Fig. 4, the cost value of the proposed cost model also maintains a relatively high level in intensive task scenes. It presents that COGA has an outstanding optimization effect on the aspects of energy and computing time. However, both the task transmitting rate and the remaining bandwidth determine how many tasks are offloaded. The fewer the number of offloading tasks, the less the cost on the end-users must be reduced (Fig. 5).

6 Related Work

In the research areas of computation offloading, the proposed approaches aim to energy [8], latency [4] and joint consideration [9]. Zhao et al. [21] discussed the task scheduling based on the consideration of computing limitation in the edge cloud. The task offloading strategy aims to reduce task latency by coordinating the heterogeneous cloud model. Li et al. [10] aim to optimize the formulated cost model in multi-users scenarios by deep reinforcement learning (DRL) method [19]. The results also achieve the proposed design purpose. The resource allocation approach in MEC is one of the key questions, and there are more studies for whole network performance progress. You et al. [20] concentrate on energy consumption and computation latency at multi-user scenarios. The proposed algorithm was designed based on priority policy to reduce the search cost. In similar task offloading scenarios, Chen et al. [5] formulate the several computation decision making among devices as a game in MEC.

From some of the recent researches above, the computation offloading is a complex problem. Each method focuses on the different aspects of MEC systems. The optimized problem ignores the task numbers and decreases the maximum cost of terminal devices which are covered in the communication area of BS. Then we proposed the COGA to optimize the number of offloading tasks and computing cost in MEC.

7 Conclusion

The computation offloading is still a hot issue in MEC, and it is hard to determine the importance of the tasks in the absence of a specific scenario. With the rapid expansion of mobile applications, more and more small computing tasks will appear in the future. It is reasonably prophesied that task computation offloading will become more and more important in the ultra dense network. Therefore, we proposed the COGA computation offloading approach based on the genetic algorithm, which decides the task offloading and adjusts the mobile terminal cost for energy efficiency and computing resource under limited channel capacity. Then, we consider the intensive tasks in BS scenarios, then we redesigned the cross operation for more rapid convergence. After plenty of simulations, several results indicated that the proposed algorithm can effectively determine the offloading tasks. The method has the flexibility for optimized targets, it still has some aspects that have not yet been discussed. For some instances, To make the offloading decision in the continuous-time slot, or some tasks with a large amount of data can not be treated fairly. The valuable problems deserve further discussions in future work.

Acknowledgement. This research was supported by China Scholarship Council (CSC), Fund of Applied Basic Research Programs of Science and Technology Department (No. 2018JY0290). The work of Lei Zhang was supported in part by the National Natural Science Foundation of China under Grant 61902257. The work of Fangxin Wang and Jiangchuan Liu is supported by a Canada NSERC Discovery Grant.

References

1. August 2018. https://iot-analytics.com/state-of-the-iot-update-q1-q2-2018-number-of-iot-devices-now-7b/
2. Bockelmann, N., et al.: Massive machine-type communications in 5G: physical and MAC-layer solutions. IEEE Commun. Mag. **54**(9), 59–65 (2016)
3. Chen, R., Liang, C.Y., Hong, W.C., Gu, D.X.: Forecasting holiday daily tourist flow based on seasonal support vector regression with adaptive genetic algorithm. Appl. Soft Comput. **26**, 435–443 (2015)
4. Chen, S., Wang, Y., Pedram, M.: A semi-Markovian decision process based control method for offloading tasks from mobile devices to the cloud. In: 2013 IEEE Global Communications Conference (GLOBECOM), pp. 2885–2890. IEEE (2013)
5. Chen, X., Jiao, L., Li, W., Fu, X.: Efficient multi-user computation offloading for mobile-edge cloud computing. IEEE/ACM Trans. Netw. **24**(5), 2795–2808 (2015)
6. Di, B., Bayat, S., Song, L., Li, Y., Han, Z.: Joint user pairing, subchannel, and power allocation in full-duplex multi-user ofdma networks. IEEE Trans. Wirel. Commun. **15**(12), 8260–8272 (2016)
7. Du, Y., Dong, B., Chen, Z., Fang, J., Yang, L.: Shuffled multiuser detection schemes for uplink sparse code multiple access systems. IEEE Commun. Lett. **20**(6), 1231–1234 (2016)
8. Huang, D., Wang, P., Niyato, D.: A dynamic offloading algorithm for mobile computing. IEEE Trans. Wirel. Commun. **11**(6), 1991–1995 (2012)
9. Kwak, J., Kim, Y., Lee, J., Chong, S.: DREAM: dynamic resource and task allocation for energy minimization in mobile cloud systems. IEEE J. Sel. Areas Commun. **33**(12), 2510–2523 (2015)
10. Li, J., Gao, H., Lv, T., Lu, Y.: Deep reinforcement learning based computation offloading and resource allocation for MEC. In: 2018 IEEE Wireless Communications and Networking Conference (WCNC), pp. 1–6. IEEE (2018)
11. Liu, X., Cao, J., Yang, Y., Qu, W., Zhao, X., Li, K., Yao, D.: Fast rfidsensory data collection: trade-off between computation and communicationcosts. IEEE/ACM Trans. Netw. (2019)
12. Liu, X., Xie, X., Wang, S., Liu, J., Yao, D., Cao, J.: Efficient range queries for large-scale sensor-augmented RFID systems. In: EEE/ACM Trans. Netw. (TON) (2019, in press)
13. Mao, Y., You, C., Zhang, J., Huang, K., Letaief, K.B.: A survey on mobile edge computing: the communication perspective. IEEE Commun. Surv. Tutor. **19**(4), 2322–2358 (2017)
14. Mao, Y., Zhang, J., Song, S., Letaief, K.B.: Stochastic joint radio and computational resource management for multi-user mobile-edge computing systems. IEEE Trans. Wireless Commun. **16**(9), 5994–6009 (2017)
15. Nordrum, A., Clark, K., et al.: Everything you need to know about 5G. IEEE Spectrum (2017)
16. Satyanarayanan, M.: The emergence of edge computing. Computer **50**(1), 30–39 (2017)

17. Teli, S.R., Zvanovec, S., Ghassemlooy, Z.: Optical internet of things within 5G: applications and challenges. In: 2018 IEEE International Conference on Internet of Things and Intelligence System (IOTAIS), pp. 40–45. IEEE (2018)
18. Wang, F., Wang, F., Ma, X., Liu, J.: Demystifying the crowd intelligence in last mile parcel delivery for smart cities. IEEE Netw. **33**(2), 23–29 (2019)
19. Wang, F., et al.: Intelligent edge-assisted crowdcast with deep reinforcement learning for personalized QoE. In: IEEE INFOCOM 2019-IEEE Conference on Computer Communications, pp. 910–918. IEEE (2019)
20. You, C., Huang, K., Chae, H., Kim, B.H.: Energy-efficient resource allocation for mobile-edge computation offloading. IEEE Trans. Wirel. Commun. **16**(3), 1397–1411 (2016)
21. Zhao, T., Zhou, S., Guo, X., Niu, Z.: Tasks scheduling and resource allocation in heterogeneous cloud for delay-bounded mobile edge computing. In: 2017 IEEE International Conference on Communications (ICC), pp. 1–7. IEEE (2017)
22. Zhao, X., Zhao, L., Liang, K.: An energy consumption oriented offloading algorithm for fog computing. In: Lee, J.-H., Pack, S. (eds.) QShine 2016. LNICST, vol. 199, pp. 293–301. Springer, Cham (2017). https://doi.org/10.1007/978-3-319-60717-7_29

Goldilocks: Learning Pattern-Based Task Assignment in Mobile Crowdsensing

Jinghan Jiang[1], Yiqin Dai[2], Kui Wu[1(✉)], and Rong Zheng[3]

[1] Department of Computer Science, University of Victoria, Victoria, BC, Canada
{jinghanj,wkui}@uvic.ca
[2] Department of Computer Science, National University of Defense Technology, Changsha, China
daiyq98@gmail.com
[3] Department of Computing and Software, McMaster University, Hamilton, ON, Canada
rzheng@mcmaster.ca

Abstract. Mobile crowdsensing (MCS) depends on mobile users to collect sensing data, whose quality highly depends on the expertise/experience of the users. It is critical for MCS to identify right persons for a given sensing task. A commonly-used strategy is to "teach-before-use", i.e., training users with a set of questions and selecting a subset of users who have answered the questions correctly the most of times. This method has large room for improvement if we consider users' learning curve during the training process. As such, we propose an interactive learning pattern recognition framework, Goldilocks, that can filter users based on their learning patterns. Goldilocks uses an adaptive teaching method tailored for each user to maximize her learning performance. At the same time, the teaching process is also the selecting process. A user can thus be safely excluded as early as possible from the MCS tasks later on if her performance still does not match the desired learning pattern after the training period. Experiments on real-world datasets show that compared to the baseline methods, Goldilocks can identify suitable users to obtain more accurate and more stable results for multi-categories classification problems.

Keywords: Mobile crowdsensing · Learning pattern recognition · Task assignment

1 Introduction

Mobile crowdsensing relies on the sensing capacity of mobile devices and the intelligence of mobile users to create innovative solutions to many real-world problems [1]. One example is environmental monitoring, where the participants are required to take photos of specific objects (e.g. some endangered species or poisonous mushrooms). Such MCS tasks normally involve both mobile users'

X. Chu et al. (Eds.): QShine 2019, LNICST 300, pp. 63–83, 2020.
https://doi.org/10.1007/978-3-030-38819-5_5

spatial-temporal information as well as their capability of securing correct, high-quality sensing data.

There is always a cost in the MCS applications of the above kind. This is because the participants (aka, crowd workers) may need to be rewarded, and even if they are purely volunteers, it would require substantial efforts for the decision maker to clean incorrect data if the crowd workers are not competent for the given tasks. As a result, "finding right people for right tasks" has become one of the most fundamental principles in MCS.

Indeed, many approaches [5,16] have been proposed to identify the qualification of crowd workers. A widely-used method is (randomly) inserting some questions with known answers during their participation. The samples with known ground truth are gold instances [2], which are used to evaluate a crowd worker's domain knowledge and accordingly take proper actions on their answers. This approach, however, has a well-known pitfall: embedding gold instances in *every* worker's annotation process may incur a high and sometimes unnecessary cost.

Another type of broadly-used method is teaching the crowd workers before assigning them a give MCS task [15,17]. This type of methods overcome the problem of embedding gold instances in the whole annotation process of crowd workers because a crowd worker without enough domain knowledge can get trained and crowd workers not performing well after the training can be excluded earlier. Nevertheless, in most existing solutions in this category, a fixed teaching set is used to train the crowd workers and the final selection of the crowd workers is mainly based on the number of questions they correctly answer in the teaching phase [15]. We, via the following illustrative example, argue that we can do much better if we consider each individual user's learning pattern.

Motivating Example. Butterflies have been widely used by ecologists as model organisms to study the impact of habitat loss and fragmentation, and climate change. To understand the ecological changes in a certain area, ecologists need to monitor different butterfly species at several specific times in a day. This is clearly too demanding if the monitored area is large. MCS fits this application perfectly but needs to solve the problem that most people do not have the expert knowledge of butterfly species. If we use the teaching-before-using method, the number of correctly answered questions during the teaching process may not be a good indicator for our final selection of crowd workers.

Consider three different learning patterns in the teaching phase, as shown in Fig. 1. The horizontal axis represents the time (or rounds of teaching), while the vertical axis denotes the capability estimation on the basis of user's correctly-answered questions over time. The three users have identical performance w.r.t. the total number of correctly-answered questions during the teaching phase (e.g. 5 in the example) and they should be treated equally in the final selection of crowd workers. 1 Nevertheless, they exhibit sharply different learning patterns: The first user correctly labels five questions in the beginning, but then makes mistakes in the follow-up questions; the performance of the second user varies all the time during the teaching process; for the third user, the number of correctly-labelled questions begins to increase after she learns a few examples and then her capability remains stable at a good level.

The reasons for different patterns could be many. For example, the first user may get confused or get tired quickly with more teaching instances; the second user may not learn effectively at all and consistently makes mistakes over time; the third user can quickly learn new knowledge and remain stable at a good capability level. Anyway, the hard-to-validate conjecture is irrelevant, since we are only interested in the observed learning patterns during the teaching phase. The point here is that the learning pattern can comprehensively reflect a user's capability of accepting, memorizing and applying new knowledge, which cannot be captured by the oversimplified metric – the total number of correctly answered questions. Clearly, users whose learning pattern in the teaching stage conforms to the third type in Fig. 1 should be a better choice than users whose learning pattern follows the other two curves, particularly when we only have limited teaching samples and cannot afford training the users for a long time.

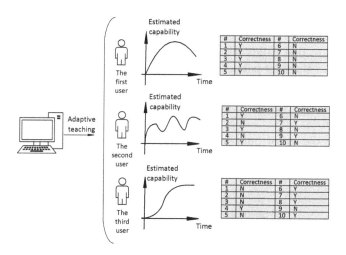

Fig. 1. Example learning patterns in the teaching phase

Motivated by the above observation, we propose Goldilocks[1], an interactive capability assessment framework for MCS, which adopts judicious user selection strategy to eliminates unsuitable users from the current MCS job at the early stage. Our goal is to select the participants whose performance follows the desired learning pattern to maximize the overall performance in an MCS task. Goldilocks adopts an adaptive teaching model to identify the users with stronger ability of generalizing new learned knowledge in the given task. The adaptive teaching strategy is tailored for each individual and is designed to exert the greatest

---

[1] The term is meant to emphasize that our ultimate goal is identifying the right people for right tasks rather than evaluating people's general learning capability.

learning potential of the user. Our philosophy is that if the "ultimate" capability of one user is still not satisfactory after the tailored teaching, we have enough evidence to believe that the user would not be a good candidate for the task and thus should be excluded from task assignment at the early stage.

This paper makes the following contributions:

1. We propose a new framework, Goldilocks, for adaptive learning pattern recognition in participatory MCS. This framework is largely different from previous work that uses either gold instance in the whole process or simplified criteria (e.g. the total number of correct answers) in the participant selection.
2. Goldilocks integrates the teaching and selection phases in a unified framework, and selects the qualified users as early as possible without assigning all the questions to each user. In this way, it significantly saves time and cost for a given MCS task.
3. Based on the work in [9], we develop a new web service over Amazon Web Services (AWS), which obtains the model parameters and automatically adjusts questions to maximize individual participants' learning performance. The web service also collects data to profile the participants' learning pattern, which can be used for task assignment over MCS. Experiments on real-world datasets show that Goldilocks outperforms the baseline methods in both user profiling and the final participant selection.

2   Related Work and Background

Based on the degree of human participation, MCS can be roughly classified into two categories: participatory sensing and opportunistic sensing, as shown in Fig. 2.

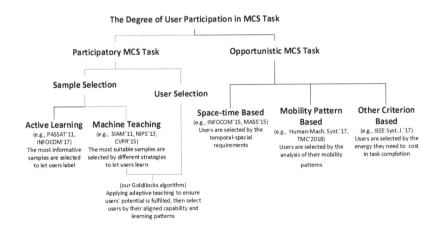

Fig. 2. Classification of MCS

2.1   Opportunistic Sensing

The user involvement is low in opportunistic sensing tasks. For example, asking for the continuous location information without the explicit action of the user is one type of opportunistic sensing [6].

Opportunistic sensing can be classified into three groups: space-time based, mobility pattern based, and others. *In the first group*, Karaliopoulos et al. [11] proposed a recruitment strategy in opportunistic networking to generate the required space-time paths across the network for collecting data from a set of fixed locations. Li et al. [12] presented a temporal-spatial model for participant recruitment in scenarios where the tasks arrive in real time and have different temporal-spatial requirements. *In the second group*, Guo et al. [8] selected crowd workers based on their movement patterns and the task's sensitivity to time. The recruitment strategy proposed in [20] is based on the user's probability of moving to a destination. *In the third group*, Liu et al. [13] considered the energy needed to complete tasks and used a participant sampling behavior model in the participant selection. Yang et al. [22] presented a personalized task recommend system which recommends tasks to users based on their preference and reliability to different tasks.

2.2   Participatory Sensing

Unlike opportunistic sensing, participatory sensing requires the active involvement of crowd workers. Active learning and machine teaching are frequently used to interact with users in their labeling process, so the performance of users can be observed in real time.

The authors in [25] introduced a method to automatically identify the most valuable unlabeled instances as well as the samples that might benefit from relabeling. Zhang et al. [24] combined both labeled and unlabeled instances in the interaction with users, and proposed a bidirectional active learning algorithm by querying users with both the informative unlabeled samples and the unreliable labeled instances simultaneously. The distributed active learning framework in [21] takes the upload and query cost into consideration when interacting with different users, with the goal of minimizing the prediction errors. In addition to the above active learning frameworks, various studies in machine teaching also provide methods to deal with the user interaction problem in the labeling process. Du et al. [3] presented a teaching strategy to achieve more effective learning, which interacts with users by using a probabilistic model based on their answers in each round. Zhu [26] employed Bayesian models to find the optimal teaching set for individuals. Johns et al. [9] developed an interactive machine teaching algorithm that enables a computer to teach users challenging visual concepts by probabilistically modeling the users' ability based on their correct and incorrect answers.

Among the machine teaching methods, adaptive teaching is directly related to our work, and hence we introduce more background in adaptive teaching in the next section.

2.3 Adaptive Teaching

Since many MCS tasks require specific domain knowledge, users usually need training before they are assigned tasks. In order to select right people for a given task, we should consider two problems: (a) how to teach people so that they can generalize the learned knowledge as soon as possible? (b) how to profile users' learning pattern so that better candidates for the MCS task can be determined?

To address the first problem, adaptive teaching [10] is a proper way to help people learn more effectively by posing training questions that are adaptively chosen based on their existing performance. In [3], the next teaching image for a user is the one that the user's answer is predicted to be the farthest from the ground truth. An offline Bayesian model is applied to select adaptive teaching samples in [17]. The teaching strategy presented in [9] chooses a teaching sample that has the greatest reduction on the future error over the rest of unlabeled samples. The goal of adaptive teaching is to stimulate a user's learning potential as much as possible. We hence have a very good reason to eliminate the users who still perform poorly for a given MCS task even after adaptive teaching.

Regarding the second problem, we need to extract users' learning styles through their training processes. Although learning pattern recognition algorithms are studied before [7], they normally assume that abundant labeling data in a given domain are available and then apply different machine learning classification models on the historical learning data to extract learning patterns. This does not match our scenario where learning profile should be built on the fly as a new question is asked and answered. In addition, the learning pattern recognition methods in existing work are more focused on predicting the accuracy of new labels only based on whether or not a user's past questions are labeled correctly.

In this paper, we consider the above two problems and propose an interactive user selection framework for participatory MCS platforms. Note that *we build on the existing solution [9] for adaptive teaching but develop a new method for profiling users' learning patterns*. Unlike other work, our work focuses on the selection of users by doing adaptive capability acquisition round by round[2] for each worker. To match the right user to right task, we firstly select the most appropriate teaching samples for each user to ensure that they can learn as much as possible according to their own learning patterns. And then we select the users for the job by fitting their learning pattern to the non-linear (sigmoid) [23] curves.

3 Overview of Goldilocks

The role of Goldilocks in the workflow of MCS is illustrated in Fig. 3: an organization or individual requests sensing data from the cloud platform (Step 1), then an adaptive teaching interface is called to teach crowd workers according to their

---

[2] A round means that the user answers a question and then is told whether her answer is correct or not as well as what the ground truth is.

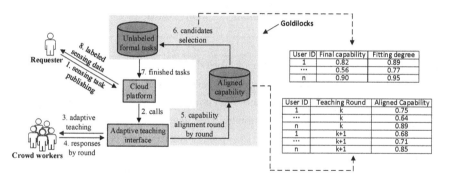

Fig. 3. The role of Goldilocks in the MCS platform; solid lines denote the sensing data requesting procedure; dash lines denote the intermediate results obtained by Goldilocks; the grey box denotes the main functions of Goldilocks.

performances (Steps 2, 3, 4). Adaptive teaching will select the questions that can maximize the user's probability of correctly answering the questions in the future round by round. After each round, we compare the user's estimated performance based on her learning performance so far with her actual performance in labeling the new question (Step 5). Steps 3, 4, and 5 will *repeat until the specified number of teaching samples are taught* to each user. Then we adopt a two-stage candidate selection strategy based on the acquired performance indicators returned by Step 5, to select the best user subset for the formal tasks (Step 6). For the users who are not selected, we will not continue to teach or hire them. Finally, the formal questions without ground truths will be completed by *the selected users*, and the sensing data from this user subset will be returned to the cloud platform, which will then be provided to the original requester (Steps 7 and 8). The above procedure is denoted by the solid lines in Fig. 3.

The core component of Goldilocks is the design of Step 5 and Step 6, denoted in the grey box in Fig. 3. They describe the learning pattern of each user by adjusting a user's estimated capability on the basis of her true performance on the teaching sample in each new round. The dash lines refer to the data stored in the "Round-by round performance indicator" database, and the high-level indicators of user's learning pattern calculated by the "Round-by round performance indicator" database.

The two core steps are denoted by the grey box in Fig. 3: "capability adjustment" and "candidate selection", which will be introduced in Sects. 4 and 5, respectively. The notations used in this paper are listed in Table 1.

4   Capability Adjustment in Goldilocks

We adjust the estimation of user's capability round by round. If we measure the user's capability with a *performance indicator*, its value should be adjusted over time, based on the questions that the user have answered and the current question at the current round. Using M_j^k to indicate user k's capability estimated

Table 1. Summary of main notations

Notation	Description
i	The question number of labeled questions ($0 < i < j$)
j	The question number of the current question
m	The number of extracted keypoint feature vector of a question
n	The number of questions in the teaching set
$\mathbf{x}_{iw}^{k}$	The wth ($0 < w < m$) keypoint feature vector of the ith question labeled by user k
$\mathbf{A}_{i}^{k}$	The vector set consists of the m keypoint feature vectors of the question i labeled by user k
d_{ij}^{k}	The value of $j - i$ of user k
s_{ij}^{k}	The similarity between question i and question j answered by user k
a_{i}^{k}	Binary value, $a_{i}^{k} = 1$ if the ith question is correctly labeled by user k, else $a_{i}^{k} = 0$
t_{i}^{k}	The time of labeling the ith question by user k
I_{i}^{k}	The ID of the ith question labeled by user k
δ_{j}^{k}	The offset on user k's capability after the jth question is labeled
α_{ij}^{k}	The impact of the user k's previously answered question i on her current to be answered question j
ϕ_{j}^{k}	The value of $\sum_{i} \alpha_{ij}^{k}$
M_{j}^{k}	The accumulated capability of user k after the jth question is labeled

after she answers the j-th question, we need to design an algorithm that calculates $\{M_{1}^{k}, M_{2}^{k}, \cdots, M_{n}^{k}\}$, where n is the total number of training questions for the user. We use superscript k to denote user k to emphasize that the sequences of teaching questions for different users are different.

Intuitively, when a user is trained with a question i, the knowledge learned from this question may have an impact on the probability that the user correctly answers a later question. This impact comes from various reasons, e.g., (1) the questions may be similar, and (2) adaptive teaching [10] raises the next question based on the user's historical answers to previous questions. In addition, the impact may become smaller as time goes. As such, we need a method to estimate the impact of all previous questions on the user's performance of answering current question (Sect. 4.1) and consider this impact when we adjust the user's performance indicator value (Sect. 4.2).

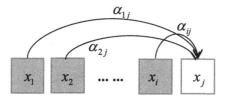

Fig. 4. The impacts of the previous questions on a user's capability of answering the current question. The shaded parts are samples that have been taught to the user

4.1 Impact of Previous Questions

We describe the teaching set for user k in the teaching phase as

$$D^k = \{(1, \mathbf{A_1^k}, t_1^k, a_1^k), \ldots, (n, \mathbf{A_n^k}, t_n^k, a_n^k)\},$$

where $\mathbf{A_i^k}$ is an extracted high-dimensional vector set to describe the features of ith question. Note that the similarity between different teaching samples and their order should be used in our model. t_i^k denotes the time that user k spends on labeling question i and a_i^k is a binary variable to record whether her answer is correct ($a_i^k = 1$ if the question is correctly labeled, otherwise $a_i^k = 0$).

As shown in Fig. 4, for each user in the teaching phase, each previously learned question has an impact on the user's ability of answering the current question j. We denote this influence value as α_{ij}^k. To estimate this influence, we need to consider parameters a_i^k and t_i^k on each previously learned question i. If question i is correctly labeled, a shorter time spent on the question implies a better skill on such type of questions, and thus user k is more likely to use the knowledge related to question i when answering the current question j. If question i is given a wrong label, the larger t_i^k implies that user k has worked harder on this question. While the reasons could vary, it is reasonable to assume that a larger t_i^k would have a more positive impact on the user's later performance compared to the situation that she spends a little time on question i with a wrong answer returned. Based on the above consideration, we suggest the following equation to calculate α_{ij}^k:

$$\alpha_{ij}^k = \frac{1}{1 + e^{-\left[\left(\frac{s_{ij}^k}{d_{ij}^k}\right)\left(1 + \frac{(-1)^{a_i^k + 1}}{t_i^k}\right)\right]}}, \tag{1}$$

where $d_{ij}^k = j - i$ is the distance between questions i and j, s_{ij}^k is the similarity between question i and question j. The calculation of s_{ij}^k depends on specific applications (e.g. image, audio, and text should use different algorithms to calculate similarity). Following the human memory curve [4], a larger d_{ij} implies a smaller likelihood that the user correctly labels question j.

When we estimate the capability of a user before she answers a current question j, we should consider the impact of *all* previous questions. As such, we calculate $\sum_i \alpha_{ij}^k$, which is denoted as ϕ_j^k for simplicity:

$$\phi_j^k = \sum_{i=0}^{j} \alpha_{ij}^k. \tag{2}$$

ϕ_j^k could be considered as a quantitative measure of *the impact of previous questions on the ability that the user can correctly answer the current question*, since ϕ_j^k encodes all the impact of previous questions before j. ϕ_j^k also implicitly reflects the knowledge that the user has gained so far and thus is useful for later adjustment of her capability estimation after we see her true answer.

Equation (2) has two advantageous properties: (a) It considers the relationship of different teaching questions. And in such context, it utilizes the user's time and correctness on those questions. (b) As the number of samples learned by the user increases, the ϕ_j^k is increased by a number in $(0, 1)$ each time. Compared to other user profiling methods, this process enables us to focus on the user's capability of applying the new knowledge she just learned, rather than simply counting the number of correctly answered questions.

Remark 1. Equation (2) is just one way, among potentially many others, of estimating ϕ_j^k. While there is no theoretical guarantee on its accuracy, it can be empirically shown to be effective in our later experimental studies.

4.2   Adjusting Capability Estimation

After the user answers the current question j, we then use ϕ_j^k and her answer to adjust the estimation of her capability. As mentioned before, we use M_j^k to indicate user k's capability estimated after she answers the j-th question, and we record $M_1^k, M_2^k, \cdots$. Essentially, we need to find the adjustment value δ_j^k to calculate $M_j^k = M_{j-1}^k + \delta_j^k$.

When the User Answers the Current Question Correctly. We propose the following formula to calculate δ_j^k when a user answers the current question j correctly (i.e., $a_j^k = 1$):

$$\delta_j^k = \frac{\frac{1}{\sigma\sqrt{2\pi}} e^{\frac{-(\phi_j^k - \mu)^2}{2\sigma^2}}}{t_j^k} \tag{3}$$

The above formula is proposed due to the following considerations: (1) Assuming that ϕ_j^k (i.e., the knowledge gained by a user) follows normal distribution, the numerator is the normal distribution's probability density function (pdf) with mean μ and variance σ^2, where μ and σ are empirical values (from our later experimental results, $\mu = 2.69, \sigma = 1$). (2) Assuming that the longer the time that the user spends on the question, the lower the increments on her capability estimation, we divide the probability value by t_j^k. It is worth noting that in our method it is the shape (i.e., the bell shape when t_j^k is fixed) rather than the absolute values that matter, and as such we believe other possible functions of the similar shape would also work well.

When the User Answers the Current Question Incorrectly. In this case, the higher the chance that she should answer the question correctly based on her historical records, the higher the reduction that should be posed to adjust her capability estimation. Due to this reason, we use a monotone decreasing function w.r.t. ϕ_j^k and t_j^k to obtain δ_j^k:

$$\delta_j^k = \frac{-\nu\left(\phi_j^k\right)^2 + c}{t_j^k} \tag{4}$$

where ν and c are parameters set with experimental results[3]. The 3-D functional image of a_j^k, t_j^k, ϕ_j^k and δ_j^k is shown in Fig. 5. From this Figure, we can also see that when a certain threshold of labeling time (e.g., 6 s) is exceeded, the longer labeling time will not lead to a significantly smaller subtraction on the alignment offset δ_j^k. This reflects a fact that there should be no much difference in the user's capability if she takes a long time and gives a wrong answer.

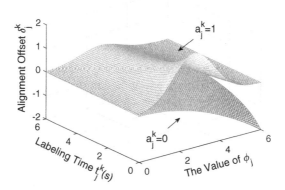

Fig. 5. The 3-D functional image of a_j^k, t_j^k, ϕ_j^k and δ_j^k, where the upper half represents the relationship of t_j^k, ϕ_j^k and δ_j^k when $a_j^k = 1$, and the other part denotes the relationship of them when $a_j^k = 0$.

4.3 Pseudocode

To summarize, the main idea of user's capability estimation includes: (a) estimating the impact of previous learned questions and (b) based on the estimation

---

[3] In our later experiments, to make Eqs. (4) and (3) have the same range values, we $\nu = 0.011$ and $c = -0.018$.

Algorithm 1. Capability Adjustment Workflow

Input: The number of question n, and the first teaching sample labeled by the kth user $T^k = \{(1, I_1^k, t_1^k, a_1^k)\}$, where I_1^k is the ID of the first question labeled by the kth user. t_1^k is the time the kth user spends on the first question. $a_1^k = 1$ if the first question is correctly labeled by user k, else $a_1^k = 0$.

Output: The user's performance indicator after each round and the final accumulated capability indicator of the user $M^k = \{M_1^k, M_2^k, \cdots, M_n^k\}$

1:   $M_1^k \leftarrow 0$
2:   **for** $j = 2 \rightarrow n$ **do**
3:       $(j, I_j^k, t_j^k, a_j^k) \leftarrow \text{EER}(j - 1, I_{j-1}^k, a_{j-1}^k)$
4:       $T^k \leftarrow T^k \cup (j, I_j^k, t_j^k, a_j^k)$
5:       $\alpha_{ij}^k \leftarrow 0$
6:       **for** $i = 1 \rightarrow j - 1$ **do**
7:          $s_{ij}^k \leftarrow \Psi(I_i^k, I_j^k)$
8:          $d_{ij}^k \leftarrow j - i$
9:          $\alpha_{ij}^k \leftarrow \alpha_{ij}^k + \text{U}(s_{ij}^k, d_{ij}^k, a_i^k, t_i^k)$
10:      **end for**
11:      $\delta_j^k \leftarrow 0$
12:      **if** $a_j^k = 0$ **then**
13:         $\delta_j^k \leftarrow \prod_0(\alpha_{ij}^k, t_j^k)$
14:      **else**
15:         $\delta_j^k \leftarrow \prod_1(\alpha_{ij}^k, t_j^k)$
16:      **end if**
17:      $M_j^k \leftarrow M_{j-1}^k + \delta_j^k$
18: **end for**
19: **return** $M^k = \{M_1^k, M_2^k, \cdots, M_n^k\}$

---

and the latest user performance to adjust the current capability estimation. The pseudocode is outlined in Algorithm 1.

In this workflow, EER($\cdot$) (i.e., Expected Error Reduction) denotes the interactive teaching algorithm [9] that we adopt to determine the next sample which can stimulate user's learning potential in the greatest extend. To be more specific, the next teaching sample is the one that, if labeled correctly, can reduce the probability of total error in the greatest level over the samples that are still not selected into the teaching set. This selection problem is formulated based on the conditional probability function and solved by a graph-based semi-supervised method named Gaussian Random Field (GRF) [27]. $\Psi(\cdot)$ represents the feature detection algorithm to obtain the similarity between any two questions. $\text{U}(\cdot)$ is the impact measure function of how the previous learning questions act on user k, which has been introduced in Sect. 4.1. $\prod_0(\cdot)$ and $\prod_1(\cdot)$ stand for the different capability adjustments when the user gives a correct or wrong answer to a new question j, respectively, as discussed in Sect. 4.2.

5 Candidate Selection in Goldilocks

To accurately select the high-quality users, we divide the selection process into two stages based on the learning curve (drawn by M^k returned by Algorithm 1) of each candidate.

– Firstly, we keep the a percentage ($p\%$) of candidates according to their final capability (i.e., M_n^k) and exclude the others, where p is a tunable parameter. We adopt this step because the final capability is a reflection of a user's final learning result, and thus we need filter out the ones whose final capability is below a certain threshold.
– Next, we fit the learning curve of each remaining candidate with our desired curve. We order these candidates according to the *degree of match* and eliminate the bottom candidates until the desired number of candidates are left.

Regarding the calculation of *degree of match*, after the first step, we only care about the shape of each remaining candidate's learning curve. For this reason, we avoid using a static, fixed curve as the benchmark. Instead, we use the shape of logistic regression (sigmoid) curve[4] $y = \frac{b}{1+ae^{-kx}}$ (where a, b, k are positive parameters) as the desired shape, and evaluate different measures on the degree of match in Sect. 6.

6 Experimental Evaluation

6.1 Implementation

To evaluate the performance of Goldilocks, we need real-world data that reflect people's learning patterns. For this, we deploy a Python-based Django website over Amazon Elastic Compute Cloud (Amazon EC2), which interacts with various users and collects the corresponding real-time data. Based on the work [9], we modify its database structure to collect more information such as a user's time spent on each question and the user's exact annotation for each question in teaching and testing phases, respectively.

Table 2. Summary of the experiment datasets

Information	Dataset	
	Butterfly	Oriole
#Teaching samples	20	16
#Testing samples	10	8
#Classes	5	4
#Samples per class	300	60

In our experiment, the user will firstly be presented a fixed number of teaching samples one by one. In the teaching phase, the user will be provided the ground truth after she submits the answer of each question, and then our website chooses the next teaching sample to her using the adaptive learning algorithm introduced

---

[4] This function is just one possible candidate, and people can adopt other desired shape here.

in [9]. In the testing phase (i.e., formal task), no ground truth will be provided for each question and the questions are selected randomly to each user. The setups of our two experiment datasets are shown in Table 2.

It is worth mentioning that in our experiments, we found that users often answered questions quickly, basically around 2 s. Small time values can lead to a steep increase in the function defined in (1) and quick fluctuations on user's capability estimated with Eq. (2). This problem can be easily avoided by using a "virtual" time system, e.g., using 2000 ms instead of 2 s or increasing the real response time by a constant. The purpose of using virtual time is to smooth the fluctuation in a way that we can easily identify a user's learning pattern. Since too-large virtual times (e.g. thousands) will take a heavy toll on using Eq. (2) to distinguish different learning patterns, in our experiment the virtual time is determined by adding a small constant (2 s) to real response time.

6.2 Data

- **Question sets:** We select two scientific image sets to evaluate the performance of Goldilocks. The first dataset, called *Butterfly* dataset, consists of a total number of 1500 butterfly images in five categories from a museum collection [9]. The second image set, called *Oriole* dataset, includes 240 oriole images in four different species from a public dataset [19]. Correctly labeling these images requires domain knowledge, which normal users might not have in advance.
- **Data processing:** The scale-invariant feature transform (SIFT) algorithm [14] is an effective algorithm for image feature detection. We apply SIFT to calculate the keypoint feature vectors of each teaching sample, and then acquire the similarity between any two teaching samples with the following function:

$$f(\rho) = \sum_{i=1}^{m} \mathbb{1}_{\{\rho_i > \theta\}} \tag{5}$$

where $\mathbb{1}_{\{\rho_i > \theta\}}$ is an indicator function:

$$\mathbb{1}_{\{\rho_i > \theta\}} = \begin{cases} 0 & \text{if } \rho_i > \theta \\ 1 & \text{otherwise} \end{cases}. \tag{6}$$

Here function $\rho_i = \left\| \mathbf{x}_{\mathbf{jw}}^{\mathbf{k}} - \mathbf{x}_{\mathbf{j'w}}^{\mathbf{k}} \right\|_2^2$ is the Euclidean distance between the w-th $(0 < w < m)$ keypoint feature vectors of teaching images j and j', and θ is a self-defined similarity threshold between two different keypoint feature vectors.

We implement the SIFT algorithm in C++. To make the labeling task non-trivial, we set the image blur-adjustment parameter λ of the Gaussian pyramid to 1.1, which introduces some difference to intra-category images and some similarity to inter-category images [14].

– **Data collection:** We share the Python-based Django website with 100 participants, we collect their performance data in the teaching phase and the testing phase, respectively, for both the *Butterfly* and *Oriole* image sets. While we have collected the data for the participants in both the teaching and testing phases, to compare Goldilocks and other baseline methods in terms of the quality of final returned sensing data, we can *pretend* that after the teaching phase, only X number of qualified users out of the 100 participants are selected in the testing phase, where X is a variable determined by the participant selection criteria. In this way, we have the ground truth regarding the data quality with and without those filtered users in the testing phase.

6.3   Baseline Algorithms

We compare our method with the following baseline methods:

– S_{acc}: This method filters the candidates based on their accuracy in the teaching phase. The candidates with more correctly-labeled questions are chosen to participate in the formal tasks.
– S_{urp}: This method [22] does not have an explicit teaching phase but it estimates users' reliability using the following *equivalent* method: After a user labels all the questions, we randomly select a small number of questions, and estimate the user's reliability based on whether or not she has correctly answered the chosen questions. In our experiment, we ask the users to label the 30 images from *Butterfly* dataset and randomly select 5 images to estimate the users' reliability. For the *Oriole* dataset, we ask the users to label the 20 images and randomly select 4 images to estimate the users' reliability. Users are then ranked based on their reliability from high to low, and we select candidates based on their reliability. We repeat this experiments 10 times and take the average over the 10 runs.
– S_{str}: STRICT [18] is an optimized algorithm that selects all the teaching samples for a user before the training, based on the use's prior. In other words, the order of teaching samples is computed offline and *fixed* in the user's training process. It finally selects the users who have the best performances on the fixed teaching set.
– S_{rnd}: It randomly selects the required number of candidates without any teaching. We take the average result over 50 random selections in all of our following experiments.

6.4   Evaluation Results and Analysis

Accuracy and F-Measure. Figure 6 shows the average labeling accuracy by users selected with different participant selection methods in the testing phase. For comparison, we set the number of selected users (i.e., ϵ), after the teaching phase, from 20 to 35 with the increment of 5. From the figure, we can see that on both datasets, all the methods perform better than the random selection. It is notable that when $\epsilon = 20$, the performance of random selected users is even worse than that of all the users. This is because the random selection might choose more unqualified users than qualified ones. We also observe that there is no fixed "second-best" across different methods and among different datasets. However, Goldilocks achieves the highest accuracy among all the five methods in all the ϵ settings on both datasets.

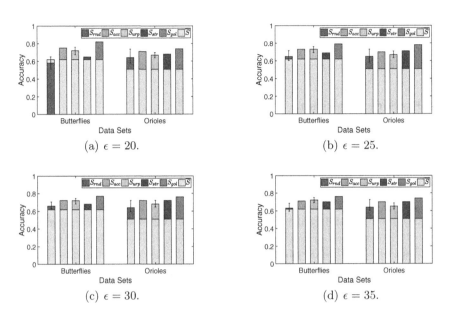

Fig. 6. Accuracy of different methods on different datasets when the number of selected users for the testing phase is different. $\mathcal{S}$ denotes the performance that all users are selected for the testing phase.

F-measure is a harmonic mean of precise and recall that ranges from 0 to 1. In addition to accuracy, this metric also reflects the stability of a model. Figure 7 shows the f-measure value of different methods under different number of the selected users on the two experiment datasets. On both image sets, $\mathcal{S}_{rnd}$ has the worst f-measure performance among all the methods. Meanwhile, $\mathcal{S}_{gol}$ outperforms all the baselines across different numbers of selected users. The maximum f-measure value of Goldilocks can reach 0.83 when $\epsilon = 20$ on the *Butterfly* dataset. Also, no baseline works consistently the second best w.r.t. f-measure. From Fig. 7, we can also observe that the f-measure performance is generally poorer on the *Oriole* dataset than on the *Butterfly* dataset. This may be because image samples of orioles are more difficult to classify due to distracting environmental background.

Response Time. If a user can answer questions quickly with a high accuracy, the user must have gained good knowledge for the task. We therefore analyze

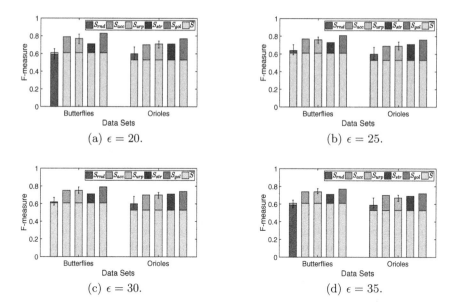

(a) $\epsilon = 20$.   (b) $\epsilon = 25$.

(c) $\epsilon = 30$.   (d) $\epsilon = 35$.

Fig. 7. F-measure of different methods on different datasets when the number of selected users for the testing phase is different. S denotes the performance that all users are selected for the testing phase.

the response time of those users who are chosen for the testing phase. Here the response time is defined as from the time when a selected user is shown the first image to the time when she submits the answer of the last image during the testing phase. Table 3 summarizes the average response time of users selected by different methods on two different datasets. We can observe that the users selected by Goldilocks tend to respond more quickly compared to other baselines. Considering Goldilocks' good performance in accuracy and F-measure, we have enough confidence to conclude that the users selected by Goldilocks have a better grasp of the knowledge. Although it can be seen that S_{rnd} and S_{urp} also perform well on the average response time in some ϵ settings, users' poorer performance on the accuracy and f-measure implies that the selected users may not be reliable.

Table 3. Average response time in the testing phase

		$\epsilon = 20$		$\epsilon = 25$		$\epsilon = 30$		$\epsilon = 35$	
		Butterfly	Oriole	Butterfly	Oriole	Butterfly	Oriole	Butterfly	Oriole
Method	S_{rnd}	**41.35**	28.05	**44.32**	28.18	47.50	27.96	47.00	28.41
	S_{acc}	47.60	34.90	46.60	35.44	45.00	34.13	47.26	33.60
	S_{urp}	46.80	28.60	46.36	27.48	43.50	**26.80**	45.26	**26.66**
	S_{str}	49.45	25.69	54.35	27.88	52.30	30.65	48.37	31.89
	S_{gol}	42.96	**21.25**	45.30	**23.12**	**42.53**	27.40	**45.08**	28.03

Note: ϵ denotes the number of selected users for test

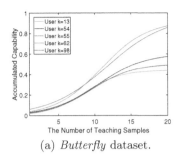

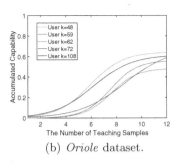

(a) *Butterfly* dataset.   (b) *Oriole* dataset.

Fig. 8. Fitted logistic regression curves of the top 5 user.

Fitting Degree of Learning Curve. Goldilocks uses the logistic function introduced in Sect. 5 to benchmark a user's learning curve. Note that a user's learning curve is obtained from the round-by-round capability adjustment (Algorithm 1). To ease illustration, we normalize the capability values with the maximum possible value. The learning curves of the selected top five users on the two datasets are shown in Fig. 8(a) and (b), respectively. We can see that all the learning curves have a similar shape of the logistic regression function, indicating the suitability of logistic regression.

Table 4. Fitting performance of Top 5 learning curves and the corresponding accuracy in the testing phase on the Butterfly dataset

User	Metrics			Accuracy
	SSE	RMSE	Adj-rsquare	
13	0.0244	0.0379	0.9638	90%
54	0.0621	0.0605	0.9702	90%
55	0.0399	0.0485	**0.9837**	**100%**
62	0.0226	0.0364	0.9721	90%
98	0.0304	0.0423	0.9715	90%

Table 5. Fitting performance of Top 5 learning curves and the corresponding accuracy in the testing phase on the Oriole dataset

User	Metrics			Accuracy
	SSE	RMSE	Adj-rsquare	
48	0.0113	0.0354	0.9869	87.5%
59	0.0146	0.0403	0.9805	87.5%
62	0.0052	0.0240	**0.9904**	**100%**
72	0.0143	0.0399	0.9776	87.5%
108	0.0080	0.0299	0.9887	87.5%

We, however, need a quantitative evaluation on the fitting degree of a learning curve towards the logistic function. Note that we only care about the shape (i.e., the trend) and thus we do not suggest a fixed logistic function. Instead, with logistic regression, different learning curves may fit to different logistic functions (i.e., the parameters in the fitted logistic functions may be different). To evaluate the fitting degree, we test the following metrics:

- *SSE*: The sum of squared errors (SSE) between the learning curve and the fitted logistic function (at discrete range values). The smaller the SSE, the better the fitting.
- *RMSE*: Root Mean Square Error. The smaller the RMSE, the better the fitting.
- *Adj-rsquare*: The adjusted R-square value according to the freedom degree of errors, where R-square is the square of the correlation coefficient between the measured data and the data obtained by the fitting curve. The higher the Adj-rsquare, the better the fitting.

Table 4 shows that in the *Butterfly* dataset, both SSE and RMSE are less than 6.5% for all the 5 users' learning curves. And the values of their Adj-rsquare are all beyond 96%. Considering the high accuracy of these 5 users, we can conclude that the users whose learning curve well follow our proposed model have high-quality answers in the testing phase. This is further validated by the fact that the user who has the highest Adj-rsquare (i.e., the 55th user) answers all the questions correctly. Table 5 shows the similar phenomena as in Table 4. For the *Oriole* dataset, the values of SSE are less than 1.5% and the values of RMSE are less than 4.1% for all the top five users' learning curves. The 62th user has the best Adj-rsquare (99.04%) and the highest accuracy (100%).

7   Conclusions

Participant selection has always been a critical problem in MCS. To "select right people for right job", existing methods usually use the number of questions that a user answered correctly during the training phase to judge the user's qualification. We proposed an enhancement method, called Goldilocks, which (1) estimates users' learning patterns using adaptive teaching and (2) selects users based on the desired learning patterns. Experiments with real-world data disclose that Goldilocks outperforms existing baselines in terms of efficiency, accuracy, and stability.

Acknowledgement. This research was supported by the Natural Sciences and Engineering Research Council of Canada (NSERC) under grant No. SPG 494083-16.

References

1. Ahlgren, B., Hidell, M., Ngai, E.C.H.: Internet of Things for smart cities: interoperability and open data. IEEE Internet Comput. **20**(6), 52–56 (2016)
2. Daniel, F., Kucherbaev, P., Cappiello, C., Benatallah, B., Allahbakhsh, M.: Quality control in crowdsourcing: a survey of quality attributes, assessment techniques, and assurance actions. ACM Comput. Surv. (CSUR) **51**(1), 7 (2018)
3. Du, J., Ling, C.X.: Active teaching for inductive learners. In: Proceedings of the 2011 SIAM International Conference on Data Mining, pp. 851–861. SIAM (2011)
4. Ebbinghaus, H.: Memory: a contribution to experimental psychology. Ann. Neurosci. **20**(4), 155 (2013)
5. Fiandrino, C., Kantarci, B., Anjomshoa, F., Kliazovich, D., Bouvry, P., Matthews, J.: Sociability-driven user recruitment in mobile crowdsensing Internet of Things platforms. In: 2016 IEEE Global Communications Conference (GLOBECOM), pp. 1–6. IEEE (2016)
6. Ganti, R.K., Ye, F., Lei, H.: Mobile crowdsensing: current state and future challenges. IEEE Commun. Mag. **49**(11), 32–39 (2011)
7. Grantcharov, T.P., Bardram, L., Funch-Jensen, P., Rosenberg, J.: Learning curves and impact of previous operative experience on performance on a virtual reality simulator to test laparoscopic surgical skills. Am. J. Surg. **185**(2), 146–149 (2003)
8. Guo, B., Liu, Y., Wu, W., Yu, Z., Han, Q.: Activecrowd: a framework for optimized multitask allocation in mobile crowdsensing systems. IEEE Trans. Hum.-Mach. Syst. **47**(3), 392–403 (2017)
9. Johns, E., Mac Aodha, O., Brostow, G.J.: Becoming the expert-interactive multiclass machine teaching. In: Proceedings of the IEEE Conference on Computer Vision and Pattern Recognition, pp. 2616–2624 (2015)
10. Jones, V., Jo, J.H.: Ubiquitous learning environment: an adaptive teaching system using ubiquitous technology. In: Beyond the Comfort Zone: Proceedings of the 21st ASCILITE Conference, vol. 468, p. 474. Perth, Western Australia (2004)
11. Karaliopoulos, M., Telelis, O., Koutsopoulos, I.: User recruitment for mobile crowdsensing over opportunistic networks. In: 2015 IEEE Conference on Computer Communications (INFOCOM), pp. 2254–2262. IEEE (2015)
12. Li, H., Li, T., Wang, Y.: Dynamic participant recruitment of mobile crowd sensing for heterogeneous sensing tasks. In: 2015 IEEE 12th International Conference on Mobile Ad Hoc and Sensor Systems, pp. 136–144. IEEE (2015)
13. Liu, C.H., Zhang, B., Su, X., Ma, J., Wang, W., Leung, K.K.: Energy-aware participant selection for smartphone-enabled mobile crowd sensing. IEEE Syst. J. **11**(3), 1435–1446 (2017)
14. Lowe, D.G.: Distinctive image features from scale-invariant keypoints. Int. J. Comput. Vis. **60**(2), 91–110 (2004)
15. Patil, K.R., Zhu, J., Kopeć, Ł., Love, B.C.: Optimal teaching for limited-capacity human learners. In: Advances in Neural Information Processing Systems, pp. 2465–2473 (2014)
16. Shah, N., Zhou, D., Peres, Y.: Approval voting and incentives in crowdsourcing. In: International Conference on Machine Learning, pp. 10–19 (2015)
17. Singla, A., Bogunovic, I., Bartók, G., Karbasi, A., Krause, A.: On actively teaching the crowd to classify. In: NIPS Workshop on Data Driven Education (2013)
18. Singla, A., Bogunovic, I., Bartók, G., Karbasi, A., Krause, A.: Near-optimally teaching the crowd to classify. In: ICML, no. 2 in 1, p. 3 (2014)

19. Wah, C., Branson, S., Welinder, P., Perona, P., Belongie, S.: The Caltech-UCSD birds-200-2011 dataset. California Institute of Technology (2011)
20. Wang, E., Yang, Y., Wu, J., Liu, W., Wang, X.: An efficient prediction-based user recruitment for mobile crowdsensing. IEEE Trans. Mob. Comput. **17**(1), 16–28 (2018)
21. Xu, Q., Zheng, R.: When data acquisition meets data analytics: a distributed active learning framework for optimal budgeted mobile crowdsensing. In: IEEE INFOCOM 2017-IEEE Conference on Computer Communications, pp. 1–9. IEEE (2017)
22. Yang, S., Han, K., Zheng, Z., Tang, S., Wu, F.: Towards personalized task matching in mobile crowdsensing via fine-grained user profiling. In: IEEE INFOCOM 2018-IEEE Conference on Computer Communications, pp. 2411–2419. IEEE (2018)
23. Yin, X., Goudriaan, J., Lantinga, E.A., Vos, J., Spiertz, H.J.: A flexible sigmoid function of determinate growth. Ann. Bot. **91**(3), 361–371 (2003)
24. Zhang, X.Y., Wang, S., Yun, X.: Bidirectional active learning: a two-way exploration into unlabeled and labeled data set. IEEE Trans. Neural Netw. Learn. Syst. **26**(12), 3034–3044 (2015)
25. Zhao, L., Sukthankar, G., Sukthankar, R.: Incremental relabeling for active learning with noisy crowdsourced annotations. In: 2011 IEEE Third International Conference on Privacy, Security, Risk and Trust and 2011 IEEE Third International Conference on Social Computing, pp. 728–733. IEEE (2011)
26. Zhu, J.: Machine teaching for Bayesian learners in the exponential family. In: Advances in Neural Information Processing Systems, pp. 1905–1913 (2013)
27. Zhu, X., Ghahramani, Z., Lafferty, J.D.: Semi-supervised learning using gaussian fields and harmonic functions. In: Proceedings of the 20th International conference on Machine learning (ICML 2003), pp. 912–919 (2003)

Cloud Resource Management and Scheduling

A Reinforcement Learning Based Placement Strategy in Datacenter Networks

Weihong Yang, Yang Qin[✉], and ZhaoZheng Yang

Department of Computer Science, Harbin Institute of Technology (Shenzhen),
Shenzhen, China
csyqin@hit.edu.cn

Abstract. As the core infrastructure of cloud computing, the datacenter networks place heavy demands on efficient storage and management of massive data. Data placement strategy, which decides how to assign data to nodes for storage, has a significant impact on the performance of the datacenter. However, most of the existing solutions cannot be better adaptive to the dynamics of the network. Moreover, they focus on where to store the data (i.e., the selection of storage node) but have not considered how to store them (i.e., the selection of routing path). Since reinforcement learning (RL) has been developed as a promising solution to address dynamic network issues, in this paper, we integrate RL into the datacenter networks to deal with the data placement issue. Considering the dynamics of resources, we propose a Q-learning based data placement strategy for datacenter networks. By leveraging Q-learning, each node can adaptively select next-hop based on the network information collected from downstream, and forward the data toward the storage node that has adequate capacity along the path with high available bandwidth. We evaluate our proposal on the NS-3 simulator in terms of average delay, throughput, and load balance. Simulation results show that the Q-learning placement strategy can effectively reduce network delay and increase average throughout while achieving load-balanced among servers.

Keywords: Datacenter networks · Placement strategy · Q-learning

1 Introduction

With the increasing scale of the Internet's users and the emergence of large-scale distributed technologies, the demand for massive data processing has promoted the development of cloud-computing services. As the core infrastructure of cloud computing, Datacenter provides vital support for growing Internet services and applications. There is an urgent need for datacenter networks to deal with massive data under delay constraints [1]. The datacenter networks play a critical role in connecting large and distributed datacenters, providing efficient management and transfer of large amounts of data. Since the centralized placement of data suffers from scalability problems and single point failure, it is necessary to disseminate data across the servers in datacenters. Therefore, how to select suitable storage servers becomes a critical issue.

© ICST Institute for Computer Sciences, Social Informatics and Telecommunications Engineering 2020
Published by Springer Nature Switzerland AG 2020. All Rights Reserved
X. Chu et al. (Eds.): QShine 2019, LNICST 300, pp. 87–101, 2020.
https://doi.org/10.1007/978-3-030-38819-5_6

There are many recent works proposed to deal with the issue of data placement from different perspectives. For example, the random-based placement strategies are simple and popular among several existing systems, such as the Google File System (GFS) [2], Cassandra [3], and the Hadoop Distributed File System (HDFS) [4]. However, random-based placement is not robust to failure and may cause an imbalanced load. On the other hand, some works make placement decisions by considering network resources and fault-tolerance, to reduce the access time and recovery time of data [5–12]. For example, based on the available storage resource, an efficient data placement strategy is proposed in [5] to achieve load balance and satisfy the fault-tolerant requirements. Similar to the existing works mentioned above, we study the data placement issue by considering the available network resource (i.e., bandwidth and storage capacity) in this paper. Moreover, we not only focus on the selection of storage nodes but also design a routing algorithm to find a suitable path to the storage node.

Due to the dynamics of the network, the data placement strategy should be adaptive to the changes in datacenter networks such as the available resource and the occurrence of faults. Reinforcement learning (RL) is agent-based learning that agents can learn by interacting with their environments. RL can explore and learn the dynamics of network and exploit limited resources based on limited knowledge. We leverage the RL method and design a Q-learning based data placement strategy. Each node, including the switch and server, is an agent that can make routing decisions toward the storage node based on the feedback from the datacenter networks.

In this paper, we propose an adaptive Q-learning placement strategy, which consists of the exploration and the exploitation phase. During the exploration phase, each node calculates the Q-value based on the information piggybacked by packets from downstream; and in the exploitation phase, the node makes routing decisions based on the Q-value. The information used for calculating Q-value consists of the available storage capacity of the server and the available bandwidth of the routing path to this server. As a result, the data can be routed along a suitable path toward the storage node. We use the NS-3 simulator to evaluate the performance of our proposal by comparing it with other placement strategies.

The rest of the paper is organized as follows. Section 2 introduces the recent works related to our work. Section 3 presents the model and detailed design of the placement strategy. The simulation results are shown in Sect. 4. Section 5 concludes this work.

2   Related Works

A simple and commonly used placement strategy is random placement, which places the replicas randomly among servers in the datacenter [2, 3, 13]. The random strategy can improve the speed of data repair; however, it is sensitive to multiple and concurrent failures. The rack-aware placement strategy (used in HDFS [4]) places replicas on the servers in both local and remote racks. Each data block is replicated at multiple servers (typically three). In the case of three replicas, one of the replicas is placed on the server of the local rack, and others are placed randomly on servers in the remote rack.

Therefore, it lacks reliability and may cause an imbalance load among the servers of the local and remote rack.

In order to balance and evenly distribute large amounts of the data block, Renuga et al. [5] proposed an efficient data placement and replication scheme to calculate the redundancy parameters accurately that satisfy fault-tolerant requirements. This scheme can improve the utilization of storage space and network bandwidth, reducing data access time and recovery time. Their work focuses on selecting nodes for storage; however, the selection of routing paths to the storage node is not considered. Zaman et al. [6] model the replica placement problem as an optimization problem that minimizing the access time of all servers and objects, given the rate of requests and capacity of servers. Then, a distributed approximation algorithm is proposed to solve the optimization problem. However, the proposed algorithm cannot well suited for the dynamic changes in the datacenter networks.

Rajalakshmi et al. [7] focus on designing an algorithm for optimal replica selection and placement in order to increase the availability of data. The proposed algorithm consists of the file application phase and the replication operation phase. Based on multidimensional locality-preserving mappings, a novel data placement scheme is proposed in [8], which aims at reducing access time of data by supporting dynamic tags. However, it may introduce extra redundancy and has poor scalability in practice. The proposal in [9] is based on the consideration of the availability and popularity of the data. This approach can be tolerant of the occurrence of faults.

AutoPlacer [10] is a self-tuning data placement in a distributed key-value store, which identifies top-k objects that generate most remote operations (i.e., hotspots) for each node of the system, and optimizes the placement of hotspots to minimize the communication between nodes. Lin et al. [11] present a novel placement algorithm that locates the optimal nodes for placing replicas in order to achieve the load balance. Moreover, they propose an algorithm to decide the minimum number of replicas. However, the traffic pattern and locality demands must be known before making the placement decision. Gao et al. [12] addressed the problem of energy cost reduction under both server and network resource constraints within the datacenter and proposed a placement strategy based on ant colony optimization incorporating network resource factors with server resources. CRUSH [14] selects the candidate nodes for storage by using a pseudo-random hashing function. CRUSH can support data placement in a heterogeneous environment; however, the issue of how to route the data toward the storage node is not studied.

3 Q-learning Based Placement

3.1 System Model

We use the Fat-tree network topology [15] as an illustrated example, as shown in Fig. 1. Note that our proposal can be adopted in any topologies of datacenter networks. Assume that the data block $b \in B$ to be placed can arrive at any server. B is the set of data blocks, and each data block is divided into many data packets. The placement strategy selects a storage server that the available capacity should not be less than m_b, where m_b is the size of data block b. Moreover, the placement strategy finds a suitable forwarding path $p \in P(s, d)$ between server s and d, where $P(s, d)$ is the set of candidate paths between server s and d. The capacity of the path should not be less than r_b, where r_b is the bandwidth requirement of block b. We assume that m_b and r_b are known when the request for placement of data block b arrives. We leverage the reinforcement learning to design distributed placement strategy. More specifically, each node (switch or server) makes a routing decision for each data packet of data block based on the information it learned from the network. We summarize the main notations used in this paper in Table 1.

Table 1. The main notations used in this paper.

Parameter	Definition
b	A data block
B	The set of data block
m_b	The size of data block b
p	A forwarding path
$P(s, i)$	The set of paths from node s to node i
r_b	The bandwidth requirement of block b
S_T^s	The total storage capacity of server s
S_O^s	The used storage capacity of server s
C_T^l	The total bandwidth of link l
C_O^l	The used bandwidth of link l

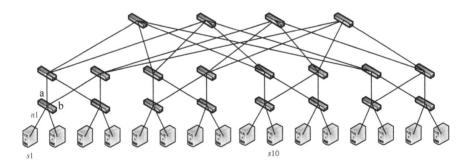

Fig. 1. Fat-tree topology.

3.2   Modeling of Placement Strategy

The goal for each node is to select the next-hop node that jointly maximizes the available storage capacity and bandwidth with constraints. Therefore, we model the placement decision problem for node i when forwarding data block b in datacenter networks as follow:

$$
\begin{aligned}
\max_{s \in D} \quad & \alpha \frac{S_T^s - S_O^s}{S_T^s} + (1 - \alpha) \max_{p \in p(i,s)} \min_{l \in p} C_T^l - C_O^l \\
\text{s.t.} \quad & S_T^s - S_O^s \geq m_b \\
& C_T^l - C_O^l \geq r_b
\end{aligned}
\tag{1}
$$

where s denotes the candidate server for storage, $p(i, s)$ is the set of paths from node i to s, and there may exits multiple paths from server i to s. We use p to represent a route between two nodes, p is consists of multiple links. S_T^s is the total storage capacity of the candidate server, S_O^s is the used storage capacity of the candidate server. C_T^l is the bandwidth of link l, and C_O^l is the used bandwidth of link l. The first constraint indicates that the size of the data being placed cannot exceed the remaining capacity of server s. The second constraint indicates that the available bandwidth of every single link must meet the bandwidth requirement of block b. The problem (1) can be interpreted as node i attempts to forward the data block to the next-hop, which has the maximum objective value and satisfies the capacity and bandwidth requirement of the data block. In this hop-by-hop forwarding manner, the data packet can be forwarded toward a suitable storage server along the path with maximum available bandwidth.

3.3   Markov Decision Process and Q-learning

A fundamental assumption based on most reinforcement learning problems is that the interaction process between agent and environment can be regarded as a Markov Decision Process. The Q-learning placement algorithm is based on Markov Decision Process (MDP) for analysis and design [16]. We can use a four-tuple to represent a finite MDP:

$$
\langle S_i, A_i, P_i, R_i \rangle_{i=1}^{|N|}
\tag{2}
$$

S is a state space of node i. At time step t, the state is denoted by $s_i(t) = (\lambda_i^1(t), \ldots, \lambda_i^{|nh|}(t))$, where $\lambda_i^k(t)$ is the information of minimum bandwidth and remaining storage capacity received via interface k of node i, and $|nh|$ is the number of next-hops. A_i is a finite set of actions performed by node i. The action of node i at time step t is $a_i(t)$, which means node i forwards the packet to the selected next-hop at time t. P_i is the transition probability from state s to state s' by performing action a. R_i is the immediate reward received by node i. The reward is defined as the objective function in optimization problem (1) if the constraints of (1) are not violated. We set the reward to zero if the next-hop cannot meet bandwidth and storage capacity.

The dynamic information of the network (state S) can be learned to make routing and placement decision (action A). The available bandwidth of the routing path and the remaining storage capacity of the server are then used as reward R to train the model.

In order to solve a specific problem, we define an objective function V whose maximum value corresponds to the optimal strategy we want to obtain. We denote a strategy by π. We hope that the system can get the optimal strategy π^* through reinforcement learning, which is a series of action-state transition sequences, which corresponds to the largest converted cumulative return value. Note that there might be more than one value function, so there may be multiple solutions to the problem. The maximum value of the calculated value function can get the optimal strategy. The optimal value function is defined as:

$$V^*(s) = \max_{\pi} E^{\pi}\left[\sum\nolimits_{t=0}^{\infty} \gamma^t r_{t+1}\right], \forall s \in S, \tag{3}$$

where $\gamma \in (0, 1)$ is the discount factor, r_t is the reward at time t, $E^{\pi}[\bullet]$ denotes the expectation value under strategy π. According to the dynamic programming, we have the following Bellman equation:

$$V^*(s) = \max_{a}\left[R^a + \gamma E[V^*(s')]\right]. \tag{4}$$

In Q-learning, the Q function is defined as follow:

$$Q^*(s, a) = \max_{\pi} Q^{\pi}(s, a), \forall s \in S, a \in A(s) \tag{5}$$

3.4 Q-learning Based Placement Algorithm

Due to the dynamic changes of the network, the self-optimization of the placement strategy is needed in the datacenter networks. The placement strategy is supposed to learn from the environment and adjust its strategy by trial and error. Q-learning can achieve good learning performance in a complex and dynamic system by learning the optimal policy without prior knowledge. The maximum value of the objective function in (1) can be obtained by the iterative method; therefore, it can be solved by Q-learning based algorithm.

A node in the datacenter networks acts as an agent and learns strategy based on the information piggybacked by the ACK packet from the downstream. The information consists of two parts: the available storage capacity of the server (the first term in the objective function of (1)), and the available bandwidth of downstream path (the second term in the objective function of (1)). The weight α adjusts the importance of bandwidth and storage capacity when making a placement decision.

Updating of Q-value and Stop Condition. Each node i with data packets to send takes action a_i at state s_i based on the strategy $\pi_i(t)$ at the beginning of the time step t. Then, the Q-value for the next time step is updated as follow:

$$
\begin{aligned}
Q_i^{t+1}(s_i, a_i) &\leftarrow (1 - \beta)Q_i^t(s_i, a_i) \\
&+ \beta(\alpha \frac{S_T^s - S_O^s}{S_T^s} + (1 - \alpha) \max_{p \in p(i,s)} \min_{l \in p}(C_T^l - C_O^l) + \gamma \max_a Q_i^t(s_i^{t+1}, a))
\end{aligned}
\tag{6}
$$

The calculation of Q-value stops when the following stop condition is met:

$$
|Q_i' - Q_i| < \frac{\varepsilon(1 - \gamma)}{2}
\tag{7}
$$

where ε is a positive number. If the difference between the two Q-values is small enough, the updating of Q-value stops.

The Detail of Q-learning based Placement. The Q-learning based placement algorithm is presented in Algorithm 1. According to (6), the calculation of Q-value needs the information from the downstream of the routing path. Therefore, we divide the placement strategy into two phases: exploration and exploitation phase.

We augment the ACK with two additional fields: *RemainCapacity* and *MinBandwith*. *RemainCapacity* field is used to record the remaining capacity of the candidate server for storage, and *MinBandwith* records the minimum bandwidth of the routing path. Based on the information in these two fields, a node only forwards the data packet to the next-hop that does not violate the constraints in (1).

Exploration (Line 2–18 in Algorithm 1): In this phase, each node will have to calculate the Q-value locally. Each node sends the request r_q for updating Q-value to its next-hops (Line 3–5). Upon receiving the request r_q, the server responds by sending back the ACK (Line 6–8). Then, the node uses the information piggybacked by the ACKs to update its local Q-values (Line 11). In this hop-by-hop manner, the Q-values along the routing path are updated. The above steps are repeated until the stop condition (7) is met, and then the phase is transited to *exploitation* (Line 12–14). Two conditions can trigger the algorithm to be in the *Exploration* phase: the change of network resources or the initialization of the network. The first condition indicates the algorithm is transited from the Exploitation to the Exploration phase due to the violation of stop condition. In this case, only the node whose Q-value is changed has to issue the request r_q. The second condition indicates that the network is initializing, and there is no Q-value that has been calculated at each node. Therefore, every node has to issue the Q-value updating request r_q.

Exploitation: In this phase, when receiving the request r_d of data block replacement, the switch selects the next-hop p that has the highest Q-value and satisfies the bandwidth and capacity requirement (Line 21–22). The switch also records the next-hop p for this request in the routing table (Line 23), and then the subsequent data packets can be routed to the storage server based on the routing table. When the server receives a placement request r_d, it sends back an ACK tagged with the available capacity (Line 25–27). The algorithm remains in the exploitation phase until the stop condition is violated; then, the phase is transited back to exploration (Line 34–36 and Line 42–44). This condition indicates that the available resource has changed, and the Q-values have to be updated. Note that when a request for data block placement arrives during the exploration phase, the request will still be forwarded to the next-hop that has the highest Q-value, even though the Q-learning based algorithm does not converge.

As a result, the data block will be routed to the storage node along the path that maximizes the objective function in (1), i.e., the selected storage node has maximum available capacity, and the routing path has maximum available bandwidth.

We here use an example to illustrate how the proposed Q-learning based placement works. When the request for data replacement arrives at the server (e.g., server $s1$ in Fig. 1), a request of the data block will be forwarded into the network via switch $n1$. This request carries information about block size m_b and bandwidth requirement r_b. Switch $n1$ will have to decide to which next-hop the request should be forwarded by looking up an Augmented Q-Table (AQT). The main format of AQT is shown in Table 2. Without violating any constraints, the interface with the largest Q-value is selected, and *MinBandwith* is updated by subtracting r_b from the current *MinBandwith*. Moreover, the routing table will be updated: the outgoing interface of the request is recorded. Then, this request is forwarded to the suitable storage server (e.g., server $s10$). Then, $s10$ sends an ACK tagged with current remaining capacity $S_T^{10} - S_O^{10} - m_b$. Upon receiving the ACK, the node updates the local Q-value and *RemainCapacity* value in the AQT. When an ACK reaches server $s1$, the AQTs of all the nodes along the routing path are updated, then the data packet of this data block will be forwarded, taking the same path as the request.

Table 2. Augmented Q-Table.

Interface	*RemainCapacity*	*MinBandwith*	Q-value
a	RC_a	MB_a	Q_a
b	RC_b	MB_b	Q_b

Algorithm 1 Q-learning Placement Algorithm

Input: parameter ε, discount factor γ, learning rate β, data block placement requests r_d, size of data block m_b, bandwidth requirement r_b, the weight α

Output: placement decision

1. phase $\leftarrow$ Exploration;
2. **while** phase $==$ Exploration **do**
3.   **for each** node i **do**
4.   Send request r_q for calculating Q-value;
5.   **end for**
6.   **while** server receives r_q **do**
7.   Send ACK;
8.   **end while**
9.   **while** node i receives ACK **do**
10.   Record RC and MB;
11.   Updated Q-value by (6);
12.   **if** $\left|Q_i'(s_i,a_i)-Q_i(s_i,a_i)\right|<\varepsilon(1-\gamma)/2$ **do**
13.   phase $\leftarrow$ Exploitation;
14.   **end if**
15.   Tag ACK packet with information;
16.   Send ACK;
17.   **end while**
18. **end while**
19. **while** node i receiving placement request r_d do
20.   **if** node i is switch **do**
21.   Select next-hop p that has the highest Q-value and satisfies the bandwidth and capacity requirements
22.   Send r_d to the next-hop p;
23.   Add next-hop p to routing table;
24.   **else** //node i is the server
25.   Calculate available storage capacity;
26.   Tag ACK packet with available storage capacity;
27.   Send ACK;
28.   **end if**
29. **end while**
30. **while** node i receiving ACK **do**
31.   Get information from ACK;
32.   Calculate Q-value by (6);
33.   Record RC and MB;
34.   **if** $\left|Q_i'(s_i,a_i)-Q_i(s_i,a_i)\right|\geq\varepsilon(1-\gamma)/2$ and phase $==$ Exploitation **do**
35.   phase $\leftarrow$ Exploration;

36. **end if;**
37. Send ACK;
38. **end while**
39. **while** node i receiving *data* **do**
40. **if** node i is switch **do**
41.   Send data to the next-hop based on routing table;
42.   **if** $\left|Q'_i(s_i,a_i)-Q_i(s_i,a_i)\right| \geq \varepsilon(1-\gamma)/2$ **do**
43.   phase $\leftarrow$ Exploration;
44.   **end if**
45. **else**   //node i is the server
46.   Store the data;
47. **end if**
48. **end while**

4   Simulation

4.1   Setup

We use the NS-3 simulator to perform the evaluation. We adopt Fat-tree as the network topology. The topology is divided into four layers. The upper layer is the core routers, followed by the aggregation routers. The following are edge routers, each of which is directly connected to two server nodes. Each group of aggregation routers, edge routers, and corresponding server nodes is called a Pod. In a k-pod Fat-tree, each pod has two layers of routers (aggregation and edge routers, respectively), each layer has $k/2$ routers, and each edge router connects to $k/2$ servers. We vary the value of k from 4 to 24 in this simulation. The bandwidth of each link is 1000 Mbps. The arrival rate of the data packet is 1 Mbps. The processing delay is 0.001 ms. The size of each data packet is 1 KB. We set the storage capacity to 10 GB for each server. Each data block consists of 1000 data packets. We compare our proposal with the random strategy and CRUSH [14] strategy in terms of delay, throughput, and server load. For the random and CRUSH strategy, we use a modified Nix-Vector algorithm that implemented in NS-3. The discount factor γ is set to 0.7, and the learning rate β is set to 0.5.

4.2   Results and Analysis

Figures 2 and 3 describe the results of the average delay of three placement algorithms. The simulation time is the running time of the simulator. Figure 4 shows the performance of the three algorithms in terms of average throughput. From Figs. 2 and 3, we can see that when simulation time increases, the Q-learning strategy performs well comparing with the other two strategies. At the beginning of the simulation, the random strategy has a low delay because it does not need to obtain the system information to make the decision. In the meantime, the Q-learning strategy will have to collect information and calculate the Q-value during its exploration phase. In this case, the delay of the Q-learning strategy can be close to or even higher than the random strategy. Later, the Q-learning strategy performs better when the calculation of Q-value converges. CRUSH strategy needs to generate the corresponding distribution function according to the system condition, and the distribution function is fixed. In the data-center where the network traffic changes dynamically, its performance of average delay is not good. The Nix-Vector is an on-demand routing strategy that calculates the routing path on the arrival of requests. To reduce the routing overhead, we record the routing information in the routing table. Then, when the subsequent request arrives, the Nix-Vector will not have to calculate the routing path again. In this case, the delay of random and CRUSH strategy drops over time.

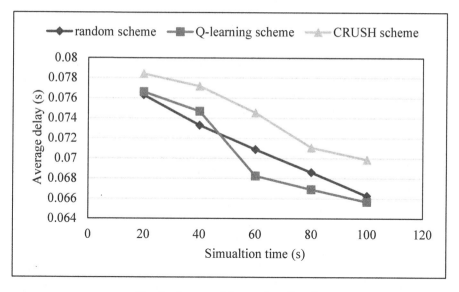

Fig. 2. Average delay vs time ($k = 4$).

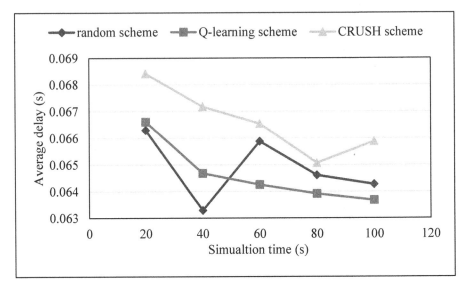

Fig. 3. Average delay vs time ($k = 8$).

Figure 4 shows the average throughput of different strategies under different values of k. The simulation runs for 100 s. From the figure, we can see that the Q-learning strategy has a slight advantage in terms of average throughput when the system runs long enough. This is because the Q-learning strategy approaches convergence and tends to the optimal solution. During the time of calculating Q-value, we consider the average bandwidth of the path and ensure that loads of each link are balanced. However, the advantage of the Q-learning algorithm in terms of average throughput is not obvious compared with the other two algorithms. This is because the Q-learning algorithm is not optimal in searching for the global optimal Q-value.

In the datacenter networks with unknown network conditions, when the system runs for a short time, the Q-learning method does not fully form a stable Q-value, so the performance of the algorithm on average delay is not good. When the running time is increasing, the Q-learning placement algorithm has a lower average delay because the Q-value in the routing table is gradually stabilized, and the algorithm can be found more accurately.

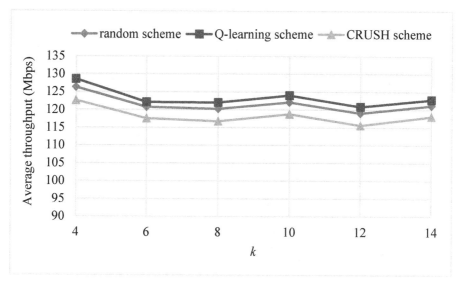

Fig. 4. Average throughput vs. k.

Figures 5 and 6 illustrate loads of each server after applying a random strategy and Q-learning strategy, respectively. The initial load of the server node is empty. Then, we apply different placement algorithms to place 10000 data blocks into the network. We set k to 8, and there are a total of 432 server nodes.

Random placement strategy randomly selects a server for storing data blocks without assessing the remaining storage capacity, which leads to uneven load among servers and unstable performance. CRUSH strategy generates a hash function based on global network information, but the hash function is relatively fixed once generated. Therefore, its performance is similar to the random placement strategy. The Q-learning strategy considers the remaining storage load of the server and the average bandwidth of path when calculating Q-value; therefore, it can avoid placing data block at a storage node with smaller bandwidth on the selected path.

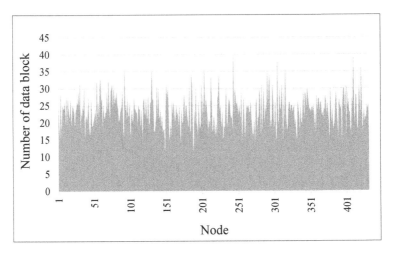

Fig. 5. Load of each node ($k = 8$, $n = 432$).

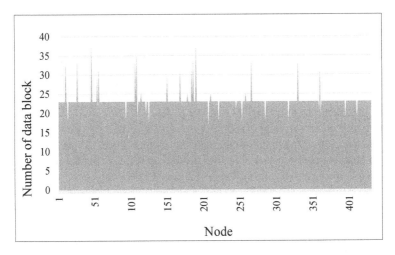

Fig. 6. Load of each node ($k = 8$, $n = 432$).

5 Conclusion

In this paper, we propose a reinforcement learning-based data placement strategy for the datacenter networks. The proposed strategy is adaptive to the network dynamic and adjusts the routing and placement decisions based on the available resource. We first model the placement problem as an optimization problem with constraints. Then, we present the detailed design of the Q-learning based data placement strategy, which consists of the exploration and exploitation phase. We perform the simulation to evaluate the performance of our proposal. The simulation results show that the proposed algorithm can effectively balance the load of nodes and improve the average throughput of the system while reducing the average delay.

References

1. Xia, W., Zhao, P., Wen, Y., Xie, H.: A survey on data center networking (DCN): infrastructure and operations. IEEE Commun. Surv. Tutor. **19**, 640–656 (2017). https://doi. org/10.1109/COMST.2016.2626784
2. Ghemawat, S., Gobioff, H., Leung, S.-T.: The Google file system. In: Proceedings of the 19th ACM Symposium on Operating Systems Principles, Bolton Landing, NY, pp. 20–43 (2003)
3. Lakshman, A., Malik, P.: Cassandra: a decentralized structured storage system. SIGOPS Oper. Syst. Rev. **44**, 35–40 (2010). https://doi.org/10.1145/1773912.1773922
4. Shvachko, K., Kuang, H., Radia, S., Chansler, R.: The hadoop distributed file system. In: 2010 IEEE 26th Symposium on Mass Storage Systems and Technologies (MSST), pp. 1–10 (2010). https://doi.org/10.1109/MSST.2010.5496972
5. Renuga, K., Tan, S.S., Zhu, Y.Q., Low, T.C., Wang, Y.H.: Balanced and efficient data placement and replication strategy for distributed backup storage systems. In: 2009 International Conference on Computational Science and Engineering, pp. 87–94 (2009). https://doi.org/10.1109/CSE.2009.27
6. Zaman, S., Grosu, D.: A distributed algorithm for the replica placement problem. IEEE Trans. Parallel Distrib. Syst. **22**, 1455–1468 (2011). https://doi.org/10.1109/TPDS.2011.27
7. Rajalakshmi, A., Vijayakumar, D., Srinivasagan, K.G.: An improved dynamic data replica selection and placement in cloud. In: 2014 International Conference on Recent Trends in Information Technology, pp. 1–6 (2014). https://doi.org/10.1109/ICRTIT.2014.6996180
8. Vilaça, R., Oliveira, R., Pereira, J.: A correlation-aware data placement strategy for key-value stores. In: Felber, P., Rouvoy, R. (eds.) DAIS 2011. LNCS, vol. 6723, pp. 214–227. Springer, Heidelberg (2011). https://doi.org/10.1007/978-3-642-21387-8_17
9. Meroufel, B., Belalem, G.: Dynamic replication based on availability and popularity in the presence of failures. J. Inf. Process. Syst. **8**, 263–278 (2012)
10. Paiva, J., Ruivo, P., Romano, P., Rodrigues, L.: AutoPlacer: scalable self-tuning data placement in distributed key-value stores. ACM Trans. Auton. Adapt. Syst. (TAAS) **9**, 19 (2015)
11. Wu, J.-J., Lin, Y.-F., Liu, P.: Optimal replica placement in hierarchical Data Grids with locality assurance. J. Parallel Distrib. Comput. **68**, 1517–1538 (2008)
12. Gao, C., Wang, H., Zhai, L., Gao, Y., Yi, S.: An energy-aware ant colony algorithm for network-aware virtual machine placement in cloud computing. In: 2016 IEEE 22nd International Conference on Parallel and Distributed Systems (ICPADS), pp. 669–676. IEEE (2016)
13. Lian, Q., Chen, W., Zhang, Z.: On the impact of replica placement to the reliability of distributed brick storage systems. In: 25th IEEE International Conference on Distributed Computing Systems (ICDCS 2005), pp. 187–196 (2005). https://doi.org/10.1109/ICDCS. 2005.56
14. Weil, S.A., Brandt, S.A., Miller, E.L., Maltzahn, C.: CRUSH: controlled, scalable, decentralized placement of replicated data. In: Proceedings of the 2006 ACM/IEEE Conference on Supercomputing, SC 2006, p. 31 (2006). https://doi.org/10.1109/SC.2006.19
15. Al-Fares, M., Loukissas, A., Vahdat, A.: A scalable, commodity data center network architecture. In: Proceedings of the ACM SIGCOMM 2008 Conference on Data Communication, pp. 63–74. ACM, New York (2008). https://doi.org/10.1145/1402958. 1402967
16. Doltsinis, S., Ferreira, P., Lohse, N.: An MDP model-based reinforcement learning approach for production station ramp-up optimization: q-learning analysis. IEEE Trans. Syst. Man Cybern.: Syst. **44**, 1125–1138 (2014). https://doi.org/10.1109/TSMC.2013.2294155

Scheduling Virtual Machine Migration During Datacenter Upgrades with Reinforcement Learning

Chen Ying[1]($\boxtimes$), Baochun Li[1], Xiaodi Ke[2], and Lei Guo[2]

[1] University of Toronto, Toronto, Canada
{chenying,bli}@ece.toronto.edu
[2] Huawei Canada, Markham, Canada
{xiaodi.ke,leiguo}@huawei.com

Abstract. Physical machines in modern datacenters are routinely upgraded due to their maintenance requirements, which involves migrating all the virtual machines they currently host to alternative physical machines. For this kind of datacenter upgrades, it is critical to minimize the time it takes to upgrade all the physical machines in the datacenter, so as to reduce disruptions to cloud services. To minimize the upgrade time, it is essential to carefully schedule the migration of virtual machines on each physical machine during its upgrade, without violating any constraints imposed by virtual machines that are currently running. Rather than resorting to heuristic algorithms, we propose a new scheduler, *Raven*, that uses an experience-driven approach with deep reinforcement learning to schedule the virtual machine migration process. With our design of the state space, action space and reward function, *Raven* trains a fully-connected neural network using the cross-entropy method to approximate the policy of a choosing destination physical machine for each migrating virtual machine. We compare *Raven* with state-of-the-art heuristic algorithms in the literature, and our results show that *Raven* effectively leads to shorter time to complete the datacenter upgrade process.

Keywords: Reinforcement learning · Virtual machine migration

1 Introduction

In modern datacenters, it is routine for physical machines to be upgraded to newer versions of operating systems or firmware versions from time to time, as part of their maintenance process. However, production datacenters are used for hosting virtual machines, and these virtual machines will have to be migrated to alternative physical machines during the upgrade process. The migration process takes time, which involves transferring the images of virtual machines between physical machines across the datacenter network.

X. Chu et al. (Eds.): QShine 2019, LNICST 300, pp. 102–117, 2020.
https://doi.org/10.1007/978-3-030-38819-5_7

To incur the least amount of disruption to cloud services provided by a production datacenter, it is commonly accepted that we need to complete the upgrade process as quickly as possible. Assuming that the time of upgrading a physical machine is dominated by the time it takes to migrate the images of all the virtual machines on this physical machine, the problem of minimizing the upgrade time of all physical machines in a datacenter is equivalent to minimizing the total migration time, which is the time it takes to finish all the virtual machine migrations during the datacenter upgrade.

In order to reduce the total migration time, we will need to carefully plan the schedule of migrating virtual machines. To be more specific, we should carefully select the best possible destination physical machine for each virtual machine to be migrated. However, as it is more realistic to assume that the topology of the datacenter network and the network capacity on each link are unknown to such a scheduler, computing the optimal migration schedule that minimizes the total migration time becomes more challenging.

With the objective of minimizing the migration time, a significant amount of work on scheduling the migration of virtual machines has been proposed. However, to the best of our knowledge, none of them considered the specific problem of migrating virtual machines during datacenter upgrades. It is common that existing work only migrated a small number of virtual machines to reduce the energy consumption of physical machines [1], or to balance the utilization of resources across physical machines [2]. Further, most of the proposed schedulers are based on heuristic algorithms and a set of strong assumptions that may not be realized in practice.

Without such detailed knowledge of the datacenter network, we wish to explore the possibilities of making scheduling decisions based on deep reinforcement learning [3], which trains a deep neural network agent to learn the policy of making better decisions from its experience, as it interacts with an unknown environment. Though it has been shown that deep reinforcement learning is effective in playing games [4], whether it is suitable for scheduling resource, especially in the context of scheduling migration of virtual machines, is not generally known.

In this paper, we propose *Raven*, a new scheduler for scheduling the migration process of virtual machines in the specific context of datacenter upgrades. In contrast to existing work in the literature, we assume that the topology and link capacities in the datacenter network are *not* known *a priori* to the scheduler, which is more widely applicable to realistic scenarios involving production datacenters. By considering the datacenter network as an unknown environment that needs to be explored, we seek to leverage reinforcement learning to train an agent to choose an optimal scheduling action, *i.e.,* the best destination physical machine for each virtual machine, with the objective of achieving the shortest possible total migration time for the datacenter upgrade. By tailoring the state space, action space and reward function for our scheduling problem, *Raven* uses the off-the-shelf cross-entropy method to train a fully-connected neural network to approximate the policy of choosing a destination physical machine for each virtual machine before its migration, aiming at minimizing the total migration time.

Highlights of our original contributions in this paper are as follows. *First*, we consider the real-world problem of migrating virtual machines for upgrading physical machines in a datacenter, which is rarely studied in the existing work. *Second*, we design the state space, action space, and reward function for our deep reinforcement learning agent to schedule the migration process of virtual machines with the objective of minimizing the total migration time. *Finally*, we propose and implement our new scheduler, *Raven*, and conduct a collection of simulations to show *Raven*'s effectiveness of outperforming the existing heuristic methods with respect to minimizing the total migration time it takes to complete the datacenter upgrade, without any *a priori* knowledge of the datacenter network.

2   Problem Formulation and Motivation

To start with, we consider two different resources, CPU and memory and we assume the knowledge of both the number of CPUs and the size of the main memory in each of the virtual machines (VMs) and physical machines (PMs). In addition, we also assume that the current mapping between the VMs and PMs is known as well, in that for each PM, we know the indexes of the VMs that are currently hosted there. It is commonly accepted that the number of CPUs and the size of main memory of VMs on a PM can be accommodated by the total number of physical CPUs and the total size of physical memory on its hosting PM.

We use the following example to illustrate the upgrade process of the physical machines, and to explain why the problem of scheduling VM migrations to minimize the total migration time may be non-trivial.

Assume there are three PMs in total, each hosting one of the three VMs. The sizes of these PMs and VMs, with respect to the number of CPUs and the amount of memory, are shown in Fig. 1. We will upgrade these PMs one by one. To show the total migration times of different schedules, we assume the simplest possible datacenter network topology, where all of these three PMs are connected to the same core switch, and the network capacity between the core switch to each PM is 1 GB/s.

In the first schedule, as shown in Fig. 1, we first upgrade PM #0 and migrate VM #0 to PM #2, and then upgrade PM #1 by migrating VM #1 to PM #0. Finally, we upgrade PM #2 with migrating VM #0 and VM # 2 to PM #0.

From the perspective of VMs, the migration process of each VM is:

◇ VM #0: PM #0 → PM #2 → PM #0;
◇ VM #1: PM #1 → PM #0;
◇ VM #2: PM #2 → PM #0.

To calculate the total migration time, we start from the VM on the PM that is upgraded first. In this schedule, we start from the migration of VM #0 from PM #0 to PM #2. As PM #0 is being upgraded now, here we cannot migrate VM #1 and VM #2 whose destination PM is PM #0. Since only VM #0 is

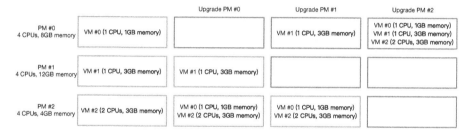

Fig. 1. Scheduling VM migration: a schedule that takes 10 s of total migration time.

being migrated, it can occupy all the network capacity through the link during its migration. Because the image size of VM #0 is 1 GB, this migration takes $1 \text{GB}/(1 \text{GB/s}) = 1 \text{s}$.

Then we come to VM #1 as PM #1 is upgraded next. Now the rest of migration processes whose migration times have not been calculated are:

◇ VM #0: PM #2 → PM #0;
◇ VM #1: PM #1 → PM #0;
◇ VM #2: PM #2 → PM #0.

Actually, all these three migration processes can be processed at the same time, because (1) for these three migration processes, no source PM is the same as any destination PMs and no destination PM is the same as any source PMs and (2) PM #0 has enough residual CPUs and memory to host these three VMs at the same time. Therefore, we can treat these three migration processes as a *migration batch*. The migration time of a migration batch is determined by the longest migration process in this batch. Since these three VMs share the link between the core switch and PM #0, each of them will get $\frac{1}{3}$ GB/s. The migration time of VM #0 is $1 \text{GB}/(\frac{1}{3} \text{GB/s}) = 3 \text{s}$. The migration time of VM #1 is $3 \text{GB}/(\frac{1}{3} \text{GB/s}) = 9 \text{s}$, which is the same as the migration time of VM #2. Thus, the migration time of this migration batch is 9 s. So the total migration time is $1 \text{s} + 9 \text{s} = 10 \text{s}$.

In contrast, a better schedule in terms of reducing the total migration time is shown in Fig. 2. We first upgrade PM #0 and migrate VM #0 to PM #1, and then upgrade PM #2 by migrating VM #2 to PM #0. Finally, we upgrade PM #1 and migrate VM #0 to PM #2 and VM #1 to VM #0.

From the perspective of VMs, the migration process of each VM is:

◇ VM #0: PM #0 → PM #1 → PM #2;
◇ VM #1: PM #1 → PM #0.
◇ VM #2: PM #2 → PM #0.

We start from VM #0 which is initially on the first migrated PM, PM #0. Since the destination PM of VM #1 is PM #0, which is the source PM of VM #0, the migration of VM #1 can not be in the current migration batch. For the

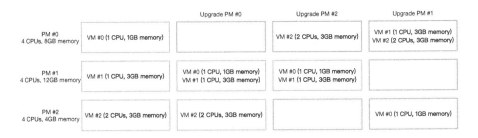

Fig. 2. Scheduling VM migration: a schedule that takes 8 s of total migration time.

same reason, the migration of VM #2 can not be in this batch either. Therefore, the migration time of this migration batch which only contains the migration of VM #0 from PM #0 to PM #1 is $1\,\mathrm{GB}/(1\mathrm{GB/s}) = 1\,\mathrm{s}$. Then we come to VM #2 because it is on PM #2 which is upgraded next. In this migration batch, we can also have the migration of VM #1 from PM #1 to PM #0. These two VMs share the link between the core switch to PM #0 with each of them having $\frac{1}{2}\,\mathrm{GB/s}$. The migration time of this batch is $3\,\mathrm{GB}/(\frac{1}{2}\mathrm{GB/s}) = 6\,\mathrm{s}$. At last, we compute the migration time of VM #0 from PM #1 to PM #2, which is 1 s. Therefore, the total migration time of this schedule is $1\,\mathrm{s} + 6\,\mathrm{s} + 1\,\mathrm{s} = 8\,\mathrm{s}$.

As we can observe from our example, even though we schedule the migration of VMs one by one, the actual migration order cannot be determined until we have the schedule of all VM migrations that will take place during the datacenter upgrade. This implies that we will only be able to compute the total migration time when the datacenter upgrade is completed. To make the scheduling problem even more difficult to solve, it is much more practical to assume that the topology and network capacities of the datacenter network is not known *a priori*, which makes it even more challenging to estimate the total migration time when scheduling the migration of VMs one by one. Therefore, we propose to leverage deep reinforcement learning to schedule the destination PM for each migrating VM, with the objective of minimizing the total migration time. The hope is that the agent of deep reinforcement learning can learn to make better decisions by iteratively interacting with an unknown environment over time.

3   Preliminaries

Before we advance to our proposed work in the *Raven* scheduler, we first introduce some preliminaries on deep reinforcement learning, which applies deep neural networks as function approximators of reinforcement learning.

Under the standard reinforcement learning setting, an agent learns by interacting with the environment E over a number of discrete time steps in an episodic fashion [3]. At each time step t, the agent observes the state s_t of the environment and takes an action a_t from a set of possible actions $\mathcal{A}$ according to its policy $\pi : \pi(a|s) \rightarrow [0, 1]$, which is a probability distribution over actions. $\pi(a|s)$ is the probability that action a is taken in state s. Following the taken action a_t, the state of the environment transits to state s_{t+1} and the agent receives a reward r_t. The process continues until the agent reaches a terminal state then a new episode begins. The states, actions, and rewards that the agent experienced during one episode form a trajectory $x = (s_1, a_1, r_1, s_2, a_2, r_2, \cdots, s_T, a_T, r_T)$, where T is the last time step in the episode. Cumulative reward $R(x) = \sum_{t \in [T]} r_t$ measures how good the trajectory is by summing up the rewards received at each time step during this episode.

As the agent's behavior is defined by a policy $\pi(a_t = a | s_t = s)$, which maps state s to a probability distribution over all actions $a \in \mathcal{A}$, how to store the state-action pairs is an important problem of reinforcement learning. Since the number of state-action pairs of complex decision making problems would be too large to store in tabular form, it is common to use function approximators, such as deep neural networks [4–6]. One significant advantage of deep neural networks is that they do not need handcrafted features. A function approximator has a manageable number of adjustable policy parameters θ. To show that the policy corresponds to parameters θ, we represent it as $\pi(a|s; \theta)$. For the problem of mapping a migrating VM to a destination PM, an optimal policy $\pi(a|s; \theta^*)$ with parameters θ^* is the mapping strategy we want to obtain.

To obtain the parameters θ^* of an optimal policy, we could use a basic but efficient method, cross-entropy [7], whose objective is to maximize the reward $R(x)$ received by a trajectory x from an arbitrary set of trajectories $\mathcal{X}$. Denote x^* as the corresponding trajectory at which the cumulative reward is maximal, and let ξ^* be the maximum cumulative reward, we thus have $R(x^*) = \max_{x \in \mathcal{X}} R(x) = \xi^*$.

Assume x has the probability density $f(x; u)$ with parameters u on $\mathcal{X}$, and the estimation of the probability that the cumulative reward of a trajectory is greater than a fixed level ξ is $l = \mathbb{P}(R(x) \geq \xi) = \mathbb{E}[1_{\{R(x) \geq \xi\}}]$, where $1_{\{R(x) \geq \xi\}}$ is the indicator function, that is, $1_{\{R(x) \geq \xi\}} = 1$ if $R(x) \geq \xi$, and 0 otherwise. If ξ happens to be set closely to the unknown ξ^*, $R(x) \geq \xi$ will be a rare event, which requires a large number of samples to estimate the expectation of its probability accurately. A better way to perform the sampling is to use importance sampling. Let $f(x; v)$ be another probability density with parameters v such that for all x, $f(x; v) = 0$ implies that $1_{\{R(x) \geq \xi\}} f(x; u) = 0$. Using the probability density $f(x; v)$, we can represent l as

$$l = \int 1_{\{R(x) \geq \xi\}} \frac{f(x; u)}{f(x; v)} f(x; v) \mathrm{d}x = \mathbb{E}_{x \sim f(x; v)} \left[1_{\{R(x) \geq \xi\}} \frac{f(x; u)}{f(x; v)} \right]. \quad (1)$$

The optimal importance sampling probability for a fixed level ξ is given by

$$f(x; v^*) \propto |1_{\{R(x) \geq \xi\}}| f(x; u), \quad (2)$$

which is generally difficult to obtain. Thus the idea of the cross-entropy method is to choose the importance sampling probability density $f(x; v)$ in a specified class of densities such that the distance between the optimal importance sampling density $f(x; v^*)$ and $f(x; v)$ is minimal. The distance $D(f_1, f_2)$ between two probability densities f_1 and f_2 could be measured by the Kullback-Leibler (KL) divergence which is defined as follows:

$$\mathcal{D}(f_1, f_2) = \mathbb{E}_{x \sim f_1(x)} \left[\log \frac{f_1(x)}{f_2(x)} \right]$$
$$= \mathbb{E}_{x \sim f_1(x)} \left[\log f_1(x) \right] - \mathbb{E}_{x \sim f_1(x)} \left[\log f_2(x) \right], \tag{3}$$

where the first term $\mathbb{E}_{x \sim f_1(x)} \left[\log f_1(x) \right]$ is called entropy, which does not reflect the distance between $f_1(x)$ and $f_2(x)$ and could be omitted during the minimization, while the second term $-\mathbb{E}_{x \sim f_1(x)} \left[\log f_2(x) \right]$ is called *cross-entropy*, which is a common optimization objective in deep learning. It turns out that the optimal parameters v^* is the solution to the maximization problem

$$\max_v \int \mathbf{1}_{\{R(x) \geq \xi\}} f(x; u) \log f(x; v) \mathrm{d}x, \tag{4}$$

which can be estimated via sampling by solving a stochastic counterpart program with respect to parameters v:

$$\hat{v} = \arg\max_v \frac{1}{N} \sum_{n \in [N]} \mathbf{1}_{\{R(x_n) \geq \xi\}} \frac{f(x_n; u)}{f(x_n; w)} \log f(x_n; v), \tag{5}$$

where $x_1, \cdots, x_N$ are random samples from $f(x; w)$ for any reference parameter w.

At the beginning of the deep neural network training, the parameters $u = \hat{v}_0$ are initialized randomly. By sampling with the current importance sampling distribution in each iteration k, we create a sequence of levels $\hat{\xi}_1, \hat{\xi}_2, \cdots$ which converges to the optimal performance ξ^*, and the corresponding sequence of parameter vectors $\hat{v}_0, \hat{v}_1, \cdots$ which converges to the optimal parameter vector. Note that $\hat{\xi}_k$ is typically chosen as the $(1 - \rho)$-quantile of performances of the sampled trajectories, which means that we will leave the top ρ of episodes sorted by cumulative reward. Sampling from an importance sampling distribution that is close to the theoretically optimal importance sampling density will produce optimal or near-optimal trajectories x^*. Typically, a smoothed updating rule with a smoothing parameter α is used, in which the parameter vector $\tilde{v}_k$ within the importance sampling density $f(x; v)$ after k-th iteration is $\tilde{v}_k = \alpha \hat{v}_k + (1 - \alpha)\tilde{v}_{k-1}$.

The probability of a trajectory $x \in \mathcal{X}$ is determined by the transition dynamics $p(s_{t+1}|s_t, a_t)$ of the environment and the policy $\pi(a_t|s_t; \theta)$. As the transition dynamics is determined by the environment and cannot be changed, the parameters θ in policy $\pi(a_t|s_t; \theta)$ are to be updated to improve the importance sampling density $f(x; v)$ of a trajectory x with $R(x)$ of high value. Therefore, the parameter estimator at iteration k could be represented as

$$\hat{\theta}_k = \arg\max_{\theta_k} \sum_{n \in [N]} \mathbf{1}_{\{R(x_n) \geq \xi_k\}} \left(\sum_{a_t, s_t \in x_n} \pi(a_t|s_t; \theta_k) \right), \tag{6}$$

where $x_1, \cdots, x_N$ are sampled from policy $\pi(a|s; \tilde{\theta}_{k-1})$, and $\tilde{\theta}_k = \alpha\hat{\theta}_k + (1 - \alpha)\tilde{\theta}_{k-1}$. The Eq. (6) could be interpreted as maximizing the likelihood of actions in trajectories with high cumulative rewards.

4   Design

This section presents the design of *Raven*. It begins with illustrating an overview of the architecture of *Raven*. We then formulate the problem of VM migration scheduling for reinforcement learning, and show our design of the state space, the action space, and the reward function.

4.1   Architecture

Figure 3 shows the architecture of *Raven*. The upgrade process starts from choosing a PM among PMs that have not been upgraded to upgrade. Then we have a queue of VMs that are on the chosen PM to be migrated. At each time step, one of the VMs in this queue is migrated. The key idea of *Raven* is to use a deep reinforcement learning agent to perform scheduling decision of choosing a destination PM for the migrating VM. The core component of the agent is the policy $\pi(a|s; \theta)$, providing the probability distribution over all actions given a state s. The parameters θ in $\pi(a|s; \theta)$ are learned from experiences collected when the agent interacts with the environment E.

An episode here is to finish the upgrade process of all physical machines in the datacenter. At time step t in an episode, the agent senses the state s_t of the environment, recognizes which VM is being migrated right now, and takes an action a_t, which is to choose a destination PM for this migrating VM based on its current policy. Then the environment will return a reward r_t which indicates whether the action a_t is good or not to the agent and transit to s_{t+1}.

We play a number of episodes with our environment. Due to the randomness of the way that the agent selects actions to take, some episodes will be better, *i.e.*, have higher cumulative rewards, than others. The key idea of the cross-entropy method is to throw away bad episodes and train the policy parameters θ based on good episodes. Therefore, the agent will calculate the cumulative reward of every episode and decide a reward boundary, and train based on episodes whose cumulative reward is higher than the reward boundary by using each state as the input and the issued action as the desired output.

4.2   Deep Reinforcement Learning Formulation

The design of the state space, action space and reward function is one of the most critical steps when applying deep reinforcement learning to a practical problem. To train an effective policy within a short period of time, the deep reinforcement learning agent should be carefully designed such that it will be able to master the key components of the problem without useless or redundant information.

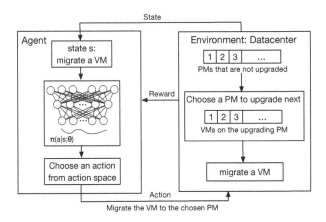

Fig. 3. The architecture of *Raven*.

State Space. To describe the environment correctly and concisely for the agent, the state should include the knowledge of the upgrade status, the total number and usage of all resources of each PM and information of the migrating VM. So we have the following design of the state.

At time step t, we denote the detailed information of PM $\#j$, $j = 0, 1, \ldots, J-1$, as $s_{tj} = \{s_{tj}^{\text{status}}, s_{tj}^{\text{total}-\text{cpu}}, s_{tj}^{\text{total}-\text{mem}}, s_{tj}^{\text{used}-\text{cpu}}, s_{tj}^{\text{used}-\text{mem}}\}$, where J is the total number of PMs in this datacenter and s_{tj}^{status} is the upgrade status of PM $\#j$. There are three possible upgrade statuses: not yet, upgrading and upgraded. $s_{tj}^{\text{total}-\text{cpu}}$ and $s_{tj}^{\text{total}-\text{mem}}$ represent the total number of CPUs and the total size of main memory of PM $\#j$, respectively. $s_{tj}^{\text{used}-\text{cpu}}$ and $s_{tj}^{\text{used}-\text{mem}}$ denote the number of used CPUs and the size of used memory of PM $\#j$, respectively. We represent the state of the environment at time step t as

$$s_t = \{s_{t0}, s_{t1}, \ldots, s_{t(J-1)}, v_t^{\text{cpu}}, v_t^{\text{mem}}, v_t^{\text{pm}-\text{id}}\}, \tag{7}$$

where v_t^{cpu}, v_t^{mem} and $v_t^{\text{pm}-\text{id}}$ denote the number of CPUs, the size of memory of and the source PM index of the migrating VM, respectively.

Action Space. Since the agent is trained to choose a destination PM for each migrating VM, the action a_t should be set as the index of the destination PM.

Even though it is intuitive to set the action space as $\mathcal{A} = \{0, 1, \ldots, J-1\}$, this setting has two major problems that (1) the destination PM may not have enough residual resources for the migrating VM and (2) the destination PM may be the source PM of the migrating VM. To avoid these two problems, we dynamically change the action space for each migrating VM, instead of keeping the action space unchanged as traditional reinforcement learning methods.

When the migrating VM is decided at time step t, the subset of PMs that are not the source PM of the migrating VM and have enough number of residual CPUs and enough size of residual memory can be determined. We denote the set of indexes of PMs in this subset as $\mathcal{A}_t^{\text{eligible}}$. The action space at this time step will be $\mathcal{A}_t^{\text{eligible}}$.

State Transition. Assume at time step t, the migrating VM on PM #m takes v_t^{cpu} number of CPUs and v_t^{mem} size of memory, and the agent takes action $a_t = n$, then we have the state of PM #m at time step $t+1$ as

$$s_{(t+1)m} = \{\text{upgraded}, s_{tm}^{\text{total}-\text{cpu}}, s_{tm}^{\text{total}-\text{mem}}, s_{tm}^{\text{used}-\text{cpu}} - v_t^{\text{cpu}}, s_{tm}^{\text{used}-\text{mem}} - v_t^{\text{mem}}\}, \tag{8}$$

and the state of PM #n at time step $t+1$ as

$$s_{(t+1)n} = \{s_{tn}^{\text{status}}, s_{tn}^{\text{total}-\text{cpu}}, s_{tn}^{\text{total}-\text{mem}}, s_{tn}^{\text{used}-\text{cpu}} + v_t^{\text{cpu}}, s_{tn}^{\text{used}-\text{mem}} + v_t^{\text{mem}}\}. \tag{9}$$

Thus the state of the environment at time step $t+1$ will be

$$s_{t+1} = \{s_{t0}, \ldots, s_{(t+1)m}, \ldots, s_{(t+1)n}, \ldots, s_{t(J-1)}, v_{t+1}^{\text{cpu}}, v_{t+1}^{\text{mem}}, v_{t+1}^{\text{pm}-\text{id}}\}, \tag{10}$$

where v_{t+1}^{cpu}, v_{t+1}^{mem} and $v_{t+1}^{\text{pm}-\text{id}}$ are the number of CPUs, size of memory and source PM index of the migrating VM at time step $t+1$.

Reward. The objective of the agent is to find out a scheduling decision to minimize the total migration time for each migrating VM. Since for our scheduling problem, we cannot know the total migration time until the schedule of all VM migrations is known. To be more specific, we can only know the total migration time after the episode is finished. This is because although we make the scheduling decision for VMs one by one, the VM migrations in the datacenter network are conducted in a different order which is not determined until we finish scheduling all the migrations, as we have discussed in Sect. 2.

Therefore, we design the reward r_t after taking action a_t at state s_t as $r_t = 0$ when $t = 1, 2, \ldots, T - 1$, where T is the number of time steps to complete this episode. At time step T, as the schedule of all VM migrations is determined, the total migration time can be computed. We set r_T as the negative number of the total migration time. So the cumulative reward of an episode will be the negative number of the total migration time of this episode. Therefore, by maximizing the cumulative reward received by the agent, we can actually minimize the total migration time.

5   Performance Evaluation

We conduct simulations of *Raven* to show its effectiveness in scheduling the migration process of virtual machines during the datacenter upgrade in terms of shortening the total migration time.

5.1   Simulation Settings

We evaluate the performance of *Raven* under various datacenter settings, where the network topology, the total number of physical machines and the total number virtual machines are different. Also, we randomly generate the mapping between the virtual machines and physical machines before the datacenter upgrade to make the environment more uncertain.

Since to the best of our knowledge, there is no existing work that studies the same scheduling problem of virtual machine migration for the datacenter upgrade as we do, we can only compare our method with existing scheduling methods of virtual machine migration designed for other migration reasons.

Here we compare *Raven* with the state-of-the-art virtual machine migration scheduler, Min-DIFF [2], which uses a heuristic based method to balance the usage of different kinds of resources on each physical machine. We also come up with a simple heuristic method to minimize the total migration time.

5.2   Simulation Results

Convergence Behaviour. The convergence behaviour of a reinforcement learning agent is a useful indicator to show that if the agent successfully learns the policy or not. A preferable convergence behaviour is that the cumulative rewards can gradually increase through the training iterations and converge to a high value.

We plot the figures of number of training iterations and cumulative rewards in different datacenters with 3, 5, 10 physical machines as Figs. 4, 5 and 6, respectively. The network topology here is that all PMs are connected to the same core switch.

As shown in these figures, *Raven* is able to learn the policy of scheduling the virtual machine migration in datacenter with various number of physical machines and virtual machines. As the number of total physical machines and virtual machines increases, the agent normally needs more iterations to converge, which is reasonable since the environment becomes more complex for the agent to learn.

However, in Fig. 4, we find that it takes fewer iterations to converge for a datacenter with 12 virtual machines than for a datacenter with 6 virtual machines or 9 virtual machines. This is due to the randomness of the initial mapping between physical machines and virtual machines before the upgrade process. We can see that some initial mappings are easier to learn for the deep reinforcement learning agent that the others.

The same situation happens when there are 10 physical machine in Fig. 5. It takes longer to converge for a datacenter with 30 virtual machines than for a datacenter with 40 virtual machines. Also, it seems difficult to converge when there are 30 virtual machines. But we find that the agent can still generate schedules with shorter total migration time than the methods we compare with before it converges, which will be presented next.

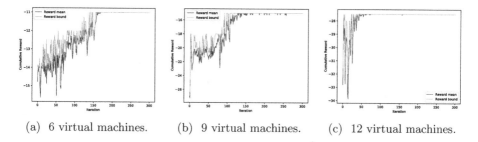

(a) 6 virtual machines.   (b) 9 virtual machines.   (c) 12 virtual machines.

Fig. 4. The learning curve of *Raven* in datacenter with 3 physical machines.

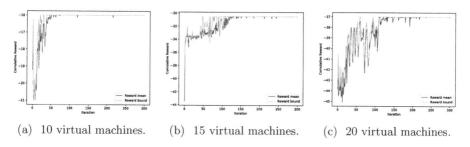

(a) 10 virtual machines.   (b) 15 virtual machines.   (c) 20 virtual machines.

Fig. 5. The learning curve of *Raven* in datacenter with 5 physical machines.

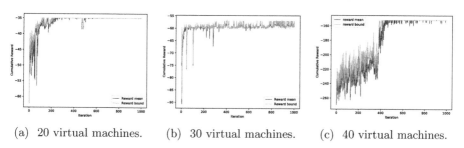

(a) 20 virtual machines.   (b) 30 virtual machines.   (c) 40 virtual machines.

Fig. 6. The learning curve of *Raven* in datacenter with 10 physical machines.

Total Migration Time. Even though we demonstrate that *Raven* is able to learn the scheduling policy of virtual machine migration, we still need to evaluate if this scheduling policy can generate the schedule that reduces the total migration time. Since we set the cumulative reward as the negative number of the total migration time, the negative number of the cumulative reward is the total migration time of the schedule generated by *Raven*.

We compute the total migration times of using Min-DIFF and the heuristic method for comparison. Different network topologies are also applied. Besides the two-layer network topology where all the physical machines are connected to the same core switch, we also have the three-layer network topology where physical machines are connected to different aggregation switches and all aggregation switches are connected to the same core switch. If the number of aggregation switches is 0, it means that the network topology is two-layer.

As we have discussed that the initial mapping between virtual machines and physical machines before the datacenter upgrade will affect the result, we conduct the simulation of each datacenter setting for 10 times and show the average total migration time in Table 1.

From Table 1, we can see that *Raven* is able to achieve shorter migration time than the other two schedulers. As the network topology becomes more complex and the number of physical machines and virtual machines increases below a certain number, *i.e.*, 50 physical machines, the superiority of *Raven* in terms of shortening the total migration time becomes more obvious. This indicates

Table 1. Average total migration time within different datacenter.

Datacenter setting			Average total migration time		
Number of PMs	Number of VMs	Number of aggregation switches	Min-DIFF	Heuristic	*Raven*
3	6	0	13.00	12.95	12.20
3	6	2	32.05	32.05	31.35
3	9	0	18.60	18.45	17.54
3	9	2	51.50	51.55	47.10
3	12	0	28.35	28.85	27.65
3	12	2	73.00	73.25	70.95
3	12	3	85.55	85.00	81.35
5	10	0	18.35	17.55	16.25
5	10	2	48.35	52.35	46.25
5	15	0	32.30	32.15	31.80
5	15	2	59.80	60.85	59.05
5	15	3	61.80	64.60	52.75
5	20	0	39.85	38.05	36.75
5	20	2	98.65	104.60	92.50
5	20	3	116.45	115.35	100.05
5	20	4	133.75	130.65	119.60
10	20	0	39.00	39.50	38.20
10	30	0	59.85	58.35	53.25
10	40	0	76.60	75.25	72.80
20	100	0	195.00	205.00	175.50
50	100	0	198.60	198.50	216.25
50	150	0	298.50	296.50	377.25
100	200	0	416.85	430.30	403.50
100	300	0	598.75	598.75	796.75

that it may be difficult for heuristic methods to handle the scheduling of virtual machine migration with minimal total migration time when the datacenter has large number of physical machines and virtual machines under complex network topology, while *Raven* can gradually learn to come up with schedules of shorter total migration time.

The results of 10 physical machines are the total migration times generated at the 1000th training iteration. Those results indicate that even when it may take a large number of iterations for *Raven* to converge its cumulative reward, *i.e.*, when there are 30 virtual machines, the schedule that *Raven* generates before the convergence can still outperform the other two methods.

However, when the number of physical machines becomes 50, we find that it is difficult for *Raven* to learn a schedule that has shorter total migration time than the other two methods. The cumulative rewards can gradually increase through training iterations, but it is hard to converge to a high value. One possible reason could be that so far we have only used fully-connected neural networks as policy approximators. It might be easier for the agent to converge when more complex and powerful deep neural networks are used. It should be noted that under the datacenter setting of 100 physical machines and 200 virtual machines, *Raven* outperforms again, which again shows the effect of the randomness of the initial mapping between physical machines and virtual machines to the result.

6   Related Work

Within a datacenter, it is common to process virtual machine migration due to various reasons, such as for the maintenance of the hosting physical machines or for the load balancing among physical machines in the datacenter. To ensure high quality of service of the datacenter, how to efficiently schedule the virtual machine migration to achieve different objectives has been extensively studied.

In order to reduce the amount of data transferred over the network during the virtual machine migration, Sapuntzakis *et al.* [8] designed a capsule-based system architecture, *Collective*.

To reduce the number of migration, Maurya *et al.* [1] proposed a minimum migration time policy which is capable of reducing the number of migration and the energy consumption of virtual machine migration proceeded to optimize resource usage and lower energy consumptions of physical machines in the datacenter.

Virtual machine migration is also studied in the field of over-committed cloud datacenter [2,9,10]. Within this kind of datacenter, the service provider allocates more resources to virtual machines than it actually has to reduce resource wastage, as study indicated that virtual machines tend to utilize fewer resources than reserved capacities. Therefore, it is necessary to migrate virtual machines when the hosting physical machines reach it is capacity limitation. Ji *et al.* [2] proposed a virtual machine migration algorithm which can balance the usage of different resources on activated physical machines and also minimize the number of activated physical machines in an over-committed cloud.

7 Conclusion

In this paper, we study a scheduling problem of virtual machine migration during the datacenter upgrade without a priori knowledge of the topology and network capacity of the datacenter network. We find that for this specific scheduling problem which is rarely studied before, it is difficult for previous schedulers of virtual machine migration using heuristics to reach the optimal total migration time.

Inspired by the success of applying deep reinforcement learning in recent years, we develop a new scheduler, *Raven*, which uses an experience-driven approach with deep reinforcement learning to decide the destination physical machine for each migrating virtual machine with the objective of minimizing the total migration time to complete the datacenter upgrade. With our careful design of the state space, the action space and the reward function, *Raven* learns to generate schedules with the shortest possible total migration time by interacting with the unknown environment.

Our extensive simulation results show that *Raven* is able to outperform existing heuristic scheduling methods under different datacenter settings with various number of physical machines and virtual machines and different network topology. However, as the number of physical machines and virtual machines becomes large, it is difficult for *Raven* to converge and outperform other methods. We discuss the possible reasons behind it and will improve it in our future work.

References

1. Maurya, K., Sinha, R.: Energy conscious dynamic provisioning of virtual machines using adaptive migration thresholds in cloud data center. Int. J. Comput. Sci. Mob. Comput. **2**(3), 74–82 (2013)
2. Ji, S., Li, M.D., Ji, N., Li, B.: An online virtual machine placement algorithm in an over-committed cloud. In: 2018 IEEE International Conference on Cloud Engineering, IC2E 2018, Orlando, FL, USA, 17–20 April 2018, pp. 106–112 (2018)
3. Sutton, R.S., Barto, A.G.: Reinforcement Learning: An Introduction, vol. 1, no. 1. MIT Press, Cambridge (1998)
4. Mnih, V., et al.: Human-level control through deep reinforcement learning. Nature **518**, 529–533 (2015)
5. Mao, H., Alizadeh, M., Menache, I., Kandula, S.: Resource management with deep reinforcement learning. In: Proceedings of the 15th ACM Workshop on Hot Topics in Networks, pp. 50–56. ACM (2016)
6. Silver, D., et al.: Mastering the game of go without human knowledge. Nature **550**, 354–359 (2017)
7. Rubinstein, R., Kroese, D.: The Cross-Entropy Method. Springer, Heidelberg (2004). https://doi.org/10.1007/978-1-4757-4321-0
8. Sapuntzakis, C.P., Chandra, R., Pfaff, B., Chow, J., Lam, M.S., Rosenblum, M.: Optimizing the migration of virtual computers. In: 5th Symposium on Operating System Design and Implementation (OSDI 2002), Boston, Massachusetts, USA, 9–11 December 2002 (2002)

9. Zhang, X., Shae, Z.-Y., Zheng, S., Jamjoom, H.: Virtual machine migration in an over-committed cloud. In: Proceedings of the IEEE Network Operations and Management Symposium (NOMS) (2012)
10. Dabbagh, M., Hamdaoui, B., Guizani, M., Rayes, A.: Efficient datacenter resource utilization through cloud resource overcommitment. In: Proceedings of the IEEE Conference on Computer Communications Workshops (INFOCOM WKSHPS) (2015)

Batch Auction Design for Cloud Container Services

Yu He[1], Lin Ma[1], Ruiting Zhou[2]([⊠]), and Chuanhe Huang[1]

[1] School of Computer Science, Wuhan University, Wuhan, China
{heyu,linma,huangch}@whu.edu.cn
[2] School of Cyber Science and Engineering, Wuhan University, Wuhan, China
ruitingzhou@whu.edu.cn

Abstract. Cloud containers represent a new, light-weight alternative to virtual machines in cloud computing. A user job may be described by a container graph that specifies the resource profile of each container and container dependence relations. This work is the first in the cloud computing literature that designs efficient market mechanisms for container based cloud jobs. Our design targets simultaneously incentive compatibility, computational efficiency, and economic efficiency. It further adapts the idea of batch online optimization into the paradigm of mechanism design, leveraging agile creation of cloud containers and exploiting delay tolerance of elastic cloud jobs. The new and classic techniques we employ include: (i) compact exponential optimization for expressing and handling non-traditional constraints that arise from container dependence and job deadlines; (ii) the primal-dual schema for designing efficient approximation algorithms for social welfare maximization; and (iii) posted price mechanisms for batch decision making and truthful payment design. Theoretical analysis and trace-driven empirical evaluation verify the efficacy of our container auction algorithms.

Keywords: Cloud container · Online auction

1 Introduction

Cloud computing offers cloud users with utility-like computing services in a pay-as-you-go fashion. Computing resources including CPU, RAM, disk storage and bandwidth can be leased in custom packages with minimal management overhead. Virtualization technologies help cloud providers pack cloud resources into a functional package for serving user jobs. Such packages used to be dominantly virtual machines (VMs), until the recent emergence of *cloud containers*, *e.g.*, Google Container Engine (largest Linux container) [6], Amazon EC2 Container Service (ECS) [2], Aliyun Container Service [1], Azure Container Service [3], and IBM Containers. Compared with general-purpose VMs, containers are more flexible and lightweight, enabling efficient and agile resource management. Applications are encapsulated inside the containers without running in a dedicated

X. Chu et al. (Eds.): QShine 2019, LNICST 300, pp. 118–137, 2020.
https://doi.org/10.1007/978-3-030-38819-5_8

operating system [25]. A representative cloud container is only megabytes in size and takes seconds to start [23,25], while launching a VM may take minutes. In the era of using VMs, VMs remain open throughout the life of the job. Because of the transient nature of a container, jobs could be separated into several containers, and resource allocation is more convenient.

A complex cloud job in practice is often composed of *sub-tasks*. For example, a social game server [19] typically consists of a front-end web server tier, a load balancing tier and a back-end data storage tier; a network security application may consist of an intrusion detection system (IDS), a firewall, and a load balancer. Different sub-tasks require different configurations of CPU, RAM, disk storage and bandwidth resources. Each sub-task can be served by a custom-made container following the resource profile defined by the cloud user [14]. Some cloud containers are to be launched after others finish execution, following the input-output relation of their corresponding tasks. Such a dependence relation among containers is captured by a *container (dependence) graph*. For example, in Amazon ECS, a cloud user submits a job definition including resource requirements, type of docker image, a container graph, and environment variables. ECS then provisions the containers on a shared operating system, instead of running VMs with complete operating systems [22] (Fig. 1).

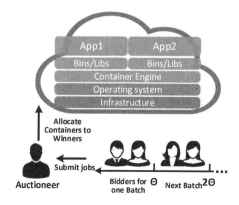

Fig. 1. Batch auction of cloud jobs running on containers.

In the growing cloud marketplace (*e.g.*, Amazon EC2 and ECS), fixed pricing mechanisms and auctions complement each other. While the former is simple to implement, the latter can automatically discover the market price of cloud services, and allocate resources to cloud users who value them the most [28]. A series of recent cloud auction mechanisms implicitly aim at non-elastic cloud jobs. These include both one-round cloud auctions [28] and online cloud auctions [21,29]. In both cases, the provider processes each bid immediately and commits to an irrevocable decision. Furthermore, even in the online auctions, users' service time window is *predefined* by start and finish times in the bid [21,29].

A large fraction of cloud jobs are elastic in nature, as exemplified by big data analytics and Google crawling data processing. They require a certain computing job to be completed without demanding always-on computing service, and may tolerate a certain level of delay in bid acceptance and in job completion. For example, since Sanger *et al.* published the first complete genome sequence of an organism in 1977, DNA sequencing algorithms around the globe currently produce 15 billion gigabytes of data per annum, for cloud processing [9]. A typical job of DNA testing takes 4 hours to complete, while the user is happy to receive the final result anytime in a few days after job submission [17].

Given that bids from cloud users can tolerate a certain level of delay in bid admission, it is natural to revise the common practice of immediate irrevocable decision making in online cloud auctions. We can group bids from a common time window into a batch, and apply batch bid processing to make more informed decisions on all bids from the same batch simultaneously. Actually, if one considers only online optimization and not online auctions, then such batch processing has already been studied in operations research, such as online scheduling to minimize job completion time [8], and scheduling batch and heterogeneous jobs with runtime elasticity in cloud computing platforms [16].

We study efficient auctions for cloud container services, where a bid submitted by a cloud user specifies: (i) the container dependence graph of the job; (ii) the resource profile of each container; (iii) the deadline of the job; and (iv) the willingness to pay (bidding price). Cloud containers can be agilely created and dropped to handle dynamic sub-tasks in cloud jobs; it becomes practically feasible to suspend and resume a sub-task. As long as a container is scheduled to run for a sufficient number of time slots, its sub-task will finish.

This work advances the state-of-the-art in the literature of cloud auctions along two directions. ***First***, while *batch algorithms* have been extensively studied in the field of online optimization, to the authors' knowledge, this work is the first that studies *batch auctions* in online auction design. ***Second***, this work is the first cloud auction mechanism designed for container services, with expressive bids based on container graphs. Our mechanism design simultaneously targets the following goals: (i) *truthfulness*, *i.e.*, bidding true valuation for executing its job on the cloud maximizes a user's utility, regardless of how other users bid; (ii) *time efficiency*, we require that all components of the auction run in polynomial time, for practical implementation; (iii) *expressiveness*; the target auction permits a user to specify its job deadlines, desired cloud containers, and inter-container dependence relations; and (iv) *social welfare maximization*; *i.e.*, the overall 'happiness' of the cloud-ecosystem is maximized.

Corresponding to the above goals, our auction design leverages the following classic and new techniques in algorithm and mechanism design. For effectively expressing and handling user bids that admit deadline specification and container dependence graphs, we develop the technique of *compact exponential Integer Linear Programs (ILPs)*. We transform a natural formulation of the social welfare optimization ILP into a compact ILP with an exponential number of variables corresponding to valid container schedules. Although such a reformulation substantially inflates the ILP size, it lays the foundation for later efficient primal-dual approximation algorithm design, helping deal with non-conventional constraints that arise from container dependence and job deadlines, whose dual variables are hard to interpret and update directly. A combinatorial sub-routine later helps identify good container schedules efficiently without exhaustively enumerating them.

Towards truthful batch auction design, we leverage the recent developments in *posted price auctions* [26]. At a high level, such an auction maintains an estimate of marginal resource prices for each resource type, based on expected supply-demand. Then upon decision making of each batch of bids, it chooses bids whose willingness to pay surpasses the estimated cost to serve them, based on resource demand of the container graph and projected marginal prices of resources. A winning user is charged with such estimated cost, which is independent from its bidding price. Truthfulness is hence guaranteed based on Myerson's celebrated characterization of truthful mechanisms [18].

The social welfare maximization problem in our container auction is NP-hard even in the offline setting, with all inputs given at once. A third key element of our cloud container auction is the classic primal-dual schema for designing efficient approximation algorithms, with rigorous guarantee on worst case performance. This is further integrated with the posted price framework, in that the marginal resource prices are associated with dual variables. The primal dual framework relies on a sub-routine that computes the optimal schedule of a given container graph, based on static resource prices (fixing dual variables, update primal solution). We apply dynamic programming [11] and graph traversal algorithms, for designing the sub-routine for (i) service chain type jobs from network function virtualization, and (ii) general jobs with arbitrary topologies in their container graphs. We evaluate the effectiveness of our cloud container auction through rigorous theoretical analysis and trace-driven simulation studies.

In the rest of the paper, we discuss related work in Sect. 2, and introduce the auction model in Sect. 3. The container auction is presented and analyzed in Sects. 4 and 5 separately. Section 6 presents simulation studies, and Sect. 7 concludes the paper.

2   Related Work

There exist a large body of studies in recent cloud computing literature on cloud auction design. Shi *et al.* [20] studied online auctions where users bid for heterogeneous types of VMs and proposed RSMOA, an online cloud auction for dynamic resource provisioning. Zhang *et al.* [27] propose COCA, a framework for truthfull online cloud auctions based on a monotonic payment rule and utility-maximizing allocation rule. These auction mechanisms are all confined to the solution space of immediately accepting or rejecting an arriving bid. To our knowledge, this work is the first that designs batch-type online auctions, both in the field of cloud computing and in the general literature of auction mechanism design.

In terms of batch-type online algorithms, Bitton *et al.* [7] study online scheduling in a batch processing system. Kumar *et al.* [16] design scheduling mechanisms for runtime elasticity of heterogeneous workloads. They propose Delayed-LOS and Hybrid-LOS, two algorithms that improve an existing dynamic programming based scheduler. These work possess a resemblance to ours in terms of postponing immediate response for more informed decision making, although they focus on algorithm design only and do not consider payments or incentive compatibility.

Along the direction of posted price algorithms and mechanisms, Huang *et al.* [15] study online combinatorial auctions with production costs. They show that posted price mechanisms are incentive compatible and achieve optimal competitive ratios. Etzion *et al.* [10] present a simulation model to extend previous analytical framework, focusing on a firm selling consumer goods online using posted price and auction at the same time. This work was inspired in part by this line of recent developments on using posted prices to achieve effective resource allocation and bid-independent charges.

3   The Cloud Container Auction Model

We consider a public cloud in which the cloud provider (auctioneer) manages a pool of R types of resources, as exemplified by CPU, RAM, disk storage and bandwidth, and the capacity of resource-r is $\mathbb{C}_r$. Integer set $\{1, 2,..., X\}$ is denoted by $[X]$. There are I cloud users arriving in a large time span $\{1, 2, ..., T\}$, acting as bidders in the auction. Each user i submits a job bid that is 4-tuple:

$$\Pi_i = \{\mathcal{W}_i, t_i, d_i, B_i\}. \tag{1}$$

Here $\mathcal{W}_i$ is the workload of user i, t_i is arrival time of user i, and its required deadline for job completion is d_i. B_i is user i's overall willingness-to-pay for finishing its job by d_i (Fig. 2).

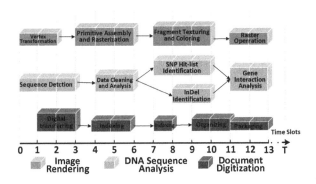

Fig. 2. Container graphs for cloud jobs from [4].

According to users workload, the detailed information will be obtained by cloud platform. Such as the number of sub-tasks of the job M, and each sub-task requires a container to process, thus m is also the number of containers. The container graph G_i that describes the dependence among sub-tasks. The number of requested time slots for each sub-task N_{im}. Each sub-task can be suspended and resumed, as long as the total execution time accumulates to N_{im}. h_{im}^r is the resource configuration of container m of user i.

A (container) schedule is a mapping from resources and time slots to cloud containers, serving accepted cloud jobs to meet their deadlines. We postpone immediate decision making on the bids, to judiciously exploit cloud jobs' tolerable delays in bid admission. We group bids from every θ time slots into a batch, resulting in Q batches within the large time span T. Let ρ_q be the number of users arriving within batch $q \in Q$. A binary variable x_i indicates whether user i's bid is accepted (1) or not (0). Another binary variable $z_{im}(t)$ indicates whether to execute user i's sub-task m at time slot t (1) or not (0); it encodes a schedule of user i's job. The cloud provider further computes a payment P_i to charge for a winning cloud user i. The holy grail of auction mechanism design is truthfulness, the property that greatly simplifies bidder strategy space and analysis of the auction mechanism (Table 1).

Table 1. List of notations

I	# of users
T	# of time slots
$\mathbb{C}_r$	capacity of type-r resource
M	# of sub-tasks/containers of one job
$\mathcal{W}_i$	Workload of user i
G_i	Dependence graph of user i's sub-tasks
N_{im}	# of time slots requested by user i's container m
h_{im}^r	Demand of type-r resource by user i's container m
t_i	User i's arrival time
d_i	Deadline of user i's bid
B_i	Bidding price of user i's bid
x_i	Accept the user i's bid(1) or not(0)
ρ_q	# of users arriving within batch q
$f_{ir}^S(t)$	Total type-r resource occupation of schedule in Γ_i for slot t
θ	# of time slots within one batch interval
$z_{im}(t)$	Allocated user i's container m at time slot t(1) or not(0)
$w_r(t)$	Amount of allocated type-r resource at time t
$y_r(t)$	Availablity of type-r resource at time slot t
$\kappa_r(t)$	Marginal price of type-r resource at time slot t
F_r	Minimum value of user's valuation per unit of type-r resource
D_r	Maximum value of user's valuation per unit of type-r resource
Γ_i	The set of valid schedules for each user
u_i	User i's utility

Lemma 1. *Let $Pr(B_i)$ denote the probability of bidder i winning an auction and B_{-i} be the bidding price except i. A mechanism is truthful if and only if the following hold for a fixed B_{-i} [12]:*

(1) $Pr(B_i)$ is monotonically non-decreasing in B_i;
(2) bidder i is charged by $B_i Pr(B_i) - \int_0^{B_i} Pr(B_i)dB$.

Lemma 1 can be explained in this orientation: the payment charged to bidder i for a fixed B_i is independent of B_i. We will use this mode to design a posted price function in Sect. 4. Since we meet the challenge that when we consider that online batch auction decisions are to be made based on hitherto information only. If user i's job is accepted, its utility is $u_i = v_i - P_i$, which equals $u_i = B_i - P_i$ under truthful bidding. The cloud provider's utility is $\sum_{i \in [I]} P_i$. The *social welfare* that captures the overall utility of both the provider and the users is $(\sum_{i \in [I]} B_i x_i - \sum_{i \in [I]} P_i) + (\sum_{i \in [I]} P_i)$. With payments cancelling themselves, the social welfare is simplified to $\sum_{i \in [I]} B_i x_i$.

Under the assumption of truthful bidding, the Social Welfare Maximization problem in our cloud container auction can be formulated into the following Integer Linear Program (ILP):

$$\text{maximize} \quad \sum_{i \in [I]} B_i x_i \tag{2}$$

subject to:

$$\theta \lceil \frac{t_i}{\theta} \rceil x_i \leq t z_{im}(t), \forall t, \forall m, \forall i : t_i \leq t, \tag{2a}$$

$$t z_{im}(t) \leq d_i x_i, \forall t, \forall m, \forall i : t_i \leq t, \tag{2b}$$

$$t z_{im}(t) \leq t' z_{im'}(t'), \tag{2c}$$

$$\forall t, t', \forall i : task\ m'\ arrives\ later\ than\ task\ m,$$

$$N_{im} x_i \leq \sum_{t \in [T]} z_{im}(t), \forall m, \forall i, \tag{2d}$$

$$\sum_{i \in [I]} \sum_{m \in [M]} h_{im}^r z_{im}(t) \leq \mathbb{C}_r, \forall r, \forall t, \tag{2e}$$

$$x_i, z_{im}(t) \in \{0, 1\}, \forall i, \forall t, \forall m. \tag{2f}$$

Constraints (2a) and (2b) ensure that user i's job is scheduled to execute only between its start time and deadline. (2c) enforces inter-task dependence of user i's sub-tasks, and (2d) makes sure that the total number of allocated time slots for each container is sufficient to finish the corresponding sub-task. Constraint (2e) states that the total amount of type-r resource utilized at time slot t is capped by system capacity.

Even in the offline setting with all inputs given, ILP (2) is still NP-hard. This can be verified by observing that with constraints (2e) and (2f) alone, and ILP (2) degrades into the classic knapsack problem known to be NP-hard. We resort to the classic primal-dual schema [24] for efficient algorithm design. We first reformulate ILP (2) into an equivalent *compact exponential* version, to hide the non-conventional constraints that arise from container dependence and job deadlines, whose dual variables would be hard to interpret and to update:

$$\text{maximize} \quad \sum_{i\in[I]}\sum_{S\in\Gamma_i} B_i x_{iS} \tag{3}$$

subject to:

$$\sum_{i\in[I]}\sum_{S:t\in S} f_{ir}^S(t) x_{iS} \le \mathbb{C}_r, \forall r \in [R], \forall t \in [T], \tag{3a}$$

$$\sum_{S\in\Gamma_i} x_{iS} \le 1, \forall i \in [I], \tag{3b}$$

$$x_{iS} \in \{0,1\}, \forall i \in [I], \forall S \in \Gamma_i. \tag{3c}$$

In the compact exponential ILP above, Γ_i represents a set of valid schedules for sub-tasks that meet constraints (2a), (2b), (2c) and (2d). B_{iS} represents the bidding price of user i for schedule $S \in \Gamma_i$. Since a time slot can serve two or more containers, we let $f_{ir}^S(t)$ represent the total type-r resource occupation of user i's schedule S in t. Constraints (3a) and (3b) correspond to (2e) and (2f) in ILP (2). We relax the integer constraints $x_i \in \{0,1\}$ to $x_i \ge 0$, and introduce dual variable vectors u_i and $\kappa_r(t)$ to constraints (3a) and (3b) respectively, to formulate the dual of the LP relaxation of ILP (3).

$$\text{minimize} \sum_{i\in[I]} u_i + \sum_{t\in[T]}\sum_{r\in[R]} \mathbb{C}_r \kappa_r(t) \tag{4}$$

subject to:

$$u_i \ge B_i - \sum_{r\in[R]}\sum_{t\in S} f_{ir}^S(t)\kappa_r(t), \forall i \in [I], \forall S \in \Gamma_i, \tag{4a}$$

$$\kappa_r(t), u_i \ge 0, \forall i \in [I], \forall r \in [R], \forall t \in [T]. \tag{4b}$$

While the reformulated ILP (3) is compact in its form, it has an exponential number of variables that arise from the exponential number of feasible job schedules. Correspondingly, the dual problem (4) has an exponential number of constraints. Even there are exponential number of schedule options are available, we only select polynomial number of them to compute the approximately optimal objective through a sub-algorithm (Sect. 4.2). We next design an efficient auction algorithm that efficiently solves the primal and dual compact exponential ILPs simultaneously, pursuing social welfare maximization (in the primal solution) while computing payments (in the dual solution).

4   Batch Auction Algorithm for Social Welfare Maximization

4.1   The Batch Algorithm

Departing from traditional online auctions that make immediate and irrevocable decisions, our auction mechanism takes a batch processing approach to handle user bids. In each batch, we aim to choose a subset of bids to accept, and to dynamically provision containers, through choosing a feasible assignment of the primal variable x_{iS}. We let $x_{iS} = 1$, if user i's bid with schedule S is accepted, then allocate time slots according to the schedule, and update the amount of resources occupied.

We now focus on batch bid processing and container provisioning for social welfare maximization. A set of dual constraints exists for each primal variable x_{iS}. We minimize the increase of the dual objective and maintain dual feasibility (4a) by leveraging *complementary slackness*. Once the dual constraint (4a) is tight with user i's schedule S (KKT conditions [29]), the primal variable x_{iS} is updated to 1. According to constraint (4b), the dual variable $u_i \geq 0$. Therefore, we let u_i be the maximum of 0 and the RHS of (4a). If $u_i = 0$, the bid is rejected.

$$u_i = \max\{0, \max_{S \in \Gamma_i}(B_i - \sum_{r \in [R]} \sum_{t \in S} f_{ir}^S(t)\kappa_r(t))\}, \forall i \in \rho_q \tag{5}$$

$\kappa_r(t)$ can be viewed as the marginal price per unit of type-r resource at t. Consequently, $\sum_{r \in [R]} \sum_{t \in S} f_{ir}^S(t)\kappa_r(t))$ represents the cost of serving user i by schedule S, and $\{B_i - \sum_{r \in [R]} \sum_{t \in S} f_{ir}^S(t)\kappa_r(t)\}$ is the utility of user i's bid. The above assignment (5) chooses the schedule which can maximize the job's utility.

Our auction strives to reserve a certain amount of resource for potential high-value bids in the future. Careful implementation of such an intuition through dual price design is crucial in guaranteeing a good competitive ratio of the auction.

Let D_r and F_r represent the maximum and minimum user valuation per unit of type-r resource respectively. $w_r(t)$ denotes the amount of allocated type-r resource at t. We define the marginal price $\kappa_r(t)$ to be an increasing function of $w_r(t)$:

$$\kappa_r(w_r(t)) = \frac{\sigma F_r}{k}(\frac{kD_r}{\sigma F_r})^{\frac{w_r(t)}{C_r}} \tag{6}$$

$$\text{where } D_r = \max_{i \in [I]} \frac{B_i}{\sum_{m \in [M]} N_{im}h_{im}^r}; F_r = \min_{i \in [I]} \frac{B_i}{\sum_{m \in [M]} N_{im}h_{im}^r}.$$

The initial price of each type-r resource should be low enough such that any user's bid can be accepted; otherwise there might be a large amount of idle resource. Thus we decrease the starting price by a coefficient k, satisfying: $k - 1 = \max_{r \in [R]} ln(\frac{kD_r}{\sigma F_r})$ and $k > 1$. The detailed explanation of k is given in Theorem 5. For all $w_r(t) < C_r$, $\kappa_r(t) < D_r$, and it will reach D_r when $w_r(t) = C_r$. In that case, the cloud provider will not further allocate any type-r resource. The parameter is defined as the minimum occupation rate of all kinds of resources within slots T, i.e.,

$$\sigma = \min_{r \in R} \frac{\sum_{i \in [I]} \sum_{m \in [M]} h_{im}^r N_{im} x_i}{C_r T}$$

We assume that there are enough cloud users to potentially exhaust resources within each slot. Thus the resource occupation rate σ is close to 1.

We design a batch auction algorithm A_{batch} in Algorithm 1 with container scheduling algorithm A_{sub} in Algorithm 2 or Algorithm 3, which can select optimal container scheduling under different circumstances. A_{batch} defines the posted price function and initializes the primal and dual variables in line 1. Upon the arrival of ρ_q users within batch q, we first select the schedule that maximize users' utility through the dual oracle (lines 4–6). $\sum_{r\in[R]}\sum_{t\in[s_i]} f_{ir}^s(t)\kappa_r(t)$ in line 7 is viewed as the weighted total resource demand by user i, thus $\frac{B_i}{\sum_{r\in[R]}\sum_{t\in[s_i]} f_{ir}^s(t)\kappa_r(t)}$ can be interpreted as the value for a unit resource of user i, and we select the bid μ with the maximum unit resource value. If user μ obtains positive utility, we update the primal variable x_μ and dual variable $\kappa_r(t)$ according to μ's schedule s_μ (lines 9–16).

Algorithm 1. A Primal-dual Posted Price Auction A_{batch}

1: Initialize $x_i = 0$, $z_{im}(t) = 0$, $w_r(t) = 0$, $u_i = 0$, $\kappa_r(t) = \frac{\sigma F_r}{k}$, $\forall i \in [I], r \in [R], t \in [T], S \in \Gamma_i, \psi = \varnothing$;

2: **Group a set of ρ_q users within θ time slots;**

3: **while** $\psi \neq \rho_q$ **do**

4:    **for all** $i \in \rho_q \setminus \psi$ **do**

5:       $(u_i, S_i, cost_i, \{f_{ir}^S(t)\}) = A_{sub}(\{\Pi_i\}, \{\mathbb{C}_r\}, \{w_r(t)\}, \{\kappa_r(t)\})$;

6:    **end for**

7:    $\mu = argmax_{i\in\rho_q\setminus\psi}\{\frac{B_i}{\sum_{r\in[R]}\sum_{t\in[s_i]} f_{ir}^s(t)\kappa_r(t)}\}$;

8:    **if** $u_\mu > 0$ **then**

9:       $x_\mu = 1$;

10:      Accept user μ's bid, allocate resources according to S_i, and charge $cost_i$ for user i;

11:      **update:** $\psi = \psi \bigcup\{\mu\}$;

12:      **for all** $t \in S_\mu$ **do**

13:         $w_r(t) = w_r(t) + f_{\mu r}^S(t)$;

14:         $\kappa_r(t) = \frac{\sigma F_r}{k}\left(\frac{kD_r}{\sigma F_r}\right)^{\frac{w_r(t)}{\mathbb{C}_r}}, \forall r \in [R]$;

15:      **end for**

16:    **else**

17:      Reject user μ's bid, and delete user μ from the set ρ_q.

18:    **end if**

19: **end while**

4.2 Sub-algorithm of Auction Mechanism

Our container scheduling algorithms A_{sub} only selects utility-maximizing schedules for each job, rather than an exponential number of schedules. Therefore, we compute a schedule that minimizes the cost of serving the job.

In our auction mechanism, dependence graph of user tasks is complicated to handle. We first focus on a relatively small, yet representative case of jobs from Network Function Virtualization [13], where each container graph is a service chain. We exploit the sequential chain structure to design A_{sub1} Algorithm 2 with polynomial time complexity, based on dynamic programming. By choosing time slots that can ensure right operating sequence and minimum payment for each sub-task, the first two nested **for** loops select minimum-cost schedule for containers (lines 3–10). Then the second **for** loop updates the cost and schedule for each container m (lines 11–15); line 17 updates the cost and utility of user i's schedule S_i at the end.

Container graphs in practice can be more complex than a chain structure. For general jobs with arbitrary container graph topology, the container scheduling problem is NP-hard, as proven in Theorem 1; we design A_{sub2} in Algorithm 3 to solve the optimization. Lines 2–8 in Algorithm 3 sort available time slots by $c_m(t)$. Then A_{sub2} employs Depth-First Search (DFS) (line 9). We adapt the DFS procedure with improvements to select available time slots with minimum cost in a recursive process that decides a container schedule. Truthfulness requires solving the problem exactly, and our algorithm runs in exponential time to the number of sub-tasks in a job, which is mostly small and can be viewed as a constant in practice.

Algorithm 2. A_{sub1}: Container Graph Scheduling - Service Chains

---

Input: bidding language $\{\Pi_i\}$, $\{\mathbb{C}_r\}$, $\{\kappa_r(t)\}$, $\{w_r(t)\}$;
Output: u_i; S_i, $cost_i$, $\{f_{ir}^S(t)\}$;
1: Initialize $S_i = \varnothing$; $f_{ir}^S(t) = 0, \forall t \in [T]$;
2: **for all** $m \in [M]$ **do**
3:     **for all** $t_s \in [\theta\lceil \frac{t_i}{\theta} \rceil + \sum_1^{m-1} N_{im}, d_i - \sum_m^M N_{im}]$ **do**
4:         **for all** $t_e \in [t_s + N_{im}, d_i - \sum_{m+1}^M N_{im}]$ **do**
5:             $c_m(t) = \sum_{r \in [R]} h_{im}^r \kappa_r(t), \forall t \in [t_s, t_e]$;
6:             Select N_{im} slots with minimum $c_m(t)$ and $w_r(t) + h_{im}^r \leq \mathbb{C}_r, \forall r \in [R]$ to τ_m;
7:             $\Delta_m = [\Delta_m\ \tau_m]$;
8:             $p_m(t_s, t_e) = \sum_{t \in \tau_m} c_m(t)$;
9:         **end for**
10:     **end for**
11:     **for all** $t_s \in [\theta\lceil \frac{t_i}{\theta} \rceil + \sum_1^{m-1} N_{im}, d_i - \sum_m^M N_{im}]$ **do**
12:         $pay = min_{t_e < t_s}\{p_{m-1}(:, t_e)\}, \tau_m \in [\Delta_m]$;
13:         $p_m(t_s, t_e) = p_m(t_s, t_e) + pay$;
14:         $S_i = [S_i\ \tau_m]$, $f_{ir}^S(t) = f_{ir}^S(t) + h_{im}^r$;
15:     **end for**
16: **end for**
17: **Update:** $cost_i = min_{t_s, t_e}(p_m(t_s, t_e))$; $u_i = B_i - cost_i$;

Theorem 1. *In each batch of container based auction, given fixed resource prices, choosing the schedule of sub-tasks with minimum cost with a general container graph is NP-hard.*

Proof: We construct a polynomial-time reduction to sub-task scheduling from the classic NP-hard problem *subset sum*: $max_{x_i} \sum_{i=1}^n c_i x_i$, subject to $\sum_{i=1}^n c_i$ $x_i \leq V, x_i \in \{0, 1\}$.

Given a set $\{c_1, c_2, ..., c_n\}$ and a objective V, our problem reduces to an instance of $K = (|M| = n, h_{im}^r = c_i, \mathbb{C}_r = V)$, in which each user's job has M types of containers with 1 slot requirement, and the resource pool contains one type of resource. We should put as many containers in one slot with lowest price as possible. If a polynomial-time algorithm solves the capacitated container scheduling problem K, it will solve the corresponding subset sum problem as well, and vice versa. Consequently, the *subset sum* problem can be viewed as a special case of the sub-task scheduling problem, which must be NP-hard as well.   □

5   Analysis of Auction Mechanism

5.1   Truthfulness of the Batch Algorithm

Theorem 2. *The batch auction in Algorithm 1 that computes resource allocation and payment is truthful.*

Proof: In Algorithm 1, upon the arrival of user i and our posted price mechanism, the payment P_i that user i needs to pay to the cloud provider (if its bid is accepted) depends only on the amount of resources that has been allocated and user i's demand. Which means, user i's bidding price does not affect its payment. Therefore, leveraging Lemma 1, our online batch auction is truthful.   □

Algorithm 3. A_{sub2}: Container Graph Scheduling - General Topology

Input: bidding language $\{\Pi_i\}$, $\{\mathbb{C}_r\}$,$\{\kappa_r(t)\}$, $\{w_r(t)\}$;
Output: u_i; S_i, $\{f_{ir}^S(t)\}$, $cost_i$;
 1: Initialize $S_i = \varnothing$; $f_{ir}^S(t) = 0, \forall t \in [T]$; c_{min}=INF;
 2: **for all** $m \in [M]$ **do**
 3:     **for all** $t \in [\theta\lceil\frac{t_i}{\theta}\rceil, d_i]$ **do**
 4:         $c_m(t) = \sum_{r \in [R]} h_{im}^r \kappa_r(t), \forall t \in [\theta\lceil\frac{t_i}{\theta}\rceil, d_i]$;
 5:         Sort slots with $w_r(t) + h_{im}^r \leq \mathbb{C}_r, \forall r \in [R]$ according to $c_m(t)$ to τ_m;
 6:         $p_m(t_s, t_e)$=$\sum_{t\in\tau_m} c_m(t)$;
 7:     **end for**
 8: **end for**
 9: Calling **Depth-First Search(m)** to find the container schedule S_i and resource allocaton $\{f_{ir}^S(t)\}$ with minimum cost c_{min};
10: **Update:** $cost_i = c_{min}$;$u_i = B_i - cost_i$;

5.2   Solution Feasibility of the Batch Algorithm

Theorem 3. *Algorithm 1 computes a feasible solution to ILP (2).*

Proof: x_i is initialized to 0 and updated to 1 only (line 10 in Algorithm A_{batch}), so the solution of our algorithm is binary valued, and satisfies constraint (2f). Container scheduling algorithms A_{sub1} and A_{sub2} guarantee that the schedule S

for each user's bid satisfies constraints (2a), (2b), (2c) and (2d). For container provisioning and scheduling, both A_{sub1} and A_{sub2} select time slots satisfying resource capacity limits, $f_{ir}^S(t) + w_r(t) \leq \mathbb{C}_r, \exists t \in [T]$. Hence constraints (2e) is satisfied. In summary, the solution we obtain is feasible for ILP (2).   □

Theorem 4. *The computational complexity of Batch Algorithm 1 to ILP (2) is polynomial time.*

Proof: We first consider the case of service chains $(A_{sub} = A_{sub1})$. Line 1 in Algorithm 1 takes linear time to initialize the price function, primal and dual variables. According to user arrivals, the while loop iterates ρ_q times to find user μ with maximum unit resource value, then updates the primal and dual variables in linear time. In the for loop (lines 4–6), Algorithm A_{sub1} iterates ρ_q^2 times to select the best schedule of users with maximum utility. Then each A_{sub1} in Algorithm 2 takes $\eta = (d_i - t_s - \sum_{m \in [M]} N_{im})^2$ steps to compute the price of each time slot and examine resource capacity limits for each container. Thus it takes $O(M\eta^2)$ to choose the utility maximization schedule for user i. In summary, the running time of A_{batch} with A_{sub1} is $O(M\eta^2\rho_q^2)$. We next consider the case of general container graphs $(A_{sub} = A_{sub2})$. The complexity of A_{sub2} is exponential to the number of containers in the container graph, which is mostly small and an be viewed as a constant.   □

5.3   Competitive Ratio of the Batch Algorithm

The *competitive ratio* is an upper-bound ratio of the optimal social welfare achieved by ILP (2) to the social welfare achieved by our batch algorithm. The primal-dual framework in our batch algorithm design enables a competitive ratio analysis based on LP duality theory [24]. Let P_i and D_i be the primal objective value (3) and dual objective value (4) after accepting user i's job, respectively. Then we let P_0 and D_0 be the initial objective values of primal (3) and dual (4) programs, and $P_0 = 0$. P_I and D_I are the final primal and dual objective values achieved by our algorithm A_{batch}. Let OPT_1 and OPT_2 be the optimal objective values of (2) and (3), respectively. Since the compact exponential ILP is equivalent to the original ILP, we have $OPT_1 = OPT_2$, which is hereafter referred to as OPT.

Lemma 2. *According to the initial marginal price of each time slot, the initial dual objective value D_0 is at most $\frac{1}{k}OPT$.*

Proof: We first show a lower bound on the optimal social welfare:

$$OPT \geq \sigma \sum_{r \in [R]} \sum_{t \in [T]} F_r \mathbb{C}_r.$$

Recall that we let σ denote the minimum resource occupation rate within slots T. F_r can be interpreted as the minimum social welfare generated by a job per unit of type-r resource and per unit of time. Therefore, $\sigma \sum_{r \in [R]} \sum_{t \in [T]} F_r \mathbb{C}_r$ is the minimum social welfare generated by all users.

According to dual (4) and marginal price function (6):

$$D_0 = \sum_{t \in [T]} \sum_{r \in [R]} \mathbb{C}_r \kappa_r(0) = \sum_{t \in [T]} \sum_{r \in [R]} \mathbb{C}_r \left(\frac{\sigma F_r}{k} \right)$$

$$= \frac{1}{k} \sum_{t \in [T]} \sum_{r \in [R]} F_r \mathbb{C}_r \sigma \leq \frac{1}{k} OPT$$

Therefore, the initial dual objective value D_0 is bounded by $\frac{1}{k} OPT$. □

Lemma 3. *If there is a constant $\alpha > 1$, and the primal and dual objective values increased by handling each user i's job satisfy $P_i - P_{i-1} \geq \frac{1}{\alpha}(D_i - D_{i-1})$, then the batch algorithm is $\frac{k}{k-1}\alpha$-competitive.*

Proof: Since the inequality is satisfied for all users, we sum up the inequality of each user i:

$$P_I = \sum_i (P_i - P_{i-1}) \geq \frac{1}{\alpha} \sum_i (D_i - D_{i-1}) = \frac{1}{\alpha}(D_I - D_0).$$

According to weak duality and Lemma 2, $D_I \geq OPT$ and $D_0 \geq \frac{1}{k} OPT$. Therefore,

$$P_I \geq \frac{k-1}{k\alpha} OPT_1 = \frac{k-1}{k\alpha} OPT_2,$$

with the fact that $P_0 = 0$. Our batch algorithm is $\frac{k}{k-1}\alpha$-competitive. □

Next we will define an *Allocation Price Relation* to identify this α. If the Allocation Price Relation is satisfied by α, the objective values achieved by our algorithm A_{batch} guarantee the inequality in Lemma 3.

Definition 1. *The Allocation Price Relation for $\alpha \geq 1$ is that $\kappa_r^{i-1}(t)(w_r^i(t) - w_r^{i-1}(t)) \geq \frac{1}{\alpha}\mathbb{C}_r(\kappa_r^i(t) - \kappa_r^{i-1}(t)), \forall i \in [I], \forall r \in [R], \forall t \in [s]$, where $\kappa_r^i(t)$ represents the price of type-r resource after processing user i's job. $w_r^i(t)$ is the total amount of allocated type-r resource after accepting user i.*

Lemma 4. *For a given $\alpha \geq 1$, if the price function $\kappa_r(t)$ satisfies $\kappa_r^{i-1}(t)(w_r^i(t) - w_r^{i-1}(t)) \geq \frac{1}{\alpha}\mathbb{C}_r(\kappa_r^i(t) - \kappa_r^{i-1}(t)), \forall i \in [I], \forall r \in [R], \forall t \in [l]$, then Algorithm A_{batch} $P_i - P_{i-1} \geq \frac{1}{\alpha}(D_i - D_{i-1}), \forall i \in [I]$.*

Proof: If bid i is rejected, $P_i - P_{i-1} = D_i - D_{i-1} = 0$. Then we assume that bid i is accepted and let s be the job schedule of user i. Knowing that our algorithm accepts a bid when constraint (4a) is tight, $B_{is} = u_i + \sum_{r \in [R]} \sum_{t \in s} f_{ir}^s(t)\kappa_r^{i-1}(t)$. So the increase of primal objective is:

$$P_i - P_{i-1} = u_i + \sum_{r \in [R]} \sum_{t \in s} \kappa_r^{i-1}(t)(w_r^i(t) - w_r^{i-1}(t))$$

According to dual (4), the increase of dual objective is:

$$D_i - D_{i-1} = u_i + \sum_{r \in [R]} \sum_{t \in s} \mathbb{C}_r(\kappa_r^i(t) - \kappa_r^{i-1}(t))$$

Since we have $u_i \geq 0$, $\alpha \geq 1$ and $\kappa_r^{i-1}(t)(w_r^i(t) - w_r^{i-1}(t)) \geq \frac{1}{\alpha}C_r(\kappa_r^i(t) - \kappa_r^{i-1}(t))$:

$$P_i - P_{i-1} = u_i + \sum_{r \in [R]} \sum_{t \in s} \kappa_r^{i-1}(t)(w_r^i(t) - w_r^{i-1}(t))$$

$$\geq u_i + \frac{1}{\alpha} \sum_{r \in [R]} \sum_{t \in s} C_r(\kappa_r^i(t) - \kappa_r^{i-1}(t))$$

$$\geq \frac{1}{\alpha}(u_i + \sum_{r \in [R]} \sum_{t \in s} C_r(\kappa_r^i(t) - \kappa_r^{i-1}(t)))$$

$$= \frac{1}{\alpha}(D_i - D_{i-1})$$

$\square$

We next try to find the α_r for type-r resource that satisfies the Allocation Price Relationship. Thus the α is the maximum value among all α_r. Since the capacity of type-r resource is larger than a user demand, we let $dw_r(t)$ denote $w_r^i(t) - w_r^{i-1}(t)$. We first prepare with the following definition.

Definition 2. *The Differential Allocation Price Relation for A_{batch} with a given parameter $\alpha_r \geq 1$ $\kappa_r(t)dw_r(t) \geq \frac{1}{\alpha_r}C_r d\kappa_r(t), \forall i \in [I], \forall r \in [R], \forall t \in [s]$.*

Lemma 5. *The marginal price defined in (5) satisfies the Differential Allocation Price Relation, and we can get $\alpha_r = ln(\frac{kD_r}{\sigma F_r})$.*

Proof: The derivative of the marginal price function is:

$$d\kappa_r(t) = \kappa_r^{'}(w_r(t))dw_r(t) = \frac{\sigma F_r}{k}(\frac{kD_r}{\sigma F_r})^{\frac{w_r(t)}{C_r}} \frac{1}{C_r}ln(\frac{kD_r}{\sigma F_r})dw_r(t).$$

Therefore: $\frac{\sigma F_r}{k}(\frac{kD_r}{\sigma F_r})^{\frac{w_r(t)}{C_r}} \geq \frac{C_r}{\alpha_r}\frac{\sigma F_r}{k}(\frac{kD_r}{\sigma F_r})^{\frac{w_r(t)}{C_r}} \frac{1}{C_r}ln(\frac{kD_r}{\sigma F_r})$

$$\geq \frac{1}{\alpha_r}(\frac{\sigma F_r}{k}(\frac{kD_r}{\sigma F_r})^{\frac{w_r(t)}{C_r}} ln(\frac{kD_r}{\sigma F_r})), \Rightarrow \alpha_r \geq ln(\frac{kD_r}{\sigma F_r})$$

Thus we can obtain $\alpha_r = ln(\frac{kD_r}{\sigma F_r})$. $\square$

Lemma 6. *The batch auction Algorithm A_{batch} is $\frac{k}{k-1}\alpha$-competitive in social welfare with $\alpha = max_{r \in [R]}ln(\frac{kD_r}{\sigma F_r})$.*

Proof: Lemma 5 implies that $\alpha = max_{r \in [R]}ln(\frac{kD_r}{\sigma F_r})$ satisfies the Differential Allocation Price Relation of all kinds of resources. Since the above mentioned, $dw_r(t) = w_r^i(t) - w_r^{i-1}(t)$,

$$d\kappa_r(t) = \kappa_r^{'}(w_r(t))dw_r(t) = \kappa_r^{'}(w_r(t))(w_r^i(t) - w_r^{i-1}(t))$$
$$= \kappa_r^i(t) - \kappa_r^{i-1}(t).$$

Thus, we can obtain $\alpha = max_{r \in [R]}ln(\frac{kD_r}{\sigma F_r})$ due to the Allocation Price Relationship. $\square$

Theorem 5. *If* k *satisfies* $k - 1 = \max_{r \in [R]} ln(\frac{kD_r}{\sigma F_r})$ *and* $k > 1$, *the competitive ratio of batch auction algorithm is minimum, and is equal to* k.

Proof: We assumpt that $\varpi = \max_{r \in [R]}(\frac{D_r}{\sigma F_r})$. By Lemma 5, the competitive ratio of our batch algorithm is $\frac{k}{k-1}\alpha = \frac{k}{k-1}ln(\frac{kD_{r*}}{\sigma F_{r*}}) = \frac{k}{k-1}ln(k\varpi)$, thus the competitive ratio is a function of k. Differentiating $\frac{k}{k-1}ln(k\varpi)$ on k is:

$$(\frac{k}{k-1}ln(k\varpi))' = \frac{k - 1 - ln(k\varpi)}{(k-1)^2}$$

It suffices to show that $(\frac{k-1-ln(k\varpi)}{(k-1)^2})'$ is positive as $k \in [1, \alpha]$. When k satisfies $k - 1 = ln(k\varpi)$ and $k > 1$, we can obtain the minimum competitive ratio:

$$\frac{k}{k-1}ln(k\varpi) = \frac{k}{ln(k\varpi)}ln(k\varpi) = k.$$

If we consider the case that competition for resource is intense, the σ is close to 1. When D_r/F_r is 2, the competitive ratio is close to 2.85, as illustrated in Fig. 3.   □

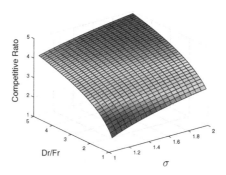

Fig. 3. Theoretical competitive ratio.

5.4   Setting the Batch Interval θ

In our batch auction, the more jobs we handle in a batch, the more information we have for social welfare maximization. Nonetheless, we can't over-extend the length of a batch given that cloud jobs have deadlines to meet. Precise optimization of the job interval length is left as future research, and we provide here a brief discussion only. Let W_i be the time required to execute a job i, and $\bar{p}$ be the expected number of user arrivals per slot. In general, an appropriate length of a batch round depends on values of W_i, deadline d_i and arrival time t_i of user

$i, i \in [I]$. We can set a target threshold on the job loss rate (*e.g.*, 10%), the ratio of jobs who cannot meet their deadlines due to delayed bid admission.

Assume that job processing time and $d_i - t_i$ are normally distributed, by $N(a_1, b_1^2)$ and $N(a_2, b_2^2)$, respectively. The max waiting time for each user equals $d_i - t_i - W_i$, and is also normally distributed as $N(a_1 - a_2, b_1^2 + b_2^2)$. If user i's maximum waiting time $\theta_i < \theta$, we will lose this job. Thus the length of batch interval θ can be set by (for $\le 10\%$ job loss):

$$\{\max \theta, s.t. \sum_{t=1}^{\theta} F(\theta) \le 0.1, \theta \in \{1, 2, 3, 4, ...\}.\}$$

where $F(\theta)$ is the Normal cumulative distribution function of θ.

6   Performance Evaluation

We evaluate our batch auction algorithm A_{batch} and its sub-algorithms by trace-driven simulation studies. We leverage Google cluster data [5], which captures rich information on user jobs, including start time, resource demand (CPU, RAM and Disk), and duration. We translate cloud job requests into bids, arriving in a one month time window. We assume that each sub-task consumes $[1, 10]$ slots, and each time slot is one hour. Job deadlines are set randomly between the arrival time and system end time. The demand of resources (CPU, RAM and Disk) is set randomly between $[0, 1]$, with the resource capacity set to 50. We use *user density* to express the number of users in one batch interval, arriving as a Poisson process.

A. Comparison with Classic Online Auctions
We compare our batch auction with a traditional online auction in terms of social welfare, as shown in Fig. 4. Under the same simulation settings, we compare the two algorithms in 10 different sets of simulation studies. Our batch auction achieves a higher social welfare in all of them. Intuitively, the online auction processes bids in a FCFS fashion, while the batch auction considers most attractive bids first in each batch. Figure 5 shows another set of comparisons. The superiority of batch auction remains clear, with different number of time slots and user density. Social welfare fluctuates with the increase of the number of users and user density. The batch auction performs better with higher user density. The influence of different batch interval θ for the batch performance is illustrated in Fig. 6. As θ grows, the cloud social welfare initially grows as well. However, when θ is too large so that more bids are lost due to delays, as we can see in Fig. 6, a gradual decrease in the percentage of winners leads to a decreasing trend in social welfare. Recall that in the analysis of θ in the previous section, a too large θ is not suitable for our batch auction.

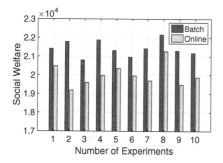

Fig. 4. Social welfare, batch vs. online auctions.

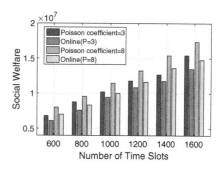

Fig. 5. Social welfare achieved by A_{batch}.

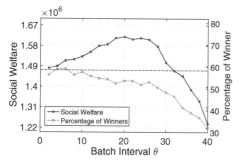

Fig. 6. Social welfare and percentage of winners, varying batch length.

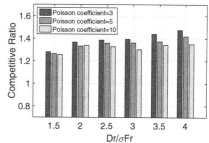

Fig. 7. Competitive ratio of auction algorithm A_{batch}.

B. Competitive Ratio of the Batch auction

Next we study the competitive ratio achieved by our batch auction. As we proved in Theorem 6, the competitive ratio depends on $D_r/\sigma F_r$. Figure 7 shows that the competitive ratio grows as $D_r/\sigma F_r$ increases. The observed competitive ratio is much better than the theoretical bound and remains smaller than 2; this can be partly explained by the fact that the theoretical bound is a pessimistic worst case scenario uncommon in practice. The ratio fluctuates with user population and sightly decreases with as $D_r/\sigma F_r$ decreases. The batch auction favors intensive user arrivals.

C. Performance of A_{batch}: The Role of System Parameters

We next examine the resource occupation ratio σ (defined in Sect. 3) of our batch auction. As we can see in Fig. 8, under different numbers of time slots and user density, the resource occupation ratio of the batch auction mechanism is constantly beyond 90% and often close to 1. Figure 9 demonstrates the variation of social welfare with different number of users. The social welfare grows mildly but steadily as the number of users and the number of time slots grow.

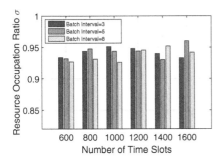
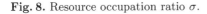
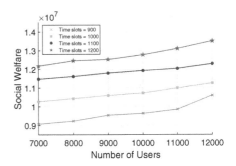

Fig. 8. Resource occupation ratio σ.

Fig. 9. Social welfare of A_{batch}, varying user population.

7   Conclusion

This work is the first in the cloud computing literature that studies efficient auction algorithm design for container services. It is also the first that designs batch online auctions, aiming at more informed decision making through exploiting the elastic nature of cloud jobs. We combined techniques from compact exponential optimization, posted price mechanisms, and primal-dual algorithms for designing a cloud container auction that is incentive compatible, computationally efficient, and economically efficient. As future directions, it will be interesting to study (i) cloud jobs that cannot be suspended and resumed; (ii) pre-processing of cloud jobs with tight deadlines to choose between immediate acceptance or delayed processing of their bids; and (iii) cloud container auctions that make revocable decisions, where a partially executed cloud job may or may not contribute towards social welfare of the cloud.

References

1. Aliyun Container Engine. http://cn.aliyun.com/product/contain-erservice
2. Amazon ECS. https://aws.amazon.com/cn/ecs/
3. Azure Container. https://azure.microsoft.com/en-us/services/container-service/
4. Batch Applications. https://github.com/Azure/azure-content/blob/master/articl es/batch/batch-hpc-solutions.md
5. Google Cluster Data. https://code.google.com/p/googlecl-usterdata
6. Google Container Engine. http://cloud.google.com/container-engine/
7. Bitton, S., Emek, Y., Kutten, S.: Efficient dispatching of job batches in emerging clouds. In: Proceedings of IEEE INFOCOM (2018)
8. Chen, B., Deng, X., Zang, W.: On-line scheduling a batch processing system to minimize total weighted job completion time. J. Comb. Optim. **8**(1), 85–95 (2004)
9. Dove, A.: Life science technologies: biology watches the cloud. Science **340**(6138), 1350–1352 (2013)
10. Etzion, H., Moor, S.: Simulation of online selling with posted-price and auctions: comparison of dual channel's performance under different auction mechanisms. In: Proceedings of HICSS (2008)

11. Golin, M.J., Rote, G.: A dynamic programming algorithm for constructing optimal prefix-free codes with unequal letter costs. IEEE Trans. Inf. Theor. **44**(5), 1770–1781 (1998)
12. Gopinathan, A., Li, Z.: Strategyproof auctions for balancing social welfare and fairness in secondary spectrum markets. In: Proceedings of the IEEE INFOCOM (2011)
13. Gu, S., Li, Z., Wu, C., Huang, C.: An efficient auction mechanism for service chains in the NFV market. In: Proceedings of IEEE INFOCOM (2016)
14. He, S., Guo, L., Guo, Y., Wu, C.: Elastic application container: a lightweight approach for cloud resource provisioning. In: Proceedings of IEEE International Conference on Advanced Information Networking and Applications (2012)
15. Huang, Z., Kim, A.: Welfare maximization with production costs: a primal dual approach. In: Proceedings of ACM-SIAM SODA (2015)
16. Kumar, D., Shae, Z., Jamjoom, H.: Scheduling batch and heterogeneous jobs with runtime elasticity in a parallel processing environment. In: Proceedings of IEEE IPDPSW (2012)
17. Mohamed, N.M., Lin, H., Feng, W.: Accelerating data-intensive genome analysis in the cloud. In: Proceedings of BICoB (2013)
18. Myerson, R.B.: Optimal auction design. Math. Oper. Res. **6**(1), 58–73 (1981)
19. RightScale: Social Gaming in the Cloud: A Technical White Paper (2013)
20. Shi, W., Wu, C., Li, Z.: RSMOA: a revenue and social welfare maximizing online for dynamic cloud resource provisioning. In: Proceedings of IEEE IWQoS (2014)
21. Shi, W., Zhang, L., Wu, C., Li, Z., Lau, F.: An online auction framework for dynamic resource provisioning in cloud computing. In: Proceedings of ACM SIGMETRICS (2014)
22. Tosatto, A., Ruiu, P., Attanasio, A.: Container-based orchestration in cloud: state of the art and challenges. In: Proceedings of Ninth International Conference on Complex, Intelligent, and Software Intensive Systems (2015)
23. Waibel, P., Yeshchenko, A., Schulte, S., Mendling, J.: Optimized container-based process execution in the cloud. In: Panetto, H., Debruyne, C., Proper, H., Ardagna, C., Roman, D., Meersman, R. (eds.) On the Move to Meaningful Internet Systems, OTM 2018 Conferences, OTM 2018. Lecture Notes in Computer Science, vol. 11230, pp. 3–21. Springer, Cham (2018). https://doi.org/10.1007/978-3-030-02671-4_1
24. Williamson, D.P.: The primal-dual method for approximation algorithms. Math. Program. **91**(3), 447–478 (2002)
25. Xu, X., Yu, H., Pei, X.: A novel resource scheduling approach in container based clouds. In: Proceedings of IEEE ICCS (2014)
26. Zhang, E., Zhuo, Y.Q.: Online advertising channel choice - posted price vs. auction (2011)
27. Zhang, H., Jiang, H., Li, B., Liu, F., Vasilakos, A.V., Liu, J.: A framework for truthful online auctions in cloud computing with heterogeneous user demands. IEEE Trans. Comput. **65**(3), 805–818 (2016)
28. Zhang, L., Li, Z., Wu, C.: Dynamic resource provisioning in cloud computing: a randomized auction approach. In: Proceedings of IEEE INFOCOM (2014)
29. Zhang, X., Huang, Z., Wu, C., Li, Z., Lau, F.: Online auctions in IaaS clouds: welfare and profit maximization with server costs. In: Proceedings of ACM SIGMETRICS (2015)

Machine Learning

A-GNN: Anchors-Aware Graph Neural Networks for Node Embedding

Chao Liu[1,2] ⓘ, Xinchuan Li[1,2], Dongyang Zhao[1], Shaolong Guo[3],
Xiaojun Kang[1,2(✉)] ⓘ, Lijun Dong[1,2] ⓘ, and Hong Yao[1,2]

[1] School of Computer Science, China University of Geosciences,
Wuhan 430074, China
kangxj@cug.edu.cn
[2] Hubei Key Laboratory of Intelligent Geo-Information Processing,
China University of Geosciences, Wuhan 430074, China
[3] Sinopec Exploration Company, Chengdu 610041, Sichuan, China

Abstract. With the rapid development of information technology, it has become increasingly popular to handle and analyze complex relationships of various information network applications, such as social networks and biological networks. An unsolved primary challenge is to find a way to represent the network structure to efficiently compute, process and analyze network tasks. Graph Neural Network (GNN) based node representation learning is an emerging learning paradigm that embeds network nodes into a low dimensional vector space through preserving the network topology as possible. However, existing GNN architectures have limitation in distinguishing the position of nodes with the similar topology, which is crucial for many network prediction and classification tasks. Anchors are defined as special nodes which are in the important positions, and carries a lot of interactive information with other normal nodes. In this paper, we propose Anchors-aware Graph Neural Networks (A-GNN), which can make the vectors of node embedding contain location information by introducing anchors. A-GNN first selects the set of anchors, computes the distance of any given target node to each anchor, and afterwards learns a non-linear distance-weighted aggregation scheme over the anchors. Therefore A-GNN can obtain global position information of nodes regarding the anchors. A-GNN are applied to multiple prediction tasks including link prediction and node classification. Experimental results show that our model is superior to other GNN architectures on six datasets, in terms of the ROC, AUC accuracy score.

Keywords: Graph Neural Network · Node embedding · Link prediction · Node classification · Global structure information

1 Introduction

Network applications are ubiquitous in the real world, such as protein-protein interaction networks [1], information networks [2] and biology networks [3]. In network analysis, it is critical to learn effective representations for nodes, which determine the performance of many downstream network tasks, such as node classification [4], link

X. Chu et al. (Eds.): QShine 2019, LNICST 300, pp. 141–153, 2020.
https://doi.org/10.1007/978-3-030-38819-5_9

prediction [5]. Recently, the use of node representation learning (also known as node embedding) to solve network application problems has received wide attention from researchers, which is aimed at preserving the structure of networks in a low-dimensional vector space.

Many node embedding methods have been proposed in recent years, which can be categorized into three types according to the category of node fusion information. The first type is unsupervised node embedding [8, 9]. This type of models integrate the connection information of each node and its neighbor nodes into the vector representation of the node. However, these models cannot capture node attributes, which is important supplementary information for nodes. The second type is attributed node embedding [6, 10], which is proposed to incorporate node attributes to node embedding. The third type is GNN node embedding [7]. In the GNN framework, the embedding of nodes can contain nodes' attribute information and network neighbor information.

However, the existing methods related to GNN node embedding and attributed node embedding cannot capture the global position information of the node within the broader context of the graph structure, which hinders the processing of downstream tasks. Take the node classification task as an example. Figure 1 shows a symmetrical structure, in which nodes v_1 and v_2 are in the identical symmetrical positions. In GNN and attributed node embedding methods, v_1 and v_2 are embedded to the same point in the low-dimensional space because they have isomorphic network neighborhoods. Thus, v_1 and v_2 cannot be distinguished in node representation vector, and they are classified into the same class.

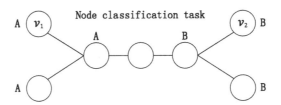

Fig. 1. A symmetrical structure example for a simple node classification task, in which nodes v_1 and v_2 are structurally symmetrical, A and B represent two different node classes respectively.

P-GNN model has partially addressed this problem of distinguishing symmetric nodes [12], which incorporates a node's global positional information with the help of anchors randomly selected in the network. However, P-GNN model has two limitations: (1) Randomly selection of anchors shows the location of the makers is uncertain, causing the P-GNN model unstable; (2) Besides, anchors are usually difficult to be selected at symmetrical locations or the distribution of them is relatively concentrated in a small part. In this case, positional information of most nodes wouldn't work, because the path between anchors and normal nodes in the symmetrical structure are identical. Actually, Anchors are the nodes with important positions and have a lot of information interaction with other nodes, which are not considered in P-GNN model.

Figure 2 gives a further explanation of limitations mentioned above. It shows a large network containing a symmetrical structure (Fig. 2, left). Similar to the notations of Fig. 1, v_1 and v_2 are in the identical symmetrical positions, A and B stand for two classes of nodes. Assume that the candidate anchor set includes α, α_1, α_2 and α_3. Firstly, we explain instability. If α is selected as the anchor, v_1 and v_2 can be distinguished by P-GNN, because the shortest path (v_1, α) is different from (v_2, α). Otherwise if α_1 or α_2 or α_3 is selected as the anchor, v_1 and v_2 wouldn't be distinguished by P-GNN, because the shortest path from v_1 and v_2 to the anchor are same. Therefore, selecting α or α_1 as anchor will lead two different results for P-GNN model. Secondly, notice that anchor α is in a symmetrical structure, while anchors α_1, α_2 and α_3 are not. But P-GNN model adopts a strategy of randomly selecting anchors, which cannot guarantee that at least one anchor is selected in each symmetric structure.

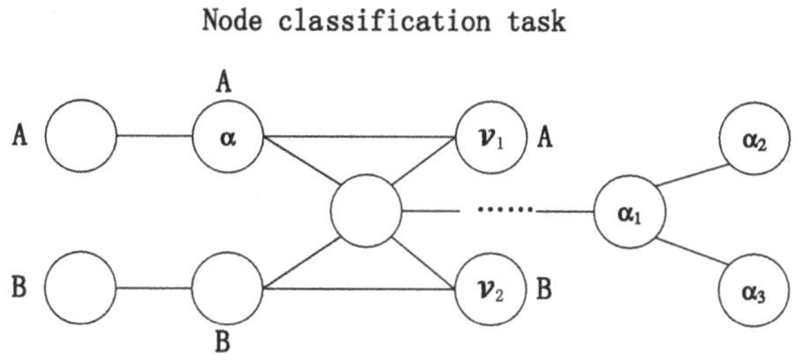

Fig. 2. An example of a large network containing a symmetrical structure.

In this paper, we propose Anchors-aware Graph Neural Networks (A-GNN), which use anchors to distinguish normal nodes with different importance. In the selection and computation of anchor nodes, we consider the following two requirements to be met: (1) Anchors should have strong information interaction with other nodes; (2) Anchors could spread as widely as possible in the whole network. We combine the Greedy Algorithm with the Minimum Point Cover Algorithm (**GA-MPCA**) to compute the anchors. Furthermore, the greedy algorithm satisfies the first requirement, and the minimum point cover algorithm satisfies the second one. Through combining with the new anchors computation strategy, A-GNN model supports for incorporating the structure information into the node vector. With the help of anchors, A-GNN learns a non-linear aggregation scheme that combines node feature information from each anchor-set and weighs it by the distance between the node and the anchors.

Overall, the main contributions of this paper are summarized as follows:

(1) We propose Anchors-aware Graph Neural Networks (A-GNN) for improving node embedding, which incorporates the global structure information of a node into its embedding vector with the help of anchors. In this case, nodes can be classified, if they obviously are different in the aspect of position, although they have similar neighborhood nodes.

(2) We propose a new algorithm to compute anchors. The anchors are selected according to the importance of the positions in the whole network. Moreover, we

apply the anchors to the learning of node embedding, which could greatly improves existed GNN architectures.

(3) We evaluate the performance of our A-GNN model for link prediction tasks and pairwise node classification tasks on eight different datasets. The experimental results show that our A-GNN model has significant improvements compared to baselines on both tasks.

The rest of the paper is organized as follows. Section 2 gives a brief review of related works. Section 3 describes the framework of our model. Section 4 reveals our proposed model in detail. In Sect. 5, we introduce the dataset, experiment settings, baseline models, experimental results and discussion. The last section is a conclusion of this paper.

2 Related Work

Anchors are the nodes with the important positions, having a lot of information interaction with other nodes. Our model A-GNN integrates the position information of nodes into the vector representation of nodes by introducing anchors. So our model is mainly related to two aspects, one is node importance evaluation, and the other is node embedding.

2.1 Node Embedding

According to the category of fusion information, the node embedding related to our work can be divided into three categories: (1) Embedding node's neighbors; (2) Embedding with node's features; (3) Embedding with positional information.

Embedding with Node's Network Neighbors. The existing GNN architectures use different aggregation schemes for a node to aggregate its neighbors in the network. For example, Graph Attention Networks aggregate neighborhood information according to trainable attention weights [13]. Message Passing Neural Networks further incorporate edge information when doing the aggregation [14]. However, as Fig. 1 shows, these models cannot distinguish nodes which have similar network neighbors or at symmetric positions in the network.

Embedding with Node's Features. Kipf and et al. proposed a heuristics method that alleviates the above issues include assigning an unique identifier to each node [12]. Hamilton and et al. proposed GraphSAGE to concatenate the node's feature in addition to mean/max/LSTM pooled neighborhood information [15]. Zhang and e al. used locally assigned node identifiers plus pre-trained transductive node features [16]. However, these models are not scalable and do not have generalization capabilities for unseen graphs.

Embedding with Positional Information. Jiaxuan and et al. proposed Position-aware Graph Neural Network (P-GNN) to capture the position/location of a given node with respect to some maker nodes generated randomly [11]. Although the model can sometimes to distinguish nodes with similar neighbors, it still has unstable limitation, due to its strategy of randomly selecting anchors.

2.2   Node Importance Evaluation

There are some traditional methods to evaluate the importance of nodes [21], among which some are based on node deletion, some are based on node affinity, and some are based on shortest paths. Besides, There also are some up-to-date methods are proposed to find important anchors, such as New metrics [22], proposing two type metrics utilized to evaluate the node importance, and GENI [17] is proposed to deal with distinctive challenges involved with predicting node importance in KGs based on GNN. Inspired by these methods and in order to ensure the selected anchors can meet the following two requirements: (1) Have strong information interaction with other nodes; (2) Spread as widely as possible in the whole network. We use **GA-MPCA** to compute the anchors, and combined with the new anchors calculation method, we propose A-GNN model.

3   The A-GNN Framework

The purpose of node representation learning is to integrate all useful information related to nodes into the vector representation of nodes. Thus, the high-quality node vectors can achieve good effects in link prediction tasks and node classification tasks. Our proposed A-GNN model can integrate useful information of nodes from three aspects: (1) node's neighborhood structure; (2) node' s attributes; (3) network global position information.

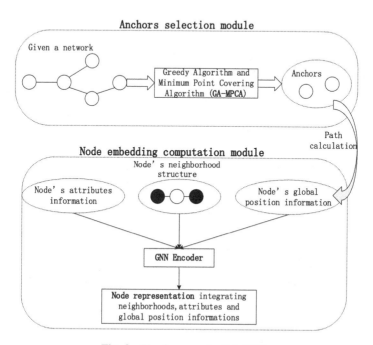

Fig. 3. The framework of A-GNN

Figure 3 gives the framework of A-GNN. As Fig. 3 shows, the A-GNN model can be divided into two mainly modules: (1) The upper layer is anchors selection module, which use GA-MPCA to compute the anchors in the network. The distribution of anchors selected is scattered and the selected anchors have strong information interaction with other nodes; (2) The lower layer is node embedding computation module. The module is used to GNN encoder, for the purpose of to integrate the node's attribute information, neighborhood structure information and global position information into the vector representation of the node.

The workflow of A-GNN model mainly includes the following steps:

- The First step is to input network datasets.
- The second step is to calculate anchors in the network by greedy algorithm and Minimum point covering algorithm.
- The third step is to extract the attribute information, neighborhood structure information contained in the path between anchors and the given node, and its position information relative to the multi-anchors of each given node. Then encode them to the low-dimensional space by GNN.
- The final step is the output the vector representation of each node, which integrates neighborhoods, attributes and global position information.

Compared with the existing node embedding models, our A-GNN model incorporates the global position information of each node, with the help of anchors. Therefore, The A-GNN model can distinguish nodes with similar neighbors or in identical symmetrical positions.

4   Proposed Approach

In this section, we mainly illustrate three key aspects of A-GNN model. The first is the strategy of selecting anchors. The second is the method mechanism of node embedding. The last is the description of algorithm implementation.

4.1   The Strategy of Anchors Selection

Anchors are the nodes in the important positions with a lot of information interaction with other nodes. Therefore, anchors have an important impact on the whole network, and can be used to provide position information to other nodes. Based on the accuracy position information provided by the anchors, A-GNN model can distinguish nodes, which have similarities in some aspects, but are in different positions. Proper and efficient selection of anchor set can provide high quality position information for nodes, thus improving the accuracy of downstream tasks. Therefore, the selection strategy of the anchor set is very crucial.

As Fig. 2 shows, the strategy of randomly selecting anchors do not satisfy two conditions: (1) one is that the information interaction with other nodes should be rich enough, and (2) the other is that the distribution should be scattered enough. The calculation process of anchors should consider that the importance of each node in a complex network is different. Inspired by previous approaches of evaluating the importance of nodes [31], our A-GNN model proposes a new method, called GA-MPCA to calculate anchors. In terms of information interaction, GA-MPCA believes that the nodes with high degree have strong information communication with other nodes, and they can influence other nodes through the shortest paths. Besides, GA-MPCA adopts first order minimum point covering method to keep the anchors scattered enough.

The strategy of anchor set selection includes three simple steps:

(1) Given a network, we first select the node with the highest degree as the first anchor, and mark it as "anchor" and its one-hop neighbors as "covered". The step belong to the greedy algorithm part.
(2) In the unmarked node geometry, the node with the most connections to the unmarked nodes is found as the next anchor, and mark it as "anchor" and its one-hop neighbors as "covered". This step still belong to the greedy algorithm part.
(3) Repeat (2), until all the nodes in the network are marked "covered" and "anchor", this step belong to minimum point covering algorithm part.

4.2   The Node Embedding Mechanism

This subsection mainly consists of two aspect of mechanisms. The one is to utilize GA-MPCA to calculate anchors, the other is to utilize GNN encoder to incorporate the node's attributes, neighborhoods and global position information into the vector representation of the node. It is responsible for the embedding computation process of nodes.

GA-MPCA. It is proposed to find anchors in network, which can satisfy the above two requirements: discrete distributions and high interaction with other nodes. To elaborate on the detail process of the algorithm, we use the example shown in Fig. 4. There are totally eight nodes and seven edges, and the red color represents anchors, the light red represents the one-hop neighbors of anchors. Given the network shown in Fig. 4, we infer that nodes v_7 and v_8 are anchors finally through GA-MPCA.

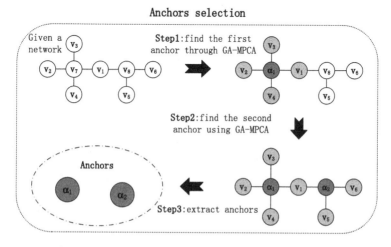

Fig. 4. The explanation of GA-MPCA (Color figure online)

For the example of Fig. 4, the steps of GA-MPCA are explained as follows:

(1) Given a network, we firstly use greedy algorithm to find node v_7 with the highest degree 4 as the first anchor, then mark it as "anchor" in red, next its one-hop neighbors v_1, v_2, v_3 and v_4 are simultaneously marked as "covered" in light red.
(2) Due to there are three nodes still not marked, we continue to calculate the degrees. As a result, the degree of v_5 and v_6 both are equal to 1, but v_8' degree is equal to 2. So we choose v_8 as the second anchor, then mark it as "anchor" in red, next its one-hop neighbors v_5 and v_6 are marked as "covered" in light red.
(3) After the step (2) is completed, all nodes have been marked. So we could extract nodes v_7 and v_8 as anchors α_1 and α_2.

Embedding Computation for Nodes. In this part, we use GNN encoder to merge the node's attributes, network neighborhood and position information into its vector representation. The calculation process is shown in Fig. 5. In the i-th layer of GNN, the input is a feature vector representation of node v. And $h_{\alpha 1}$, …, $h_{\alpha n}$ are the vector of anchors. Function F_1 combines the position information into node representation, which is marked as A. Function AGG_M is a trainable function that can transform anchors' features into the given node v, represented by M. Then, M_1, …, M_n are joined together getting M. We perform two-step operation for M. The one is applying function AGG_S to M, and getting the input vector of next layer. The other is the use of the trainable vector w for projecting M to the output anchors-aware vector $\mathbf{z}_v$ of node v.

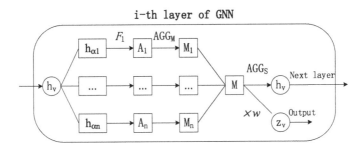

Fig. 5. Embedding computation for node v

4.3 Algorithm Implementation

In this part, we elaborate the algorithm of anchors selection and GNN encoder in detail.

Anchors Selection Algorithm (GA-MPCA). For Algorithm 1, the input can be one or several networks, and the output is the anchors set. We use $G = (\mathcal{V}, \mathcal{E})$ to represent a network, wherein $\mathcal{V}$ represents the node set, $\mathcal{E}$ represents the edge set. Firstly, we go through all the nodes in the network to look for the one with the highest degree. Next, mark it as "anchor" and its neighbors as "covered". Besides, we add them to the set $\mathcal{A}$.

Secondly, we still find the node with the highest degree in V but not in $\mathcal{V}$, and mark it and its neighbors as well. In addition, we add them to $\mathcal{A}$. Moreover, we repeat step 2, until all nodes in the network are marked. Finally, we go through the network, and add all the nodes marked "anchor" to anchor set S = $\{\alpha_1, ...\}$.

Algorithm 1 Anchors selection algorithm (**GA-MPCA**)

Input: Network $G = (\mathcal{V}, \mathcal{E})$

Output: Anchor set S = $\{\alpha_1, ...\}$

while $\mathcal{V} \neq \mathcal{A}$ **do**

  for $v \in \mathcal{V}$ and $v \notin \mathcal{A}$ **do**

    if v' degree is the highest **do**

      mark v "anchor" and its neighbors "covered", and add them to the clique $\mathcal{A}$

    End if

  End for

End while

for $v \in \mathcal{V}$ **do**

  i = 1

  if v is marked "anchor" **do**

    $\alpha_i \leftarrow v$

    i = i + 1

  End if

End for

GNN Encoder to Calculate Node's Embedding. In Algorithm 2, we also represent network with $G = (\mathcal{V}, \mathcal{E})$. Nodes features are represented by $\{y_v, ...\}$. There are L layers for GNN, and Anchor set is represented by S = $\{\alpha_1, ..., \alpha_n\}$. Firstly, we assign features vectors $\mathbf{h}_{z\{1,...\}}$ to nodes $\mathbf{h}_{v\{1,...\}}$, and regard it as the initial node vector of the first layer neural network. Secondly, we apply the function F_1 to combine the given node and anchors' feature information with their network distance to produce A. In Eq. (2), $d_{sp}^q(v, \alpha)$ represents the shortest path distance between the given node v and anchor α. Note that when the distance is over q, it won't be included in the calculation. Function $s(v, \alpha)$ maps the distance to a (0,1) range.

$$F_1(v, \alpha, \mathbf{h}_v, \mathbf{h}_\alpha) = s(v, \alpha) \, \text{Concat} \, (\mathbf{h}_v, \mathbf{h}_\alpha) \tag{1}$$

$$s(v, \alpha) = \frac{1}{d_{sp}^q(v, \alpha) + 1} \tag{2}$$

Next, trainable aggregation function AGG_M is applied to A. We transform anchors' features to the given node, which is represented by $M_{\{1,...\}}$. Then, we combine them into the matrix M. Finally, we perform two operations on M. The one is using AGG_S message aggregation function to transform M to the next layer input vector $\mathbf{h}_v$. The other is projecting M to the anchors-aware vector $\mathbf{z}_v$ of node v by using the trainable vector $\mathbf{w}$.

5   Experiments

The experiment section includes four parts. The first part introduces datasets used for link prediction and node classification tasks. The second part presents the experimental setup, containing inductive learning settings. The third part explains some baseline models, and the last part analyzes the experiment results.

Algorithm 2 GNN encoder with anchors algorithm

Input: Network $G = (\mathcal{V}, \mathcal{E})$; Node input features $\{y_v\}$; Layer $l \in [1, L]$; Anchor set $S = \{\alpha_1, ..., \alpha_n\}$

Output: Anchors-aware embedding z_v for every node

$h_v \leftarrow y_v$

for $l = 1, ..., L$ **do**

  for $v \in \mathcal{V}$ **do**

    for $i = 1 ..., n$ **do**

      $A \leftarrow \{F_l(v, \alpha, h_v, h_\alpha), \forall \alpha \in S_i\}$

      $M_i \leftarrow AGG_M(A)$

    End for

    $z_v \leftarrow \sigma(M \bullet w)$

    $h_v \leftarrow AGG_S(\{M_v[i], \forall i \in [1, n]\})$

  end for

end for

$z_v \in R^n, \forall v \in \mathcal{V}$

5.1   Datasets

We choose some typical synthetic and real datasets (Table 1) to perform our experiments. **Grid**, **Communities** [18], and **PPI** [3] are used for link prediction task, while **Communities**, **Emails** [19], and **Protein** [20] are used to node classification tasks. Note that only nodes in dataset **PPI**, and **Protein** have attributes.

Table 1. Statistics on the datasets.

Dataset	$|G|$	$|\mathcal{V}|$	$|\mathcal{E}|$	#train	#test
Grid	1	400	1216	973	243
Communities	1	400	6080	4864	1216
PPI	24	56658	1269770	1015816	253954
Email	7	920	14402	11522	2880
Protein	1113	17996	68632	54906	13726

5.2   Experimental Setup

The proposed A-GNN model is evaluated by two variants. Their differences are reflected in the path calculation of a given node and anchors. (1) P-GNN-F: the variant of P-GNN using truncated 2-hop shortest path distance; (2) P-GNN-E: the variant of P-GNN using exact shortest path distance.

Table 2. AUC value for link prediction.

	Grid	Communities	PPI
GCN	0.456 ± 0.037	0.512 ± 0.008	0.769 ± 0.002
GraphSAGE	0.532 ± 0.050	0.516 ± 0.010	0.803 ± 0.005
GAT	0.566 ± 0.052	0.618 ± 0.025	0.783 ± 0.004
GIN	0.499 ± 0.054	0.692 ± 0.049	0.782 ± 0.010
P-GNN-F	0.694 ± 0.066	0.991 ± 0.003	0.805 ± 0.003
P-GNN-E	0.940 ± 0.027	0.985 ± 0.008	0.808 ± 0.003
P-GNN-F (repetition)	0.685 ± 0.029	0.980 ± 0.007	0.786 ± 0.006
P-GNN-E (repetition)	0.932 ± 0.031	0.973 ± 0.000	0.793 ± 0.005
A-GNN-F	0.736 ± 0.066	0.988 ± 0.006	0.818 ± 0.005
A-GNN-E	**0.969 ± 0.005**	**0.993 ± 0.000**	**0.820 ± 0.003**

In the experiments of A-GNN model, 80% of the graphs are used to train our A-GNN model and the remaining graphs for testing. For the pairwise node classification task, whether a pair of nodes belongs to the same community is predicted by our model. Note that a pair of nodes that do not belong to the same community are negative.

5.3   Baseline Models

In order to prove the validity of our proposed A-GNN model, the classic GNN models and P-GNN model are used as baseline for comparison. Therefore, all above model are trained for the same number of epochs and are set to the same model parameters. The experimental results on both link prediction and pairwise node classification tasks show that our model is about 3% better than the state-of-art P-GNN model in many tasks. Furthermore, in some datasets, the accuracy of our model achieves almost 100%.

GNN Related Classical Models. We consider four GNN related classical models, including GCN [12], Graph-SAGE [15], Graph Attention Networks(GAT) [13], and Position-aware Graph Neural Networks (P-GNN) [11].

A-GNN Model. Our model consider two variants of A-GNN: (1) A-GNN using truncated 2-hop shortest path distance(A-GNN-F); (2) A-GNN using exactly shortest path distance (A-GNN-E).

5.4   Results and Analysis

Link Prediction. Link prediction is intended to predict the missing edges in the graph. If two nodes in a low-dimensional vector space are close, they are generally more likely to be linked by an edge. The performance of baseline models and A-GNN model are summarized in Table 2 on link prediction tasks. It can be seen that our A-GNN model achieves better results than any other baseline model of the link prediction tasks. Comparing the datasets, the effect of our model on their improvement is different, ranging from 1% to 4%. The improvements are minimal for both communities and Grid datasets, while obvious for PPI dataset. The reason is that both communities and Grid are small graphs with only 400 network nodes. Therefore, the nodes with similar network neighbors or at symmetric positions can be distinguished by a few makers instead of anchors. However, since each graph in PPI is a large graph, which has about 3000 nodes and 50000 edges on average, and have a lot of symmetrical structures. Thus, anchors can better help A-GNN model to distinguish nodes with similar local structures, compared to randomly selected makers.

Table 3. AUC value for pairwise node classification.

	Communities	Email	Protein
GCN	0.520 ± 0.025	0.515 ± 0.019	0.515 ± 0.002
GraphSAGE	0.514 ± 0.028	0.511 ± 0.016	0.520 ± 0.003
GAT	0.620 ± 0.022	0.502 ± 0.015	0.528 ± 0.011
GIN	0.620 ± 0.102	0.545 ± 0.012	0.523 ± 0.002
P-GNN-F	0.997 ± 0.006	0.640 ± 0.037	0.729 ± 0.176
P-GNN-E	1.0 ± 0.001	0.640 ± 0.029	0.631 ± 0.175
P-GNN-F(repetition)	0.987 ± 0.002	0.676 ± 0.050	0.675 ± 0.001
P-GNN-E(repetition)	0.988 ± 0.005	0.668 ± 0.021	0.512 ± 0.000
A-GNN-F	0.988 ± 0.006	**0.754 ± 0.002**	**0.708 ± 0.003**
A-GNN-E	**1.0 ± 0.002**	0.721 ± 0.009	0.633 ± 0.002

Pairwise Node Classification. In pairwise node classification tasks, we predict whether a pair of nodes belongs to the same community/class. In this case, a pair of nodes that do not belong to the same community are a negative example. The performance of baseline models and A-GNN model are summarized in Table 3 on pairwise node classification tasks. Our A-GNN model achieves the best experimental results in all datasets. Because GNNs focus on learning structure-aware embeddings, these models cannot perform well in distinguishing nodes belonging to different communities but have similar neighbourhood structures. Furthermore, the results of GNNs are about 30% lower than the other two models. A-GNN results are better than P-GNN's, indicating that the anchors adopted by our model are more efficient than randomly generated makers.

6   Conclusion

We propose A-GNN model, a new class of GNNs for incorporating the global structure information into the node vector, and utilize node features. We show that A-GNN consistently outperform existing baselines in link prediction and pairwise node classification tasks and both synthetic and real datasets.

Acknowledgements. This work was supported in part by the National Key R&D Program of China (Grant No. 2018YFB1004600), the National Science and Technology Major Project of China (Grant No. 2017ZX05036-001) and the National Natural Science Foundation of China (NSFC) (Grant No. 61972365, 61772480, 61672474, 61673354, 61501412).

References

1. Damian, S., John, H., Helen, C.: quality-controlled protein–protein association networks, made broadly accessible. Nucleic Acid Res., 937 (2016)
2. Ying, R., He, R., Chen, K.: Graph convolutional neural networks for web-scale recommender systems. In: 2018 International Proceedings on ACM SIGKDD Knowledge Discovery and Data Mining, pp. 1576–1585 (2018)
3. Zitnik, M., Leskovec, J.: Predicting multicellular function through multi-layer tissue networks. Bioinformatics 33(14), i190–i198 (2017)
4. Kipf, T.N., Welling, M.: Semi-supervised classification with graph convolutional networks. In: 2017 International Proceedings on Learning Representation (2017)
5. Grover, A., Leskovec, J.: node2vec: Scalable feature learning for networks. In: 22th International Proceedings on ACM SIGKDD, pp. 855–864 (2016)
6. Sun, G., Zhang, X.: A novel framework for node/edge attributed graph embedding. In: Yang, Q., Zhou, Z.-H., Gong, Z., Zhang, M.-L., Huang, S.-J. (eds.) PAKDD 2019. LNCS (LNAI), vol. 11441, pp. 169–182. Springer, Cham (2019). https://doi.org/10.1007/978-3-030-16142-2_14
7. Scarselli, F., Gori, M., Tsoi, A.C., Hagenbuchner, M., Monfardini, G.: The graph neural network model. IEEE Trans. Neural Netw. 20(1), 61–80 (2009)
8. Sun, M., Tang, J., Li, H.: Data poisoning attack against unsupervised node embedding methods. arXiv preprint arXiv:1810.12881 (2018)
9. Grover, A., Leskovec, J.: node2vec: scalable feature learning for networks. In: 22nd International Proceedings on ACM SIGKDD Knowledge Discovery and Data Mining, pp. 855–864 (2016)
10. Cheng, Y., Zhi, L., Deli, Z.: Network representation learning with rich text information. In: 2015 International Proceedings on IJCAI (2015)
11. Jiaxuan, Y., Rex, Y., Jure, L.: Position-aware graph neural networks. In: 36th International Proceedings on International Conference on Machine Learning (2019)
12. Kipf, T.N., Welling, M.: Semi-supervised classification with graph convolutional networks. In: 2017 International Proceedings on International Conference Learning Representations, pp. 1–14 (2017)
13. Velickovic, P., Cucurull, G., Casanova, A.: Graph attention networks (2018)
14. Battaglia, P.W., Hamrick, J.B., Bapst, V.: Relational inductive biases, deep learning, and graph networks. arXiv preprint arXiv:1806.01261 (2018)
15. Hamilton, W., Ying, Z., Leskovec, J.: Inductive representation learning on large graphs. In: Advances in Neural Information Processing Systems, pp. 1024–1034 (2017)
16. Zhang, M., Chen, Y.: Link prediction based on graph neural networks. Advances in Neural Information Processing Systems (2018)
17. Qin, Q., Wang, D.: Evaluation method for node importance in complex networks based on eccentricity of node. In: Advances in Neural Information Processing Systems, pp. 1324–1334 (2019)
18. Watts, D.J.: Networks, dynamics, and the small-world phenomenon. Am. J. Sociol. 105(2), 493–527 (1999)
19. Leskovec, J., Kleinberg, J., Faloutsos, C.: Graph evolution: densification and shrinking diameters. ACM Trans. Knowl. Discov. Data (TKDD) 1(1), 2 (2007)
20. Borgwardt, K.M., Ong, C.S., Schonauer, S.: Protein function prediction via graph kernels. Bioinformatics 21(suppl 1), i47–i56 (2005)
21. Xiqing, S., Shoukui, S.: Complex Network Algorithms and Applications, 2nd edn. National Defense Industry Press (2016)
22. Xinbo, A.: New metrics for node importance evaluation in occupational injury network. IEEE Access 7, 61874–61882 (2019)

Accelerating Face Detection Algorithm on the FPGA Using SDAccel

Jie Wang[✉] and Wei Leng

Dalian University of Technology, Dalian 116620, China
wangjie1003@163.com

Abstract. In recent years, with the rapid growth of big data and computation, high-performance computing and heterogeneous computing have been widely concerned. In object detection algorithms, people tend to pay less attention to training time, but more attention to algorithm running time, energy efficiency ratio and processing delay. FPGA can achieve data parallel operation, low power, low latency and reprogramming, providing powerful computing power and enough flexibility. In this paper, SDAccel tool of Xilinx is used to implement a heterogeneous computing platform for face detection based on CPU +FPGA, in which FPGA is used as a coprocessor to accelerate face detection algorithm. A high-level synthesis (HLS) approach allows developers to focus more on the architecture of the design and lowers the development threshold for software developers. The implementation of Viola Jones face detection algorithm on FPGA is taken as an example to demonstrate the development process of SDAccel, and explore the potential parallelism of the algorithm, as well as how to optimize the hardware circuit with high-level language. Our final design is 70 times faster than a single-threaded CPU.

Keywords: FPGA · Heterogeneous · Face detection · Architecture · High-level synthesis · SDAccel

1 Introduction

In the Internet industry, with the popularization of information technology, the explosion of data makes people have a new requirement on storage space. At the same time, the rise of machine learning, artificial intelligence, unmanned driving, industrial simulation and other fields makes the general CPU encounter more and more performance bottlenecks in processing massive computing, massive data and pictures, such as low parallelism, insufficient bandwidth and high delay. In order to meet the demand of diversified computing, more and more scenarios begin to introduce GPU, FPGA and other hardware for acceleration, resulting in the emergence of heterogeneous computing, which refers to the computing mode of a system composed of different types of instruction sets and computing units of the system architecture.

Two common heterogeneous computing platforms are CPU+GPU or CPU+FPGA architectures. The biggest advantage of these typical heterogeneous computing architectures is that they have higher efficiency and lower latency than traditional CPU parallel computing. CPU belongs to general computing and is good at management and

© ICST Institute for Computer Sciences, Social Informatics and Telecommunications Engineering 2020
Published by Springer Nature Switzerland AG 2020. All Rights Reserved
X. Chu et al. (Eds.): QShine 2019, LNICST 300, pp. 154–165, 2020.
https://doi.org/10.1007/978-3-030-38819-5_10

scheduling. Therefore, the algorithms-intensive part can be unloaded onto FPGA or GPU for parallel calculation, so as to realize algorithm acceleration. FPGA has hardware programmability, which means that FPGA can make customized design according to algorithm, which increases the flexibility of FPGA and enables FPGA to enter the market quickly. Compared with GPU, FPGA tends to show a better energy efficiency ratio, and the processing delay is much lower than GPU. This paper uses SDAccel to implement a heterogeneous computing platform for face detection based on CPU+FPGA. CPU transmits data to FPGA through PCIe bus. The face detection algorithm is accelerated by the FPGA. Finally, the results are transmitted back to CPU from FPGA through PCIe bus, detection results and pictures display are performed on CPU.

The SDAccel environment uses a standard programming language, providing a framework for developing and delivering FPGA accelerated data center applications. Nowadays, the application of FPGA has turned to the field of high-performance heterogeneous computing and massive data processing, and the object of using FPGA is not necessarily the traditional hardware engineer, it is likely that the programmer who works for developing software. SDAccel enables application developers to use familiar software programming workflows to accelerate with FPGA, even though there has been little experience in FPGA or hardware design before. Programs running on CPU are developed using c/c++ and opencl [1] APIs, while programs running on hardware can be developed using c/c++, opencl or RTL. When we have finished our design on SDAccel, we need to first carry out software simulation to verify the functionality of the design, then carry out hardware simulation to see the rationality of the resources and architecture needed for the design, and finally generate the FPGA bitstream. The hardware program of this paper is synthesized by Vivado HLS with c/c++ high-level language. The benefit of this approach is that it shortens the development cycle and allows developers to focus more on the architecture of the design.

The rest of the paper is organized as follows: Sect. 2 examines the related work; Sect. 3 provides an overview of face detection based on the Viola Jones algorithm; Sect. 4 describes the implementation of the real-time face detection system in an FPGA and the optimization methods; Sect. 5 presents performance and area results, followed by conclusions in Sect. 6.

2   Related Work

Face detection is the key technology of pattern recognition and computer vision. The improvement of algorithm speed is often at the cost of increasing hardware resources or power consumption. However, with the further development of face detection in various fields and the consideration of the trend of miniaturization and portability for energy saving, the requirement of hardware and power consumption for face detection has gradually become more and more important. Many researches are based on hardware-accelerated face detection algorithms [4–7, 13–16]. Most of which use Viola Jones face detection algorithm [3], because it not only has advantages in accuracy and speed, but also is more suitable for hardware implementation. Lai et al. [4] proposed a FPGA hardware architecture for face detection using feature cascade classifiers, which achieved the detection speed of 143 frames per second (FPS) at VGA (640 × 480) resolution. But they only used 52 Haar feature classifiers, which greatly reduced the accuracy of face detection and could not be used in actual detection tasks. Hiromoto [5] made a thorough analysis of the algorithm, studied the effects of various parallel schemes, different image downscaling methods and fixed-point on the detection speed and resource consumption, and proposed a partial parallel face detection architecture. This greatly reduced the total processing time without greatly increasing the circuit area. Cho [6] used each detection window to generate integral image for face detection. Instead of upscaling Haar features, they used image pyramid to detect faces. Kyrkou [7] combined image downscaling and feature upscaling to realize viola jones face detection algorithm.

There are many studies on high-level synthesis (HLS) tools [2, 8–12]. Srivastava [13] explored how to implement viola jones face detection algorithm with high-level synthesis method. They implemented their design with SDSOC and achieved a rate of 30 frames per second (FPS) at 320 × 240 resolution. In this paper, we implement a face detection algorithm based on heterogeneous computing platform using high-level synthesis method and SDAccel tool.

3   Face Detection Algorithm

Haar features is first proposed by Papageorgiou [17]. But it is too much calculation to be applied. Later, Paul Viola and Michael Jones proposed a method of fast calculating Haar features by using integral image in [3], three types and four forms of Haar features are used. Haar-like features were widely used together with Adaboost algorithm. Common Haar features are shown in the Fig. 1.

Fig. 1. Five common haar features

The haar features is calculated by the sum of pixels in the white rectangle by their weight minus the sum of pixels in the black rectangle by their weight. Because of the translation and enlargement of variety of Haar features in the picture, there will be a huge number of single features. The numerical calculation of each feature involves the sum of many pixel values. If the calculation is carried out directly, the amount of calculation is very huge, which brings trouble to the practical application of Haar features. In order to solve this problem, Paul Viola and Michal Jones put forward a fast method of calculating Haar features by integral image. The pixel value of a point in the integral image is equal to the sum of all the pixel values corresponding to the upper left of this point in the original image. As shown in Fig. 2, to calculate the total value of pixels in area D, we only need to subtract the total value of pixels in the upper left of point 2 and point 3 from point 4, and add the total value of pixels in the upper left of point 1. The calculation process is expressed as sum (x4, y4) - sum (x3, y3) - sum (x2, y2) + sum (x1, y1) by the pixel values in the integral image, where xi and yi represent the horizontal and vertical coordinates of point i. Using the integral image, we can quickly calculate the pixel values in any rectangular area of the image. A small detection window contains tens of thousands of Haar features. It is impractical to calculate all the Haar features by integral image. Moreover, not all Haar features can be used as classifiers. In order to find the most suitable features for constructing classifiers among the numerous Haar features and improve the accuracy of these classifiers, Haar features are combined with Adaboost algorithm. Adaboost algorithm is a kind of boosting algorithm, and boosting algorithm is an algorithm that upgrades weak learning algorithm to strong learning algorithm. Adaboost algorithm was proposed by Freund et al. [18] in 1995, namely, Adaptive Boosting learning. It can adjust the hypothesis error rate adaptively according to the learning results of the weak learning algorithm, so it does not need to get the lowest hypothesis error rate in advance. That is to say, Adaboost does not need to know the performance of the weak classifier in advance like other boosting algorithms, and the learning efficiency keeps the same as other boosting algorithms. This is why Adaboost algorithm is widely used.

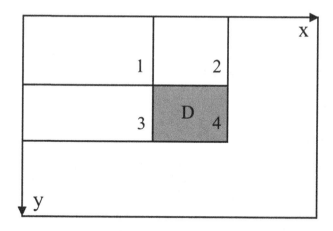

Fig. 2. Integral image.

4   Implementation

4.1   Data Transmission

The image used for detection is transmitted to DDR on the FPGA through the PCIe bus. The image pixel value needs to be extracted from DDR by AXI bus. In order to reduce the time of data transmission, we should adopt burst transmission method to extract data from DDR through AXI bus. Because the lowest bit width transmitted by AXI bus is 32 bits in SDAccel, and the bit width of image pixel value is 8 bits, in order to make full use of the data width of AXI, we can combine four pixels into a 32-bit data. When the 32-bit data is transmitted to the FPGA chip, the data is divided into four pixels. The data transmission process is shown in Fig. 3.

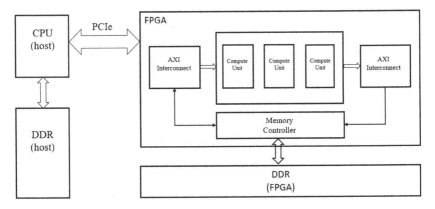

Fig. 3. Data transfer model

4.2 Image Storage

The module takes out the image transferred from PC to FPGA from DDR and stores it into BRAM on chip. Then pass the image from BRAM to the image scaling module and detection module. The advantage of storing images in BRAM is that the latency of data transmission is small and the speed is fast. The image resolution used in this paper is 320×240.

4.3 Image Scaling Module

When the sliding window method is used for face detection, in order to detect faces with different scales in the image, it is usually necessary to constantly expand the window size or reduce the image, and the scaling factor is usually 1.2 or 1.25. This paper uses the method of image pyramid, and scaling method is the nearest neighbor, the scaling factor is 1.25 (Fig. 4). This module is pipelined by adding a #pragma HLS pipeline instruction, which greatly speeds up image scaling.

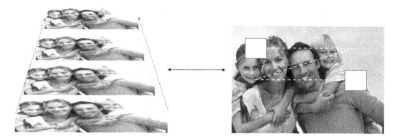

Fig. 4. Image pyramid and sliding window

4.4   Classification Module

Integral Image

In order to calculate the characteristic value of Haar quickly, we need to calculate the integral image of the image first. The calculated Haar feature values often need to be normalized by dividing the standard deviation of the pixels in the current window, so a square integral image is needed. The square integral image is the sum of squares of all the pixel values in the image. Taking the image of 320×240 resolution as an example, if we want to store the whole integral image on the FPGA, the data bit width of each storage unit of the integral graph is $\log_2(320 \times 240 \times 255)$, at least 25 bits are needed to store one data in the integral image, and the whole integral image needs $320 \times 240 \times 25$bits, that is, 2 M storage unit. But in the process of each detection of sliding window, only the data in the window is needed, every data in the integral image is useless in most of the time. Moreover, with the improvement of image resolution, the space occupied by the integral image will increase rapidly. Therefore, we used the method of dynamically generating integral image, which only generates one integral image of detecting window size at a time.

The integral image detection window in this paper consists of 25×25 registers, each of which stores the integral values corresponding to each pixel position in the detection window. The width of the register is 18 bits ($\log_2(255 \times 25 \times 25)$). The reason why register is used instead of RAM or ROM is that the integral image data at any position in the detection window can be accessed and updated at the same time, so as to improve the detection efficiency. Because it only stores the integral image of the current detection window, the consumption of hardware is not large. By taking advantage of the relevance between adjacent windows and the read-on-call characteristics of registers, we design a pipeline based quick update method of single clock integral image. Only the first detection window requires several clock delays to fill the empty integral image window. After that, only one clock can get the integral image of adjacent window, and the data can be updated very quickly. The update of integral image is divided into two parts: get the column integral value of the detection window, and get the integral value of the whole window from the column integral value. Taking

3×3 window as an example, the updating process of integral image is shown in Fig. 5. To compute the squared integral image, the same procedure is followed.

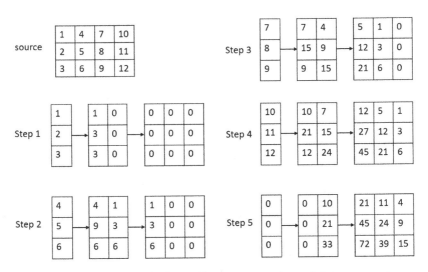

Fig. 5. Illustration of the integral image computation and data movement

Classifier

The classifier used in this paper comes from opencv. This classifier is trained by Adaboost algorithm with 24×24 frontal face, in which each haar feature is a weak classifier, multiple weak classifiers are combined to form a strong classifier, and multiple strong classifiers are cascade to form the final cascade classifier. The classifier finally trained consists of 25 strong classifiers and 2913 weak classifiers, and its specific components are shown in the Table 1.

Table 1. Number of weak classifiers in each stage

Stage	Classifier	Stage	Classifier	Stage	Classifier
0	9	9	91	18	169
1	16	10	99	19	196
2	27	11	115	20	197
3	32	12	127	21	181
4	52	13	135	22	199
5	53	14	136	23	211
6	62	15	137	24	200
7	72	16	159	Total	2913
8	83	17	155		

The formula for calculating the value of weak classifier is shown in (1).

$$F_{Haar} = \frac{E(R_{white}) - E(R_{black})}{w \cdot h \cdot \sqrt{|E(R_u)^2 - E(R_u^2)|}} \tag{1}$$

$E(R_u)^2$ represents the square of the average pixel values in the window, and $E(R_u^2)$ represents the average sum of squares of pixel values in the window. $w \cdot h \cdot \sqrt{|E(R_u)^2 - E(R_u^2)|}$ can be converted to $\sqrt{w \cdot h \cdot sqsum - sum \cdot sum}$, sqsum is expressed as the sum of squares of the pixels in the window, and sum is expressed as the sum of the pixels in the window. These two values can be obtained by the square integral image and the integral image respectively. Each weak classifier has a threshold, a left value and a right value. If the Haar feature value is greater than the threshold, the right value is output, otherwise the left value is output. The input of weak classifier module has coordinate of the upper left corner of the rectangle, length, width, weight, left and right values. Since these values are fixed and do not need to be changed, we can store these values in each ROM of the FPGA according to the category, thus eliminating the initialization time and extracting all attributes of a weak classifier in parallel in one clock cycle. In SDAccel, we can define arrays through static int when writing kernel code, and fill the values of various attributes of the weak classifier into different arrays, so that vivado HLS will synthesize these arrays into ROM in FPGA when compiling kernel code.

These weak classifiers will eventually form a strong classifier. Each strong classifier also has a threshold, which we store in ROM. If the sum of the output of all weak classifiers in the strong classifier is less than this threshold, the current detection window is excluded, otherwise the current detection window is passed. These strong classifiers are cascaded to form the final face detection classifier. The working mode of the classifier is shown in the Fig. 6. We also store the number of weak classifiers in each strong classifier in ROM. Thus, in SDAccel, we can complete the detection module through two for loops. But it does not give full play to the characteristics of FPGA parallel computing. We can make vivado HLS design this code into pipeline mode on hardware by adding # pragma HLS pipeline instruction in the inner loop. By pipelining 2913 weak classifiers, the speed of image detection is greatly accelerated.

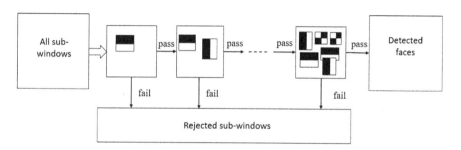

Fig. 6. Illustration of the Classification process

4.5   Optimization

There are many factors that affect the speed of face detection, such as image scaling factor, sliding window step size, initial sliding window size and so on. Although the values of these factors can be changed, they can only be changed in a certain range, otherwise, the accuracy of face detection will be affected. The image scaling factor used in this paper is 1.25, the sliding window step is 1, and the window size is 24 × 24. For a 320 × 240 resolution image, a total of 157433 detection windows can be generated. In the worst case, each detection window will be detected by 2913 classifiers, which shows that the computation of the detection algorithm is very large. However, except for the target area in the image, very few areas will be detected by all the classifiers, most of which are usually excluded in the first few layers of the cascade classifier. This is also the advantage of cascaded classifiers. If we want to speed up the algorithm, we usually use hardware area in exchange for time. In VJ face detection algorithm, the most extreme example is to parallelize all weak classification detection. But this approach requires a lot of hardware resources, increases power consumption and increases the cost of products. We made a compromise between area and speed. Since most of the detection windows are excluded by the first three layers of cascade classifier, we only expand the first three layers of cascade classifier. The latter 22-layer classifier still adopts pipeline parallel method and achieves good results. In order to expand the first three layers of strong classifiers, the 12 coordinate values required by weak classifiers should be written into the code manually when writing the kernel code in SDAccel, rather than from ROM. Because ROM can only read two values in one clock cycle at most, it is obviously not able to fully expand a strong classifier.

We should also note the various floating-point operations in fpga. Because FPGA is not suitable for floating-point operation, we should convert floating-point into fixed-point as much as possible, such as the weights and thresholds of classifiers. This saves hardware resources and speeds up computing.

When writing software algorithms, we are often used to defining integer variables as int types. When we want to implement an algorithm on hardware, we should try to be as accurate as possible about the bit width of the data. Vivado HLS provides ap_ [u] int, ap_[u]fixed type so that we can accurately declare the data bit width. For example, in our algorithm, we use an integral image of 25 × 25, which has a bit width of 18bits ($\log_2$ (25 × 25 × 255)), much less than 32bits. This saves hardware resources, improves clock frequency, speeds up algorithms, and makes vivado easier to route.

In addition to the hardware architecture, we can also consider increasing the speed of the algorithm by changing the algorithm. Variance is the necessary data for VJ face detection algorithm. Through the variance statistics of face frontal images, we find that the variance of face is mostly in the range of 200 to 6000. So we also put the variance as a strong classifier into the first layer of the cascade classifier. Since the variance calculation does not need to consume extra time to calculate, and the classification process is only compared with the threshold value, this method speeds up the face detection algorithm. The speed comparison between adding variance classifier and not adding variance classifier will be given in the results section.

5 Experimental Results

Our design is implemented on inrel i7-8700 CPU and KCU1500 FPGA. The software environment is SDAccel 2018.2. SDAccel generates kernel programs by calling Vivado HLS 2018.2, and develops host programs by calling opencl API. We designed a single thread cpu-based face detection algorithm for comparison with our hardware implementation. We tested the performance of the software algorithm on the Intel i7-8700 CPU, and the hardware performance was tested at the clock frequency of 100 MHz.

Table 2. Performance of proposed face detection system

	Resolution	Variance classifier(No)	Variance classifier(Yes)
SW Classifier	320 × 240	0.78fps(1279 ms)	–
HW Classifier	320 × 240	58.8fps(17 ms)	66.6fps(15 ms)

Table 2 shows the performance of the implemented face detection algorithm in software and hardware. It can be seen that CPUs based single thread face detection algorithm is extremely time consuming, with a speed of less than one frame per second. After acceleration by FPGA, the speed can be increased 70 times to 58 frames per second (FPS), which meets the demand of video real-time processing. We can also see that when adding variance classifier, our speed can be increased by at least 10%, and in some cases, the variance classifier can achieve quite better performance. Table 3 shows the resource utilization of the system.

Table 3. Resource Utilization of our proposed face detection system

Logic	Total used	Total available	Utilization (%)
LUT	84137	663360	12
FF	52735	1326720	3
DSP48E	68	5520	1
BRAM_18K	194	4320	4

6 Conclusions

In this paper, we implement VJ face detection algorithm by using SDAccel, and implement a heterogeneous computing platform of CPU+FPGA. We discuss the parallelism of the algorithm and the hardware architecture, and try some optimization methods. According to the experimental results, our design can meet the requirements of real-time face detection. We demonstrate the efficiency of SDAccel, and it is clear that SDAccel's products are of good quality and greatly reduce the development cycle of FPGA products. But there is still room for improvement in the synthesized fine control of design.

References

1. Stone, J.E., Gohara, D., Shi, G.: OpenCL: a parallel programming standard for heterogeneous computing systems. Comput. Sci. Eng. **12**(1–3), 66–73 (2010)
2. Guidi, G., et al.: On how to improve FPGA-based systems design productivity via SDAccel. In: Proceedings of 2016 IEEE 30th International Parallel and Distributed Processing Symposium, IPDPS 2016, pp. 247–252 (2016)
3. Viola, P., Jones, M.J.: Robust real-time face detection. Int. J. Comput. Vis. **57**(2), 137–154 (2004)
4. Lai, H.C., Savvides, M., Chen, T.: Proposed FPGA hardware architecture for high frame rate (>00 Fps) face detection using feature cascade classifiers. In: IEEE Conference on Biometrics: Theory, Applications and Systems, BTAS 2007 (2007)
5. Hiromoto, M., Sugano, H., Miyamoto, R.: Partially parallel architecture for AdaBoost-based detection with haar-like features. IEEE Trans. Circuits Syst. Video Technol. **19**(1), 41–52 (2009)
6. Cho, J., Benson, B., Mirzaei, S., Kastner, R.: Parallelized architecture of multiple classifiers for face detection. In: 2009 20th IEEE International Conference on Application-specific Systems, Architectures and Processors, pp. 75–82. IEEE (2009)
7. Kyrkou, C., Theocharides, T.: A flexible parallel hardware architecture for AdaBoost-based real-time object detection. IEEE Trans. Very Large Scale Integr. (VLSI) Syst. **19**(6), 1034–1047 (2011)
8. Casseau, E., Gal, B.L.: High-level synthesis for the design of FPGA-based signal processing systems. In: International Symposium on Systems, Architectures, Modeling, and Simulation (SAMOS) (2009)
9. Skalicky, S., Wood, C., Łukowiak, M., Ryan, M.: High-level synthesis: where are we? A case study on matrix multiplication. In: International Conference on Reconfigurable Computing and FPGAs (ReConFig) (2013)
10. Winterstein, F., Bayliss, S., Constantinides, G.A.: High-level synthesis of dynamic data structures: a case study using Vivado HLS. In: International Conference on Field-Programmable Technology (FPT) (2013)
11. Neuendorffer, S., Li, T., Wang, D.: Accelerating OpenCV applications with Zynq-7000 all programmable SoC using Vivado HLS video libraries. Xilinx Inc., August 2013
12. Edwards, S., et al.: The challenges of synthesizing hardware from c- like languages. IEEE Des. Test Comput. **23**(5), 375–386 (2006)
13. Srivastava, N.K., Dai, S., Manohar, R., Zhang, Z.: Accelerating face detection on programmable SoC using C-based synthesis. In: Proceedings of the 2017 ACM/SIGDA International Symposium on Field-Programmable Gate Arrays - FPGA 2017, pp. 195–200 (2017)
14. Zemcik, P., Juranek, R., Musil, P., Musil, M., Hradis, M.: High performance architecture for object detection in streamed videos. In: Proceedings of 2013 23rd International Conference on Field Programmable Logic and Applications, FPL 2013, pp. 4–7 (2013)
15. Musil, P., Juranek, R., Musil, M., et al.: Cascaded stripe memory engines for multi-scale object detection in FPGA. IEEE Trans. Circuits Syst. Video Technol., 1–1 (2018)

16. Kyrkou, C., Bouganis, C., Theocharides, T., Polycarpou, M.M.: Embedded hardware-efficient real-time classification with cascade support vector machines. IEEE Trans. Neural Netw. Learn. Syst. **27**(1), 99–112 (2016)
17. Papageorgiou, C.P., Oren, M., Poggio, T.: General framework for object detection. In: Proceedings of the IEEE International Conference on Computer Vision, February 1998, pp. 555–562 (1998)
18. Freund, Y., Schapire, R.E.: A decision-theoretic generalization of on-line learning and an application to boosting BT. In: Proceedings of Computational Learning Theory: Second European Conference, EuroCOLT 1995, Barcelona, Spain, 13–15 March 1995, pp. 23–37 (1995). Journal of Computer & System Sciences

Telecommunication Systems

Hybrid NOMA/OMA with Buffer-Aided Relaying for Cooperative Uplink System

Jianping Quan[1], Peng Xu[1(✉)], Yunwu Wang[1], and Zheng Yang[2]

[1] Chongqing Key Laboratory of Mobile Communications Technology,
School of Communication and Information Engineering,
Chongqing University of Posts and Telecommunications, Chongqing 400065, China
quanjianp@163.com, xupeng@cqupt.edu.cn, wangyunw@163.com
[2] Fujian Provincial Engineering Technology Research Center
of Photoelectric Sensing Application, Key Laboratory of OptoElectronic Science and
Technology for Medicine of Ministry of Education, Fujian Normal University,
Fuzhou 350007, China
zyfjnu@163.com

Abstract. In this paper, we consider a cooperative uplink network consisting of two users, a half-duplex decode-and-forward (DF) relay and a base station (BS). In the relaying network, the two users transmit packets to the buffer-aided relay using non-orthogonal multiple access (NOMA) or orthogonal multiple access (OMA) technology. We proposed a hybrid NOMA/OMA based mode selection (MS) scheme, which adaptively switches between the NOMA and OMA transmission modes according to the instantaneous strength of wireless links and the buffer state. Then, the state transmission matrix probabilities of the corresponding Markov chain is analyzed, and the performance in terms of sum throughput, outage probability, average packet delay and diversity gain are evaluated with closed form expressions. Numerical results are provided to demonstrate that hybrid NOMA/OMA achieves significant performance gains compared to conventional NOMA and OMA in most scenarios.

Keywords: Hybrid NOMA/OMA · Buffer-aided relaying ·
Cooperative uplink system

1 Introduction

Non-orthogonal multiple access (NOMA) technology, is recognized to be a promising mobile communication technology in future communication systems

The work of J. Quan and P. Xu was supported by the National Natural Science Foundation of China under Grant 61701066, in part by Chongqing Natural Science Foundation Project under Grant cstc2019jcyj-msxm1354, in part by Chongqing College Students' Innovative Entrepreneurial Training Plan Program under Grant S201910617032, and in part by Special Funded Undergraduate Research Training Program under Grant A2019-39. The work of Z. Yang was supported by National Natural Science Foundation of China under Grant 61701118.

X. Chu et al. (Eds.): QShine 2019, LNICST 300, pp. 169–183, 2020.
https://doi.org/10.1007/978-3-030-38819-5_11

since it can significantly enhance spectrum efficiency [2]. Different to orthogonal multiple access (OMA) technology which serves multiple users in orthogonal time/frequze/code domain, NOMA allows multiple users to share communication resources in the same time/frequze/code domain with different power levels, and achieves better performance than conventional OMA [4,13].

Cooperative communication enables efficient utilization of communication resources, which has many advantages in improving system efficiency and reliability, and expanding the coverage of wireless communication networks. The work in [3] first exploited cooperation between the users, i.e., the stronger users help the other weaker users by using the decode-and-forward (DF) scheme, such that the performance of NOMA can be enhanced and the optimal diversity gain can be achieved. On the other hand, the work in [6] investigated cooperative NOMA with a single relay, where multiple users were helped by a dedicated relay node using the DF and amplify-and-forward (AF) schemes. In addition, relay selection scheme has also been proposed for cooperative NOMA networks with multiple relays in some existing works (e.g., [15,16]).

For the Buffer-aided relaying system, the data buffer enables the relay to transmit when the source-to-relay link is in outage and to receive when the relay-to-destination link is in outage, which can provide additional freedom for wireless cooperative communication networks and overcome the bottleneck effect of conventional cooperative communication technologies [17,19]. Exiting works related to buffer-aided cooperative communication mainly considered the design of adaptive link or mode selection (MS) schemes for single-relay systems (e.g., [5,20]), and the design of relay selection (RS) schemes for multiple-relay systems [7,9,10,14]. In addition, buffer-aided cooperative NOMA for downlink transmission has also been investigated in recent existing works [8,11,17]. The works in [8] and [17] considered cooperative NOMA with a single buffer-aided relay. In [8], adaptive and fixed rates were assumed for the source-to-relay and relay-to-user transmissions, respectively, and the sum throughput was maximized based on the optimal MS scheme. In [17], fixed rate was assumed for both the source-to-relay and relay-to-user transmissions, and a relay decision scheme was proposed to enhance outage performance. Recently, the work in [11] proposed a hybrid buffer-aided NOMA/OMA RS scheme, which is shown to significantly outperform NOMA and OMA RS schemes, but its performance is hard to be analyzed with closed-form expressions.

In previous works [8,11,17], downlink buffer-aided relay systems has been widely considered. In this paper, we focus on an uplink buffer-aided relay system with two users, a DF relay, and a base station (BS). For the considered system, we propose a buffer-aided hybrid NOMA/OMA based MS scheme, which adaptively switches between the NOMA and OMA transmission modes according to the instantaneous channel state information (CSI) and buffer state. The basic idea of the proposed hybrid NOMA/OMA MS scheme is to give priority to the NOMA transmission mode, i.e., NOMA will be adopted to transmit the two users' messages simultaneously. However, NOMA transmission mode might not be successful, especially for weak channel conditions; in this case, the transmission mode will switch to OMA.

The Markov chain (MC) of the proposed hybrid NOMA/OMA based MS scheme is formulated, and the corresponding state transmission matrix probabilities are analyzed. Then, we evaluate the performance of the proposed scheme. In particular, closed-form expressions for sum throughput, outage probability, and average delay are obtained, and it is demonstrated that the proposed scheme can achieve a diversity gain of 2 as long as the buffer size is not smaller than 3. It is worth noting that performance analysis of the proposed hybrid NOMA/OMA scheme is non-trivial since NOMA and OMA have different requirements of the channel state and buffer state. Numerical results are provided to demonstrate that hybrid NOMA/OMA can significantly outperform conventional NOMA and OMA in most scenarios, especially for sum throughput and outage probability.

2   System Model and Preliminaries

2.1   System Model

Consider a buffer-aided uplink DF relaying system which consists of two users, a relay, and a BS, as shown in Fig. 1. We assume that the direct links between the two users and the are sufficiently weak to be ignored, since they are blocked due to long-distance path loss or obstacles [7,16,17]. It is assumed that the time duration is partitioned into slots with equal length and each transmitted packet spans one time slot. In each time slot, the users or the relay may be selected to transmit packets. When each user is selected, it assembles an information symbol intended for the BS into a packet with r_0 bits, where r_0 denotes the target transmission rate, i.e., the same target rate is assumed for each user to guarantee fairness [17]. The relay is equipped with two buffers, i.e., B_1 and B_2. Each buffer consists of $L \geq 2$ storage units and each storage unit can store a data packet received from any user. A storage unit at buffer B_u is used to store an information symbol transmitted by user u, $u = 1, 2$. If the relay is selected, it retrieves information symbols from the buffers and transmits them to the BS. Assume that each user always has information symbols to transmit. The channel gain from user u to the relay is denoted as h_u. The channel gain from the relay to the BS is denoted as h_R. These channels are assumed to be independent flat Rayleigh block fading channels which remain constant during one time slot and change randomly from one time slot to anther. Denote $H_u \triangleq |h_u|^2$ and $H_R \triangleq |h_R|^2$ for the sake of brevity, which follow exponential distributions and their expectations are denoted by

$$\mathbb{E}[H_1] = \frac{1}{\Omega_1}, \ \mathbb{E}[H_2] = \frac{1}{\Omega_2} \text{ and } \mathbb{E}[H_R] = \frac{1}{\Omega_R}. \tag{1}$$

In addition, it is assumed that each transmitter is constrained by the maximum transmit power P, and each receiver has the same noise power σ^2.

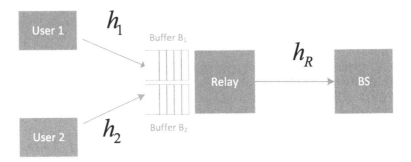

Fig. 1. System Model of an uplink buffer-aided relaying system.

Table 1. Necessary requirements for each transmission mode (T: Transmit; R: Receive; S: Silent)

Mode	User 1	User 2	Relay	BS	CSI requirement	Buffer requirement
$\mathcal{M}_1$	T	S	R	S	$\mathcal{R}_1 \triangleq \{H_1 \geq \epsilon_0\}$	$l_1 < L$
$\mathcal{M}_2$	S	T	R	S	$\mathcal{R}_2 \triangleq \{H_2 \geq \epsilon_0\}$	$l_2 < L$
$\mathcal{M}_3$	T	T	R	S	$\mathcal{R}_3 \triangleq \begin{Bmatrix} H_{\pi_1} \geq \epsilon_0 2^{r_0} \\ H_{\pi_2} \geq \epsilon_0 \end{Bmatrix}$	$\max\{l_1, l_2\} < L$
$\mathcal{M}_4$	S	S	T	R	$\mathcal{R}_4 \triangleq \{H_R \geq \epsilon_R\}$	$\min\{l_1, l_2\} > 0$
$\mathcal{M}_5$	S	S	S	S	$\forall H_1, H_2, H_R$	$\forall l_1, l_2$

2.2 Transmission Modes and CSI Requirements

For the proposed system, we consider five possible transmission modes, denoted by $\mathcal{M}_1, \cdots, \mathcal{M}_5$. Specifically, $\mathcal{M}_1$, $\mathcal{M}_2$, and $\mathcal{M}_3$ denote the user-to-relay modes, where the opportunistic hybrid NOMA/OMA is utilized: $\mathcal{M}_1$ and $\mathcal{M}_2$ utilize OMA for which only one of the users is selected to transmit a packet to the relay, and $\mathcal{M}_3$ utilizes NOMA for which the two users transmit packets to the relay simultaneously. $\mathcal{M}_4$ denotes the relay-to-BS mode, where the relay selects a packet from each user's buffer and blends the two packets into a mixed packet with $2r_0$ bits and then transmits it to the BS[1]; and $\mathcal{M}_5$ denotes the silent mode.

The instantaneous CSI requirement for each mode is summarized in Table 1, where the CSI region of mode $\mathcal{M}_k$ is defined as $\mathcal{R}_k$. Specifically, for the mode $\mathcal{M}_u$, $u = 1, 2$, it requires $H_u \geq \epsilon_0$ so that the relay can decode packets correctly, where $\epsilon_0 \triangleq \frac{2^{r_0}-1}{\rho}$ and $\rho \triangleq \frac{P}{\sigma^2}$ is the transmit signal-to-noise-ratio (SNR). For the mode $\mathcal{M}_4$, the transmission rate from the relay to the BS should be $2r_0$ bits per channel use (BPCU), so $H_R \geq \epsilon_R$ is required, where $\epsilon_R \triangleq \frac{2^{2r_0}-1}{\rho}$. For

---

[1] Note that, different to the user-to-relay transmission, we consider only one mode for the relay-to-BS transmission (i.e. $\mathcal{M}_4$), where the relay transmits both the two users' messages simultaneously, such that the two users' messages can reach the BS at the same time slot and short-term user fairness can be guaranteed [13].

the NOMA mode $\mathcal{M}_3$, the relay receives the following signal:

$$y_R = h_1 \sqrt{P_1} x_1 + h_2 \sqrt{P_2} x_2 + n_r, \tag{2}$$

where $P_u \leq P$ is the transmit power at user u, $u = 1, 2$, and n_r is the additive Gaussian noise at the relay with zero mean and variance σ^2. In addition, some existing modulation classification algorithms [18] can be more piratical in existing complex networks, which is out the scope of this paper.

The relay uses successive interference cancellation (SIC)[2] to decode the two users' messages. Specifically, assume that the users are sorted according to their channel qualities, i.e., $|h_{\pi_1}| \geq |h_{\pi_2}|$, where $\pi_1, \pi_2 \in \{1, 2\}$. The relay first decodes the message of the stronger user π_1 by treating the other user's signal as pure noise, which requires $\frac{H_{\pi_1} P_{\pi_1}}{\sigma^2 + H_{\pi_2} P_{\pi_2}} \geq \rho\epsilon_0$; then, it cancels the signal of the stronger user π_1 from the observed signal, and decodes the message of the weaker user π_2, which requires $H_{\pi_2} P_{\pi_2} \geq P\epsilon_0$.

Remark 1. *For user π_1, we set $P_{\pi_1} \triangleq P$; for user π_2, we set the minimum required transmit power, i.e., $P_{\pi_2} \triangleq \frac{P\epsilon_0}{H_{\pi_2}}$ if $\frac{\epsilon_0}{H_{\pi_2}} \leq 1$, and $P_{\pi_2} \triangleq 0$, otherwise, in order to control the inter-user interference power when decoding user π_1's messages. Using this power setting, the required CSI region $\mathcal{R}_3$ can be easily obtained as shown in Table 1. Such a power setting requires the weaker user π_2 to know the perfect CSI of h_{π_2} at the beginning of each time slot. Hybrid NOMA with imperfect CSI would be an interesting future topic.*

2.3   The Buffer Requirements

Let l_u denote the number of packets in buffer B_u at the end of each time slot, $l_u \in \{0, 1, ...L\}$. The buffer requirement for each mode is also summarized in Table 1, where mode $\mathcal{M}_u$ requires that buffer B_u is not full, i.e., $l_u < L$, $u = 1, 2$; mode $\mathcal{M}_3$ requires that both the two buffers are not full, i.e., $\max\{l_1, l_2\} < L$; and mode $\mathcal{M}_4$ requires that both the two buffers are not empty, i.e., $\min\{l_1, l_2\} > 0$.

3   Hybrid NOMA/OMA Mode Selection

The design of optimal buffer-aided relaying schemes for delay-constrained networks is still a challenging issue, which has not been solved even for the single-user case [19]. Alternatively, a heuristic but efficient delay-constrained buffer-aided MS scheme will be proposed in this section.

The basic idea is to allocate each mode $\mathcal{M}_k$ a weight, denoted by W_k, to determine the priority of each mode, which is given in Table 2, where $0 < \delta < 1/2$ is used to differentiate two weights with the same integer part. In addition, α_1, α_2 and α_3 denote three layers of the corresponding transmission modes, where $\alpha_1 \ll \alpha_2 \ll \alpha_3$. In particular, when $\min\{l_1, l_2\} \geq 2$, $\mathcal{M}_4$ lies in layer α_3, which

---

[2] Compared to "joint decoding" [1], SIC enjoys much lower decoding complexity, and hence this paper adopts the SIC detection at the relay.

enjoys the highest priority. The motivation of the threshold of 2 is to achieve the tradeoff between outage probability minimization and average packet delay minimization [9,17]. In this case, each buffer will be prone to remain at the size of 1 or 2 especially at high SNRs, which means that each buffer is neither full nor empty in most time slots as long as $L \geq 3$. When $\min\{l_1, l_2\} = 1$, $\mathcal{M}_4$ falls down to layer α_2, the same layer with $\mathcal{M}_3$. Moreover, the OMA modes $\mathcal{M}_1$ and $\mathcal{M}_2$ lies in layer α_1, and the silent mode $\mathcal{M}_5$ will be selected only if the weight of any other mode is smaller than 2δ or its CSI requirement is not satisfied.

Table 2. Weight for Each Mode, where $0 < \delta < 1/2$, $0 \ll \alpha_1 \ll \alpha_2 \ll \alpha_3$

Mode	Weight for each mode, i.e., W_k
$\mathcal{M}_1$	$\alpha_1(L - l_1)$
$\mathcal{M}_2$	$\alpha_1(L - l_2) + \delta$
$\mathcal{M}_3$	$\alpha_2(L - \max\{l_1, l_2\}) + \delta$
$\mathcal{M}_4$	$\alpha_3(\min\{l_1, l_2\} - 1) + \alpha_2$
$\mathcal{M}_5$	2δ

With the allocated weights, the hybrid NOMA/OMA based MS scheme can be mathematically expressed as follows. In particular, mode $\mathcal{M}_{k^*}$ is selected in each time slot, where

$$k^* = \arg \max_{k \in \mathcal{R}_k, W_k \geq 2\delta} W_k. \tag{3}$$

Remark 2. *Hybrid NOMA/OMA will reduce to NOMA, if we disable the transmission mode $\mathcal{M}_1$ and $\mathcal{M}_2$ by setting $W_1 = W_2 = 0$, i.e., only modes $\mathcal{M}_3$ and $\mathcal{M}_4$ are used to receive and transmit messages at the relay, respectively. In addition, if we disable mode $\mathcal{M}_3$ by setting $W_3 = 0$, hybrid NOMA/OMA will reduce to OMA where the users transmit messages to the relay in orthogonal time slots.*

4   Performance Analysis

In this section, the performance of the proposed hybrid NOMA/OMA based MS scheme will be analyzed by formulating a MC as well as its transition matrix to model the evolution of the relay buffers.

4.1   State Transmission Matrix

Let $s_n = (l_1, l_2)$, $n \in \{1, 2, ..., (L+1)^2\}$, denote the states in the MC, which describes the queues of the two buffers at the relay. Let $\mathbf{A}$ denote the $(L+1) \times (L+1)$ state transition matrix, whose entry $\mathbf{A}_{i,j} = p(s_j \rightarrow s_i) = \mathbb{P}\{(l_1(t + 1), l_2(t + 1)) = s_i | (l_1(t), l_2(t)) = s_j\}$ is the transition probability to move from state s_j at time t to s_i at time $t+1$. The transition probabilities for the proposed scheme can be summarized in the following proposition.

Proposition 1. *The transition probabilities of the states of the MC for the proposed hybrid NOMA/OMA based MS scheme are given in (5)–(9), shown in the next page, where $P_{(l_1,l_2)}^{(l_1,l_2+1)}$ is identical to $P_{(l_1,l_2)}^{(l_1+1,l_2)}$, after switching "1" and "2" in (7). Note that, for the sake of brevity, $\phi(\Omega_1, \Omega_2)$ in (7)–(9) is defined as follows:*

$$\phi(\Omega_1, \Omega_2) \triangleq e^{-\epsilon_0(\Omega_1 2^{r_0} + \Omega_2)} + e^{-\epsilon_0(\Omega_2 2^{r_0} + \Omega_1)} - e^{-(\Omega_1 + \Omega_2)\epsilon_0 2^{r_0}}. \tag{4}$$

Proof. Please refer to Appendix A.

$$P_{(l_1,l_2)}^{(l_1',l_2')} = 0,$$

$$\text{if } |l_1' - l_1| \geq 2 \vee |l_2' - l_2| \geq 2 \vee \{l_1' = l_1 - 1 \wedge l_2' \neq l_2 - 1\} \vee \{l_1' \neq l_1 - 1 \wedge l_2' = l_2 - 1\}. \tag{5}$$

$$P_{(l_1,l_2)}^{(l_1,l_2)} = \begin{cases} (1 - e^{-\Omega_1 \epsilon_0})(1 - e^{-\Omega_2 \epsilon_0})(1 - e^{-\Omega_R \epsilon_R}) & \text{if } \max\{l_1, l_2\} < L \wedge \min\{l_1, l_2\} > 0, \\ (1 - e^{-\Omega_1 \epsilon_0})(1 - e^{-\Omega_2 \epsilon_0}) & \text{if } \max\{l_1, l_2\} < L \wedge \min\{l_1, l_2\} = 0, \\ (1 - e^{-\Omega_2 \epsilon_0})(1 - e^{-\Omega_R \epsilon_R}) & \text{if } l_1 = L \wedge 0 < l_2 < L, \\ (1 - e^{-\Omega_1 \epsilon_0})(1 - e^{-\Omega_R \epsilon_R}) & \text{if } l_2 = L \wedge 0 < l_1 < L, \\ 1 - e^{-\Omega_1 \epsilon_0} & \text{if } l_1 = 0 \wedge l_2 = L, \\ 1 - e^{-\Omega_2 \epsilon_0} & \text{if } l_2 = 0 \wedge l_1 = L, \\ 1 - e^{-\Omega_R \epsilon_R} & \text{if } l_1 = l_2 = L, \\ 0 & \text{otherwise.} \end{cases} \tag{6}$$

$$P_{(l_1,l_2)}^{(l_1+1,l_2)} = \begin{cases} e^{-\Omega_1 \epsilon_0}(1 - e^{-\Omega_2 \epsilon_0})(1 - e^{-\Omega_R \epsilon_R}) & \text{if } 0 < l_2 \leq l_1 < L, \\ [e^{-\Omega_1 \epsilon_0} - \phi(\Omega_1, \Omega_2)](1 - e^{-\Omega_R \epsilon_R}) & \text{if } 0 < l_1 < l_2 < L, \\ e^{-\Omega_1 \epsilon_0}(1 - e^{-\Omega_R \epsilon_R}) & \text{if } 0 < l_1 < l_2 = L, \\ e^{-\Omega_1 \epsilon_0}(1 - e^{-\Omega_2 \epsilon_0}) & \text{if } 0 = l_2 \leq l_1 < L, \\ e^{-\Omega_1 \epsilon_0} - \phi(\Omega_1, \Omega_2) & \text{if } 0 = l_1 < l_2 < L, \\ e^{-\Omega_1 \epsilon_0} & \text{if } l_1 = 0, l_2 = L, \\ 0 & \text{otherwise.} \end{cases} \tag{7}$$

$$P_{(l_1,l_2)}^{(l_1+1,l_2+1)} = \begin{cases} (1 - e^{-\Omega_R \epsilon_R})\phi(\Omega_1, \Omega_2) & \text{if } \max\{l_1, l_2\} < L \wedge \min\{l_1, l_2\} \geq 2, \\ \phi(\Omega_1, \Omega_2) & \text{if } \max\{l_1, l_2\} < L \wedge \min\{l_1, l_2\} < 2, \\ 0 & \text{otherwise.} \end{cases} \tag{8}$$

$$P_{(l_1,l_2)}^{(l_1-1,l_2-1)} = \begin{cases} e^{-\Omega_R \epsilon_R}(1 - \phi(\Omega_1, \Omega_2)) & \text{if } \max\{l_1, l_2\} < L \wedge \min\{l_1, l_2\} = 1, \\ e^{-\Omega_R \epsilon_R} & \text{if } \min\{l_1, l_2\} \geq 2 \vee \{\min\{l_1, l_2\} = 1 \wedge \max\{l_1, l_2\} = L\}, \\ 0 & \text{otherwise.} \end{cases} \tag{9}$$

4.2   Performance of the Proposed Scheme

One can verify that the transition matrix $\mathbf{A}$ is column stochastic and irreducible[3], so the stationary state probability vector can be obtained as follows [7]:

$$\boldsymbol{\pi} = (\mathbf{A} - \mathbf{I} + \mathbf{B})^{-1}\mathbf{b}, \tag{10}$$

---

[3] Column stochastic means that all entries in any column sum up to one; irreducible means that it is possible to move from any state to any state [12].

where $\boldsymbol{\pi} = [\pi_{s_1}, \cdots, \pi_{s_{(L+1)^2}}]^T$, $\mathbf{b} = [1, 1, \cdots, 1]^T$ and $\mathbf{B}_{i,j} = 1$, $\forall i, j$. In the next, we will use $\pi_{(l_1,l_2)}$ to denote the stationary state probability of the buffer state $s_n = (l_1, l_2)$ for simplicity.

In the following, the performance of the sum throughput, the outage probability, and the average delay will be analyzed.

Throughput. Over a long time of period, obviously the sum receive and the transmit throughputs at the relay will be the same, and the sum throughput of the system can be expressed as follows:

$$
\begin{aligned}
\bar{R}_{\text{sum}} &= r_0 \sum_{l_1=0}^{L-1} \sum_{l_2=0}^{L-1} (P_{(l_1,l_2)}^{(l_1+1,l_2)} + P_{(l_1,l_2)}^{(l_1,l_2+1)} + 2P_{(l_1,l_2)}^{(l_1+1,l_2+1)}) \pi_{(l_1,l_2)} \\
&= 2r_0 \sum_{l_1=1}^{L} \sum_{l_2=1}^{L} P_{(l_1,l_2)}^{(l_1-1,l_2-1)} \pi_{(l_1,l_2)}.
\end{aligned}
\tag{11}
$$

Outage Probability. Since the target sum rate is r_0 BPCU ($r_0/2$ BPCU for each user), the outage probability of the system can be expressed as follows:

$$
P_{\text{sys}}^{\text{out}} = 1 - \bar{R}_{\text{sum}}/r_0.
\tag{12}
$$

Proposition 2. *The diversity gain of 2 can be achieved by the proposed hybrid NOMA/OMA MS scheme, i.e.,* $-\lim_{\text{SNR}\to\infty} \frac{\log P_{\text{sys}}^{\text{out}}}{\log \text{SNR}} = 2$, *as long as* $L \geq 3$.

Proof. Please refer to Appendix B.

Average Delay. Denote P_k as the probability that mode $\mathcal{M}_k$ is selected. Over a long period of time, based on (11), we obtain

$$
P_1 + P_2 + 2P_3 = 2P_4 = 1 - P_{\text{sys}}^{\text{out}}.
\tag{13}
$$

Moreover, denote η_U and η_R as the transmit sum throughputs (in number of packets) of the users and the relay, respectively, which can be expressed as

$$
\eta_U = \eta_R = \bar{R}_{\text{sum}}/r_0 = 1 - P_{\text{sys}}^{\text{out}}.
\tag{14}
$$

Since in each time slot, at most two packets are transmitted from the two users, the average sum queuing length (in number of time slots) at two users can be obtained as

$$
Q_U = 2 - (P_1 + P_2 + 2P_3) = 1 + P_{\text{sys}}^{\text{out}}.
\tag{15}
$$

Thus, the average delay at the two users is

$$
D_U = \frac{Q_U}{\eta_U} = \frac{1 + P_{\text{sys}}^{\text{out}}}{1 - P_{\text{sys}}^{\text{out}}}.
\tag{16}
$$

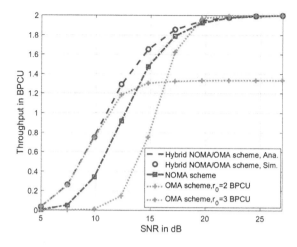

Fig. 2. Sum throughput vs. transmit SNR, where $L = 5$.

In addition, the average delay at the relay is $D_R = \bar{Q}_R/\eta_R$, where $\bar{Q}_R$ is the average sum queuing length of the two buffers, which can be expressed as

$$\bar{Q}_R = \sum_{l_1=0}^{L} \sum_{l_2=0}^{L} (l_1 + l_2)\pi_{(l_1,l_2)}. \tag{17}$$

In summary, the total average packet delay of the system is $D_U + D_R$.

5 Numerical Results

In this section, we evaluate the performance of the proposed hybrid NOMA/OMA based MS scheme by using computer simulations, in terms of sum throughput, outage probability and average delay. NOMA and OMA mentioned in Remark 2 are taken as the comparative ones. Each channel is modeled as $h_i = d_i^{-\beta/2} g_i$, where the small scale fading gain is Rayleigh distributed, i.e., $g_i \sim \mathcal{CN}(0,1)$, $i \in \{1, 2, R\}$. Furthermore, asymmetric distances are considered, which are set as $d_1 = 1$, $d_2 = 2$ and $d_R = 1$, and the path loss exponent is chosen as 2 to reflect a favorable propagation condition. This means that $\Omega_1 = 1$, $\Omega_2 = 4$, and $\Omega_R = 1$. In addition, the target rate is set as $r_0 = 2$ BPCU unless stated otherwise. In Fig. 2, sum throughput comparison is presented for hybrid NOMA/OMA, NOMA and OMA schemes, where the buffer size is set as $L = 5$. One can observe that, when $r_0 = 2$, hybrid NOMA/OMA and NOMA achieve the maximum sum throughput of 2 BPCU at high SNRs, whereas OMA can only achieve about 1.3 BPCU in this case. This is because only one packet can be transmitted from the users to the relay in one time slot for OMA. If we set $r_0 = 3$, OMA can achieve the sum throughput of 2 BPCU at high SNRs, but has a very poor performance at low or moderate SNRs. In addition, one can also

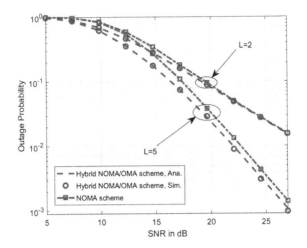

Fig. 3. System outage probability vs. transmit SNR, where $r_0 = 2$ BPCU.

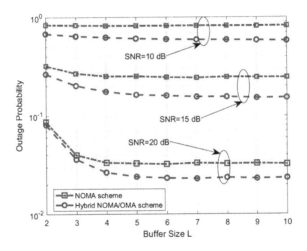

Fig. 4. System outage probability vs. buffer size L, where $r_0 = 2$ BPCU.

observe that hybrid NOMA/OMA outperforms NOMA significantly especially at low or moderate SNRs. For example, when SNR=10 dB, hybrid NOMA/OMA and NOMA achieve the sum throughputs of 0.75 and 0.35 BPCU, respectively, i.e., there is a improvement of more than 100%.

The outage probability performance of hybrid NOMA/OMA and NOMA schemes are presented in Figs. 3 and 4 versus transmit SNR and buffer size L, respectively. In Fig. 3, one can observe that the gap between the two schemes is slight when $L = 2$, especially at high SNRs, but significant performance gap exists when $L = 5$. In Fig. 4, one can observe that hybrid NOMA/OMA achieves lower outage probability compared to NOMA for different buffer sizes and SNRs.

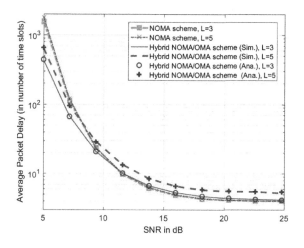

Fig. 5. Average packet delay vs. transmit SNR, where $r_0 = 2$ BPCU.

In particular, hybrid NOMA/OMA can benefit from enlarging L significantly, whereas the outage probability of NOMA almost does not decrease when $L \geq 5$.

In Fig. 5, we present average packet delay comparison of hybrid NOMA/OMA and NOMA schemes when $L = 3$ and $L = 5$. One can observe that, at low SNRs, hybrid NOMA/OMA achieves a much shorter average delay. This is because the average delay at the users is the dominant factor when the outage probability is high at low SNRs (shown in Sect. 4.2). At high SNRs, hybrid NOMA/OMA suffers from a longer average delay especially when $L = 5$. This is because the average delay at the relay is the dominant factor at high SNRs. For hybrid NOMA/OMA, a single packet is transmitted when an OMA transmission mode ($\mathcal{M}_1$ or $\mathcal{M}_2$) is selected, which may obstruct the following received packets in the same buffer. However, it can be seen that the average delay of hybrid NOMA/OMA is just slightly longer than NOMA at high SNRs.

6   Conclusion

This paper has investigated a cooperative uplink system with two users, a buffer-aided relay, and a BS. A hybrid NOMA/OMA based MS scheme has been proposed, which combines NOMA and OMA, and all possible transmission modes are allocated layered weights according to the buffer states in order to determine their priorities. Then, we have also analyzed the state transmission matrix probabilities of the corresponding MC, and derived closed form expressions for sum throughput, outage probability, and average delay. A diversity gain of 2 can be achieved when the buffer size is not smaller than 3. Numerical results have shown that hybrid NOMA/OMA significantly outperforms conventional NOMA and OMA in most scenarios.

Appendix A

Proof of Proposition 1

To prove this proposition, we first analyze the probability of the required CSI region for each mode $\mathcal{M}_k$ (shown in Table 1), denoted by $P_{\mathcal{R}_k}$, $k = [1:4]$, which is given as follows:

$$P_{\mathcal{R}_1} = e^{-\Omega_1 \epsilon_0}, \ P_{\mathcal{R}_2} = e^{-\Omega_2 \epsilon_0} \tag{18}$$

$$P_{\mathcal{R}_3} = \phi(\Omega_1, \Omega_2), \ P_{\mathcal{R}_4} = e^{-\Omega_R \epsilon_R}. \tag{19}$$

We then consider the following cases:

1. Since each buffer at most receives or transmits only one packet in one time slot, $P_{(l_1,l_2)}^{(l_1',l_2')} = 0$ if $|l_u' - l_u| \geq 2$, $u = 1, 2$. Moreover, the two buffers transmit at the same time slot in the proposed scheme, and hence (5) can be easily obtained.

2. $P_{(l_1,l_2)}^{(l_1,l_2)}$ corresponds to the case that m ode $\mathcal{M}_5$ is selected. Since weight W_5 has the smallest value when $\max\{l_1, l_2\} < L \wedge \min\{l_1, l_2\} > 0$ compared to the other modes' weights, mode $\mathcal{M}_5$ can only be selected if all channels are so weak that the other modes' CSI requirements (shown in Table 1) cannot be satisfied. In this subcase, $P_{(l_1,l_2)}^{(l_1,l_2)} = (1 - P_{\mathcal{R}_1})(1 - P_{\mathcal{R}_2})(1 - P_{\mathcal{R}_4})$. The values of $P_{(l_1,l_2)}^{(l_1,l_2)}$ in the other subcases can be obtained similarly shown in (6).

3. $P_{(l_1,l_2)}^{(l_1+1,l_2)}$ corresponds to the case that mode $\mathcal{M}_1$ is selected. Take the subcase $0 < l_2 \leq l_1 < L$ for example. In this subcase, $W_5 < W_1 < \min\{W_2, W_3, W_4\}$, so mode $\mathcal{M}_1$ can be selected only if the CSI requirement of $\mathcal{M}_1$ can be satisfied but the CSI requirement of $\mathcal{M}_i$ cannot be satisfied, $i = 2, 3, 4$, and thus $P_{(l_1,l_2)}^{(l_1+1,l_2)} = P_{\mathcal{R}_1}(1 - P_{\mathcal{R}_2})(1 - P_{\mathcal{R}_4})$. $P_{(l_1,l_2)}^{(l_1+1,l_2)}$ can be calculated for the other subcases shown in (7).

4. $P_{(l_1,l_2)}^{(l_1+1,l_2+1)}$ corresponds to the case that mode $\mathcal{M}_3$ is selected. If $\max\{l_1, l_2\} < L \wedge \min\{l_1, l_2\} = 2$, $W_3 > W_i$, $i = 1, 2, 5$, and $W_3 < W_4$, so mode $\mathcal{M}_3$ can be selected only if the CSI requirement of $\mathcal{M}_3$ can be satisfied but the CSI requirement of $\mathcal{M}_4$ cannot be satisfied, and thus $P_{(l_1,l_2)}^{(l_1+1,l_2+1)} = P_{\mathcal{R}_3}(1 - P_{\mathcal{R}_4})$. If $\max\{l_1, l_2\} < L \wedge \min\{l_1, l_2\} < 2$, W_3 has the largest value, and hence $P_{(l_1,l_2)}^{(l_1+1,l_2+1)} = P_{\mathcal{R}_3}$.

5. $P_{(l_1,l_2)}^{(l_1-1,l_2-1)}$ corresponds to the case that mode $\mathcal{M}_4$ is selected, and (9) can be easily obtained, following similar derivation steps for the previous case.

Appendix B

Proof of Proposition 2

The transition matrix $\mathbf{A}$ is too complicated (shown in Proposition 1) to obtain an explicit approximation of the outage probability $P_{\text{sys}}^{\text{out}}$ in (12) at high SNRs.

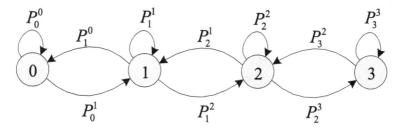

Fig. 6. Diagram of the MC of the simplified NOMA scheme with $L = 3$.

Alternatively, we wish to derive an upper bound on $P_{\text{sys}}^{\text{out}}$ in order to obtain an achievable diversity gain of the proposed scheme. In particular, it should be noted that the throughput achieved by NOMA (mentioned in Remark 2) is just a lower bound of hybrid NOMA/OMA. This is because the relay can still receive messages by using modes $\mathcal{M}_1$ and $\mathcal{M}_2$ for hybrid NOMA/OMA, even if the CSI requirements of $\mathcal{M}_3$ and $\mathcal{M}_4$ cannot be satisfied. Thus, the outage probability of NOMA, denoted by $P_{\text{NOMA}}^{\text{out}}$, is an upper bound of $P_{\text{sys}}^{\text{out}}$.

Using NOMA, there exists only three modes ($\mathcal{M}_k$, $k = 3, 4, 5$) and ($L + 1$) states since the two buffers have the same size in each time slot. The MC of the simplified NOMA scheme for the case $L = 3$ is presented in Fig. 6, where each transition probability from state i to state j, denoted by P_i^j, can be easily approximated as

$$P_0^0 \approx \epsilon_0(\Omega_1 + \Omega_2), \ P_1^1 \approx \epsilon_0 \epsilon_R \Omega_R(\Omega_1 + \Omega_2), \tag{20}$$

$$P_3^3 \approx \epsilon_R \Omega_R, \ P_0^1 \approx 1 - \epsilon_0(\Omega_1 + \Omega_2), \tag{21}$$

$$P_2^3 \approx \epsilon_R \Omega_R, \ P_3^2 \approx 1 - \epsilon_R \Omega_R, \tag{22}$$

$$P_1^0 \approx \epsilon_0(\Omega_1 + \Omega_2), \tag{23}$$

at high SNRs. Based on the above transition probabilities, the stationary state probabilities of the MC can be obtained, which are approximately given by

$$\pi_0^{\text{NOMA}} \approx \frac{1}{2}\epsilon_0(\Omega_1 + \Omega_2), \pi_1^{\text{NOMA}} \approx \frac{1}{2}, \tag{24}$$

$$\pi_2^{\text{NOMA}} \approx \frac{1}{2}, \pi_3^{\text{NOMA}} \approx \frac{1}{2}\epsilon_R \Omega_R, \tag{25}$$

at high SNRs. Thus, the outage probability of NOMA can be obtained as follows:

$$P_{\text{sys}}^{\text{NOMA}} \approx \frac{1}{2}[\epsilon_0(\Omega_1 + \Omega_2) + \epsilon_R \Omega_R]^2. \tag{26}$$

Furthermore, it is easy to prove that the diversity gain regarding to $P_{\text{sys}}^{\text{NOMA}}$ is 2. On the other hand, increasing L obviously benefits to decrease the outage probability, and hence hybrid NOMA/OMA achieves the diversity gain of 2 as long as $L \geq 3$.

References

1. Cover, T.M., Thomas, J.A.: Elements of Information Theory, 2nd edn. Wiley-Interscience, New York (2006)
2. Ding, Z., Lei, X., Karagiannidis, G.K., Schober, R., Yuan, J., Bhargava, V.K.: A survey on non-orthogonal multiple access for 5G networks: research challenges and future trends. IEEE J. Sel. Areas Commun. **35**(10), 2181–2195 (2017)
3. Ding, Z., Peng, M., Poor, H.: Cooperative non-orthogonal multiple access in 5G systems. IEEE Commun. Lett. **19**(8), 1462–1465 (2015)
4. Ding, Z., Yang, Z., Fan, P., Poor, H.V.: On the performance of non-orthogonal multiple access in 5G systems with randomly deployed users. IEEE Signal Process. Lett. **21**(12), 1501–1505 (2014)
5. Jamali, V., Zlatanov, N., Schober, R.: Bidirectional buffer-aided relay networks with fixed rate transmission-part II: delay-constrained case. IEEE Trans. Wireless Commun. **14**(3), 1339–1355 (2015)
6. Kim, J.B., Lee, I.H.: Non-orthogonal multiple access in coordinated direct and relay transmission. IEEE Commun. Lett. **19**(11), 2037–2040 (2015)
7. Krikidis, I., Charalambous, T., Thompson, J.S.: Buffer-aided relay selection for cooperative diversity systems without delay constraints. IEEE Trans. Wireless Commun. **11**(5), 1957–1967 (2012)
8. Luo, S., Teh, K.C.: Adaptive transmission for cooperative NOMA system with buffer-aided relaying. IEEE Commun. Lett. **21**(4), 937–940 (2017)
9. Luo, S., Teh, K.C.: Buffer state based relay selection for buffer-aided cooperative relaying systems. IEEE Trans. Wireless Commun. **14**(10), 5430–5439 (2015)
10. Nomikos, N., Charalambous, T., Krikidis, I., Skoutas, D.N., Vouyioukas, D., Johansson, M.: A buffer-aided successive opportunistic relay selection scheme with power adaptation and inter-relay interference cancellation for cooperative diversity systems. IEEE Trans. Commun. **63**(5), 1623–1634 (2015)
11. Nomikos, N., Charalambous, T., Vouyioukas, D., Karagiannidis, G.K., Wichman, R.: Hybrid NOMA/OMA with buffer-aided relay selection in cooperative networks. IEEE J. Sel. Top. Signal Process. **13**(3), 524–537 (2019)
12. Norris, J.R.: Markov Chains. Cambridge University Press, Cambridge (1997). https://doi.org/10.1017/CBO9780511810633
13. Xu, P., Cumanan, K.: Optimal power allocation scheme for non-orthogonal multiple access with alpha-fairness. IEEE J. Sel. Areas Commun. **35**(10), 2357–2369 (2017)
14. Xu, P., Ding, Z., Krikidis, I., Dai, X.: Achieving optimal diversity gain in buffer-aided relay networks with small buffer size. IEEE Trans. Veh. Technol. **65**(10), 8788–8794 (2016)
15. Xu, P., Yang, Z., Ding, Z., Zhang, Z.: Optimal relay selection schemes for cooperative NOMA. IEEE Trans. Veh. Technol. **67**(8), 7851–7855 (2018)
16. Yang, Z., Ding, Z., Wu, Y., Fan, P.: Novel relay selection strategies for cooperative NOMA. IEEE Trans. Veh. Technol. **66**(11), 10114–10123 (2017)
17. Zhang, Q., Liang, Z., Li, Q., Qin, J.: Buffer-aided non-orthogonal multiple access relaying systems in Rayleigh fading channels. IEEE Trans. Commun. **65**(1), 95–106 (2017)
18. Zhang, Z., Wang, C., Gan, C., Sun, S., Wang, M.: Automatic modulation classification using convolutional neural network with features fusion of SPWVD and BJD. IEEE Trans. Signal Inf. Process. Netw. **5**(3), 469–478 (2019)

19. Zlatanov, N., Ikhlef, A., Islam, T., Schober, R.: Buffer-aided cooperative communications: opportunities and challenges. IEEE Commun. Mag. **52**(4), 146–153 (2014)
20. Zlatanov, N., Schober, R., Popovski, P.: Buffer-aided relaying with adaptive link selection. IEEE J. Sel. Areas Commun. **31**(8), 1530–1542 (2013)

UltraComm: High-Speed and Inaudible Acoustic Communication

Guoming Zhang, Xiaoyu Ji, Xinyan Zhou, Donglian Qi, and Wenyuan Xu[✉]

Zhejiang University, Hang Zhou, China
{realzgm,xji,xinyanzhou,qidl,wyxu}@zju.edu.cn

Abstract. Acoustic communication has become a research focus without requiring extra hardware on the receiver side and facilitates numerous near-field applications such as mobile payment, data sharing. To communicate, existing researches either use audible frequency band or inaudible one. The former gains a high throughput but endures being audible, which can be annoying to users. The latter, although inaudible, falls short in throughput due to the limited available (near) ultrasonic bandwidth (18–22 kHz). In this paper, we achieve both high speed and inaudibility for acoustic communication by modulating the coded acoustic signal (0–20 kHz) on ultrasonic carrier. By utilizing the nonlinearity effect on microphone, the modulated audible acoustic signal can be demodulated and then decoded. We design and implement UltraComm, an inaudible acoustic communication system with OFDM scheme based on the characteristics of the nonlinear speaker-to-microphone channel. We evaluate UltraComm on different mobile devices and achieve throughput as high as 16.24 kbps, meanwhile, keep inaudibility.

Keywords: Ultrasound · Inaudible acoustic communication · Nonlinearity · Device-to-device communication

1 Introduction

With the widespread use of mobile devices equipped with audio interfaces, acoustic communication has attracted an increasing amount of attention [14,16–19,25,31–34]. Unlike Wi-Fi, Near Field Communication (NFC) or Bluetooth, acoustic communication doesn't need extra hardware on the receiver side and provides a communication channel with only built-in microphones. In addition, it is not necessary to go through pairing handshake before establishing connection. The universality and convenience of acoustic communication makes it a lightweight communication scheme for mobile devices and facilitate numerous applications such as mobile payment, near-field file transferring and even interactive gaming.

W. Xu—Supported by National Key R&D Program of China (2018YFB0904900, 2018YFB0904904).

X. Chu et al. (Eds.): QShine 2019, LNICST 300, pp. 184–204, 2020.
https://doi.org/10.1007/978-3-030-38819-5_12

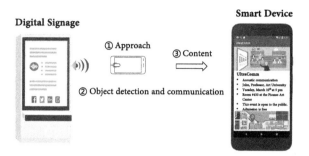

Fig. 1. Inaudible acoustic communication for information sharing. In a school, for example, the detailed information of activities on the screen of a digital signage can be conveniently transmitted to smartphones using the acoustic channel.

Current acoustic communication schemes can be divided into two categories: audible acoustic communication (roughly <18 kHz) [14,16,17,25,29] and inaudible acoustic communication (18–20 kHz) [28,31,33,34]. In general, the throughput for the former is always higher than the latter since it could utilize a wider frequency band, i.e., the audible frequency band. However, audible acoustic communication can be perceived by human ears, which could be annoying. Besides, audible communication also leaks information during transmission. Although information-hiding techniques [17,29] can alleviate the security problem, the sound in which the information is hidden is still audible. On the contrary, inaudible acoustic communication uses near-ultrasonic or ultrasonic sound to achieve inaudibility, while the available frequency band is limited, e.g., less than 4 kHz. We summarize representative literatures in Table 1. We can note that existing schemes fail to accomplish the seemingly conflicting goal of throughput and inaudibility.

We look into the seemingly contradictory goal of being both high-speed and inaudibility. We scrutinize the problem and find that the essence for the contradiction originates from a common belief: people take it for granted that acoustic communication must be within the cutoff frequencies of hardware components, e.g., ADC (analog-to-digital converter). Designed to capture audible sound, the cutoff frequency for an ADC is around 22 kHz, which is only 2 kHz higher than the human-perceivable sound frequency. As a result, the maximum inaudible frequency band is 4 kHz (plus the 18–20 kHz near-ultrasonic frequency band) in an ideal condition, not to mention the losses due to poor frequency responses.

In this paper, we investigate and explore a new approach for acoustic communication, whereby the high-speed and inaudible properties can be simultaneously achieved. We exploit the nonlinearity effect of electronic components (e.g., ADC and operational amplifier) to recover the low-frequency (<20 kHz) signals that are modulated onto a high-frequency (>22 kHz) carrier. That is, the low-frequency signals can be easily "**reproduced**" during the demodulation process caused by the nonlinearity effect of microphones. Utilizing the nonlinearity effect, we first theoretically investigate the throughput of inaudible communication and analyze the maximum throughput. Guided by the formulation, we

Table 1. Comparison with other acoustic communication schemes.

Existing work	Modulation type	Inaudibility	Throughput (bps)
Near-Ultrasound Screen [31]	Chirp QOK	$\checkmark$	15
Chirp [33]	Chirp	$\checkmark$	16
Acoustic OFDM [25]	OFDM	$\times$	40
Dolphin [17]	OFDM	$\times$	500
MCLT [29]	MCLT	$\times$	600
Multi-Tone [28]	MFSK	$\checkmark$	800
PriWhisper [16]	FSK	$\times$	1k
Dhwani [14]	OFDM	$\times$	2.4k
U-wear [34]	GMSK	$\checkmark$	2.76k
BackDoor [27]	FM	$\checkmark$	4k
Ultrasound Proximity [3]	OFDM	$\checkmark$	4.9k
Ultracomm	**OFDM**	$\checkmark$	**16.24k**

develop UltraComm, an inaudible acoustic communication system that modulates audible signals on inaudible frequency. UltraComm is able to: (1) utilize the entire sound frequency band, to satisfy the high-speed requirement, and (2) transmit in high frequency, to maintain inaudibility.

With the increase of communication rate, UltraComm can be applied not only to the payment and authentication but also to some lightweight image and file transfer scenarios. For example, with UltraComm, any type of displaying content, such as activities, exhibitions, and advertising, can be delivered to the user's smartphone when approaching the digital signage. According to the new market research report [2], the digital signage market is expected to grow from USD 20.8 billion in 2019 to USD 29.6 billion by 2024, and it has been widely used in school, museums, transportation systems, and other public spaces, etc. However, the digital signages don't equip with convenient and efficient data transmission channel and cannot send the contents of interest to users to the smartphone. With UltraComm, the user can quickly get the information they want. As shown in Fig. 1, the information of activities can be broadcast to students who put their smartphones close to the digital signage.

The design of UltraComm addresses the following key challenges. First, to approach the theoretical throughput, we specially design the data symbol and use OFDM (Orthogonal frequency-division multiplexing) to increase the frequency efficiency. We exploit 2ASK (2 Amplitude Shift Keying) to modulate each "1" or "0" bit onto a subchannel and carefully choose the duration of symbol and guard interval time. Second, in order to reduce the crosstalk between subchannels caused by the nonlinear distortion, nonlinearity effect should be avoided as much as possible. However, UltraComm needs to demodulate the high-frequency modulated signal by using the nonlinearity effect. So how to utilize the nonlinearity effect while reducing the interference is a challenge. In order to suppress the high bit-error-rate (BER), UltraComm adopt an anti-distortion

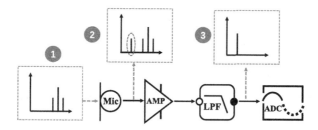

Fig. 2. The hardware structure inside a microphone system. If a modulated signal on high frequency carrier (>20 kHz) is inputted to the microphone ①, a new low-frequency (<20 kHz) signal is generated ②, the high-frequency signals are finally filtered by the LPF with the modulated signals low-frequency signal left ③.

strategy when designing the OFDM symbol. Third, like other electric devices, the speaker-to-microphone channels are high frequency selective due to the non-optimal response on both the speaker and microphone sides. As a result, the demodulated signals at the microphone side are distorted heavily. To maintain equivalent response at each subchannel, UltraComm proposes a differentiated gain control (DGC) mechanism by assigning different power coefficients to each subchannel, i.e., transmitting using various power levels at each subchannel. Fourth, to maximize the nonlinearity effect on the microphone side, we experimentally validate AM (Amplitude Modulation) parameters such as modulation depth and carrier frequency to deduce the proper ones.

In summary, our contributions are summarized as follows:

- We propose UltraComm, an inaudible communication system from a new perspective, which fundamentally addresses the conflict between high-speed and inaudibility for acoustic communication.
- We analyze the characteristic of the nonlinear speaker-to-microphone channel and propose an anti-distortion strategy to find the best subcarriers combination to improve communication performance.
- We implement the UltraComm prototype, evaluate its performance on unmodified mobile devices and achieve a throughput as high as 16.24 kbps.

2   Acoustic Nonlinearity Effect Background

In this section, we first describe the microphone system in mobile devices, and then elaborate the nonlinearity effect.

2.1   Microphone System

A microphone system converts acoustic waves into electrical signals. Microphones on mobile devices can be either Electret Condenser Microphone (ECM) or Micro Electrical Mechanical System (MEMS). Nowadays, MEMS microphones dominate the market of mobile devices such as smartphones, Pads and wearable devices like smart watch due to the miniature package sizes and low power consumption. Thus, we focus mainly on MEMS microphones in this paper yet the analysis suits for both MEMS and ECM microphones.

In order to capture audible sounds, microphones, low-pass filters (LPFs), and analog-to-digital converter (ADC) in the microphone system are used to suppress signals out of the frequency range of audible sounds (i.e., 20 Hz to 20 kHz). The typical structure of signal processing components in a microphone system is shown in Fig. 2. Most sound communication systems are assumed to only accept the audible frequency bands due to suppression of signals above 20 kHz.

2.2   Nonlinearity Effect Principle

Nonlinearity is a phenomenon that demodulated signals can be produced in low-frequency range. It is reported to appear in many electric components, such as operational amplifiers [21–24, 26]. For a microphone, nonlinearity means when a modulated high-frequency signal (e.g. >20 kHz) passes through the microphone system, low-frequency signal (e.g. <20 kHz) can be generated and received by the microphone.

Nonlinearity effect has been regarded as distortions of devices and avoided [20]. In UltraComm, however, we attempt to exploit the nonlinearity effect to transmit modulated data on frequency above 20 kHz and recover it in the audible frequency band.

Without loss of generality, let S be a single frequency signal with a frequency of f_S. Theoretically, the output signal under nonlinearity effect can be modeled as:

$$S_{out} = \begin{cases} a_0 S & , f_S \leq f_{rcv} \\ \sum\limits_{i=1}^{\infty} a_i S^i & , f_S > f_{rcv} \end{cases} \quad (1)$$

where a_0 is the gain coefficient for signals of a frequency less than f_{rcv} and f_{rcv} is the maximum receiving frequency of the receiver. In Eq. (1), when $f_S > f_{rcv}$, $S_{out} = a_1 S + a_2 S^2 + \cdots + a_n S^n$. Typically, the values of $a_i, (i \geq 1)$ are related to f_S, and a_i decreases with the increase of i. According to the basic trigonometric theory, the frequency of S^i is higher than f_{rcv} when $i \geq 1$. As a result, the nonlinearity response, i.e., $a_1 S^1, a_2 S^2, a_3 S^3, \ldots$, can be eliminated by the LPF in the microphone system. What is more, a_i becomes small when $i \geq 3$, thus we often consider the nonlinearity response as $S_{out} = a_1 S + a_2 S^2$ when $f_S > f_{rcv}$.

Nonlinearity Response for Microphone System. For a microphone system, the nonlinearity effect can be utilized for inaudible communications. Define a signal to microphone as $S_{in} = S_1(1 + S_2)$ where $S_1 = sin\omega_1 t$ is the carrier signal with frequency $f_{S_1} > f_{rcv}$ and $S_2 - sin\omega_2 t$ is the baseband signal with frequency $f_{S_2} < f_{rcv}$. According to Eq. (1), the nonlinearity response through a microphone S_{out} should be:

$$S_{out} = \sum_{i=1}^{\infty} a_i (S_1 + S_1 * S_2)^i \quad (2)$$

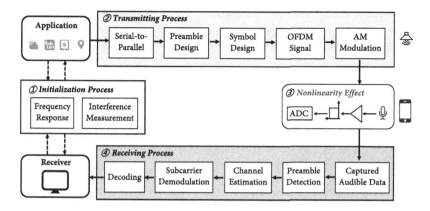

Fig. 3. Overview of the UltraComm system.

After neglecting the high-order harmonics ($i \geq 3$), S_{out} can be represented as:

$$S_{out} = a_1(sin\omega_1 t + sin\omega_1 t * sin\omega_2 t) + a_2(sin\omega_1 t + sin\omega_1 t * sin\omega_2 t)^2 \quad (3)$$

We then expand Eq. (3), and the output of the signal contains the baseband signal frequency f_{S_2}, the carrier signal frequency f_{S_1}, and other harmonics such as $(f_{S_1} - f_{S_2})$, $(f_{S_1} + f_{S_2})$ and other cross frequencies (i.e., $2f_{S_1}, 2f_{S_2}, 2(f_{S_1} + f_{S_2}), 2f_{S_1} + f_{S_2}, 2f_{S_1} - f_{S_2}$).

As mentioned above, the resulting signals from nonlinearity effect with frequency lower than the cut-off frequency of LPF (f_{LPF}, which is often set to 25 kHz) will remain while others are filtered. That is to say, the signal S_2 ($f_{S_2} < f_{rcv}$) modulated on S_1 will be reproduced and output from the microphone. Figure 2 illustrates the whole process where a signal from nonlinearity effect is generated.

3   UltraComm System Design

In this section, we analyze and verify the characteristics of nonlinear speaker-to-microphone channel, and design UltraComm based on them. The design of UltraComm mainly involves three components: initialization process, transmitter, and receiver design. The whole system is shown in Fig. 3 in detail.

The initialization process aims to get the status of the current speaker-to-microphone channel and then select appropriate communication parameters, such as the available bandwidth.

In the transmitter process, the high rate serial data is mapped to lower rate paralleled data by the S/P converter. After the S/P process, the data is modulated onto subcarriers with 2ASK scheme and then adds the preamble. Before the final transmission, we modulate the UltraComm data symbols on an ultrasonic carrier (in ultrasound frequency band, e.g., 40 kHz) with AM modulation. In this way, we transform the originally audible signal into an inaudible signal successfully.

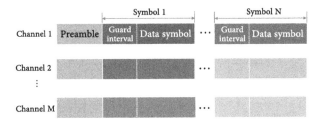

Fig. 4. The frame structure specified in UltraComm.

At the receiver side, demodulation that produces the low-frequency (baseband) signal happens due to the nonlinearity effect on microphones. A preamble in front of a frame is used for synchronization and channel estimation. Once the preamble is matched at the receiver side, the receiver demodulates the OFDM signal and then decodes it to obtain the data.

3.1 Initialization Process

Initialization process is the first step to initialize parameters for transmission, including (1) the frequency response of the speaker-to-microphone channel, (2) the noise level. All the above device-related and environment-dependent parameters are measured before data transmission.

To get the frequency response at each subchannel, we transmit each modulated single tone signal which lasts for 100 ms, and measure the results at the microphone side. The attenuation coefficients can therefore be derived and they are delivered back to the transmitter using existing communication schemes, such as Chirp [33]. According to those measured results, all communication parameters will be elaborately selected at the transmitter side which will be described in the following section and starts the data transmission.

In the following part, we only elaborate the key modules in both transmitter and receiver side.

3.2 Frame Structure

Preamble Design. In UltraComm, data frames are transmitted in the form of OFDM symbols. Figure 4 shows the structure of a frame, which is composed of symbols with a preamble in the front.

In UltraComm, preamble is used for synchronization between the transmitter and the receiver, and channel estimation in frequency–selective environments. As we can see from the Fig. 7(a), the frequency response decreases roughly with the increase of frequency. In order to predict channel state information (CSI) more accurately, we use the combination of two sinusoidal signals as preamble and the frequencies of sinusoidal signals are 5.1 and 15.1 kHz respectively. To estimate the fast-varying channel, preamble is assembled in the front of each frame to facilitate channel estimation [13].

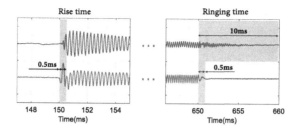

Fig. 5. Rise and ringing time measured at the microphone side using a single-tone 4 kHz signal (the top one) and an AM-modulated (carrier frequency 40 kHz) single-tone signal (the bottom one).

3.3 Symbol Design

As the most important part in transmitter, UltraComm symbol mainly considers subchannel design, subchannel modulation and duration of a symbol as well as the guard interval time.

How Long Should the Duration of Symbol (t_{symbol}) be? In UltraComm, we utilize a guard interval between adjacent data symbols to eliminate the inter symbol interference (ISI). Theoretically, the time duration of guard interval (t_{gi}) depends on the multipath effect as well as the rise and ringing time [14] in the nonlinear speaker-to-microphone channel.

Rise and Ringing Time. In order to obtain a proper value for t_{gi}, we investigate and observe the rise and ringing time using an iPhone 7 which has a MEMS microphone. Figure 5 shows the results with different stimulation. To be specific, with the single-tone input (a), the rise and ringing time are about 0.5 ms and 10 ms respectively but only 0.5 ms and 0.5 ms for the AM-modulated signal (b). This proves that modulated signal (AM) can utilize smaller t_{gi}, e.g., $t_{gi} \geq 0.5$ ms is enough. Actually, the larger value of t_{gi} used in existing acoustic communication system is one of the most important reasons for the low throughput.

The time duration of data symbol: t_{data} is mainly determined by t_{gi} and the lowest frequency of subcarrier. To avoid excessive transmission rate loss, we require the value of $t_{gi}/t_{data} \leq 0.1$.

$$10 * t_{gi} \leq t_{data} \tag{4}$$

Based on Eq. (4), the minimum value of t_{symbol} can be set to 5.5 ms.

Subchannel Design. UltraComm adopts OFDM to transmit data efficiently. An OFDM signal is the sum of multiple subcarriers that are modulated independently with phase-shift keying (PSK), ASK, or Quadrature Amplitude Modulation (QAM). In UltraComm, each subcarrier is modulated with the 2ASK. Due to the unique characteristics of the nonlinear speaker-to-microphone channel, the design of subcarrier should consider the following questions:

– What is the available frequency for subchannels?
– What is the width of frequency spacing for subcarrier, namely how many subchannels should be divided?

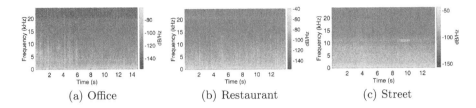

(a) Office   (b) Restaurant   (c) Street

Fig. 6. Empirical study of ambient noise and its spectrum in three scenarios.

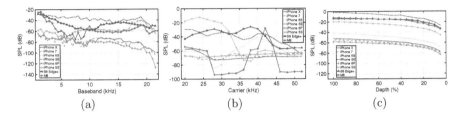

(a)   (b)   (c)

Fig. 7. Frequency-selectivity of nonlinearity for microphones. (a) Frequency response of modulated signal under nonlinearity differs across devices and the response becomes worse for higher frequency baseband; (b) Frequency response of modulated signal vs. different carrier frequencies at 2 kHz; (c) Frequency response of modulated signal vs. AM depth.

– How to deal with distortion products?
– How to deal with frequency selectivity?

Frequency Range for Subchannels. To achieve a high throughput, the available frequency band Δf should be wide enough. Unfortunately, Δf is often limited in reality.

Minimum Frequency f_{min}. The floor frequency of subcarrier (f_{min}) should be above the ceiling frequency of ambient noise to avoid interference. We conduct an experiment to get a sense of the ambient noise and show the result in Fig. 6. From the figure, the intensity of noises shows the difference for the three scenes (office, restaurant and street). Noise in the street is louder than that of office and restaurant, which is attributed to the crowded people and other sources such as vehicles. Nevertheless, the strength of noise dims when frequency increases, the majority of noise lies below 1 kHz. Thus, f_{min} can be empirically set to 1 kHz to avoid interference. To eliminate the interference of ambient noise, one can also amplify transmitting power to improve the signal-to-noise ratio (SNR) in the lower frequency range, therefore, the f_{min} can also be set lowly.

Maximum Frequency f_{max}. The upper limit frequency of subcarrier f_{max} depends on several factors: (1) Sampling rate of ADC in a microphone. f_{max} should be less than half of the sampling rate of ADC (f_{ADC}) to avoid aliasing. (2) The frequency response of microphone under nonlinearity effect. Microphones may have different frequency-selectivity with the increase of frequency. We will

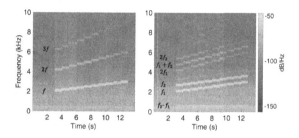

Fig. 8. Harmonic and intermodulation distortion of AM signal over speaker-to-microphone channel. The baseband signals are f and f_1, f_2 respectively.

elaborate the details later. (3) The relation between baseband signal and carrier signal. According to Eq. (3), $f_c - f_{max} > 20$ kHz, where f_c is the carrier frequency, should be satisfied. This is to ensure only the baseband signal can be received by microphone under nonlinearity effect. For instance, if we modulate a 14 kHz baseband signal on a 30 kHz carrier, the lower sideband of the AM signal is 16 kHz, which is also audible.

Frequency-Selectivity for Baseband. To investigate the frequency-selectivity of microphones under nonlinearity effect, we conduct an experiment. We use a signal generator to generate a modulated signal and feed it into 8 smartphones respectively to test the frequency responses. As Fig. 7(a) shows, frequency responses vary across the 8 microphones and the responses roughly get worse when frequency increases. Denote the maximum acceptable frequency f_{worst}. In order to guarantee low BER, $f_{max} < f_{worst}$ should be satisfied.

Take all the aforementioned constraints into consideration, the frequency of any subchannel f_{sc} should satisfy the following conditions:

$$f_{min} \leq f_{sc} \leq f_{max}$$
$$f_{min} > f_{Noise} \tag{5}$$
$$f_{max} < min(f_{ADC}/2, \ f_c - 20k, \ f_{worst})$$

Subcarrier Spacing f_{sp}. To ensure the signal can be demodulated accurately, f_{sp} should be an integral multiple of the f_{res}, which is represented as:

$$f_{sc} \mod f_{res} = 0 \tag{6}$$

Besides Eq. (6), f_{sp} is also determined by the f_{min}, i.e., the harmonic distortion and intermodulation distortion (IMD) to be specific.

Dealing with Harmonic Distortion and IMD. Due to the nonlinearity of microphone circuits, the output of the circuits will contain harmonic components. Considering an input signal that contains one single frequency components at f, the output signal will contain higher harmonics with frequencies that are multiple of the frequency of the input signal, which can be expressed as:

$$f_{HAR} = \sum_{k=2}^{\mathbb{N}} k * f \tag{7}$$

In the same time, the output of microphone circuits also contains IMD products which are the result of two or more signals interacting in a nonlinear device to produce additional unwanted signals. For two input signals, the IMD products can be expressed as:

$$f_{IMD} = k_1 * f_1 + k_2 * f_2 \tag{8}$$

Where, k_1, k_2 are integers. The order of the intermodulation product is the sum of the integers $|k_1| + |k_2|$. In UltraComm, the interference of higher order IMD products is generally slight and can be ignored because they have lower amplitudes and are more widely spaced. However, the second-order components, $f_1 \pm f_2$ will interfere with the original signals. For example, if the frequencies of subcarriers are $f_1 = 200\,\mathrm{Hz}$, $f_2 = 400\,\mathrm{Hz}$, the frequencies of second-order products will contain 200 and 600 Hz, which is the same as one of the original frequency.

To verify the distortion in the case of AM signal as input, we modulated two different signals onto carrier respectively. As depicted in Fig. 8, the received signals include not only the original one (f and f_1, f_2), but also the second–order harmonics ($2f$ and $2f_1, 2f_2$), IMD products ($f_2 - f_1, f_1 + f_2$), even third order harmonics ($3f$), which will bring a considerable challenge for accurate decoding. Especially, as the number of baseband signals increases, the received signal is worse and can't be decoded.

In our case, the subcarriers can be represented as:

$$f_{sc} = f_{min} + n * f_{sp}, \ n \in \{0, 1, 2, \ldots, \Delta f / f_{sp}\} \tag{9}$$

Based on Eqs. (7), (8) and (9), we find the second–order product may have the same frequency as the subcarrier. To avoid interference caused by IMD and harmonics, we proposed the value of f_{sp} should meet the following condition:

$$f_{sc} \notin n * f_{sp}, \ n \in \{0, 1, 2, \ldots, \Delta f / f_{sp}\} \tag{10}$$

Based on Eqs. (6), (9) and (10), we have:

$$\begin{aligned} f_{min} \quad &\mathrm{mod}\ f_{sp} \neq 0 \\ f_{min} \quad &\mathrm{mod}\ f_{res} = 0 \\ f_{sp} \quad &\mathrm{mod}\ f_{res} = 0 \end{aligned} \tag{11}$$

In our implementation, we empirically set $f_{sp} = 200\,Hz$, thus f_{min} can be set to $300 + 200 * i$, where i is non-negative integer.

Subcarrier Modulation. With the selected parameters for subcarriers and symbols, we elaborate subcarrier modulation with 2ASK as follows.

3.4   Modulating Symbols on Inaudible Frequency

In order to achieve inaudibility, the OFDM signal should be modulated on carriers of higher frequency ($>20\,\mathrm{kHz}$) before transmission. To fully leverage the

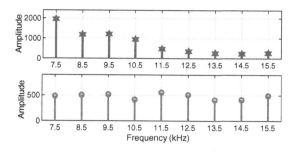

Fig. 9. Performance of DGC in terms of frequency response improvement. The top figure is without DGC while the bottom one utilizes DGC.

nonlinearity of microphone and recover the OFDM signal successfully, Ultra-Comm utilizes AM for baseband (audible sound) modulation.

In the following, we will describe how to select proper AM parameters and cope with the audibility in UltraComm.

Carrier Frequency. Carrier frequency f_c mainly depends on two factors: the available frequency range of ultrasound and the frequency response of the microphone. Note that f_c should be larger than 20 kHz for inaudibility. Besides, f_c has to satisfy the condition of $f_c - f_{max} > 20$ kHz. For instance, given a baseband of 6 kHz, the carrier frequency has to be higher than 26 kHz to ensure the lower sideband of the AM signal is above 20 kHz and inaudible.

Frequency-Selectivity for Carrier. However, microphones are also frequency-selective. For the high-frequency carrier signals, the carrier frequency f_c, therefore, should utilize the carrier with good frequency response.

To discover the frequency-selectivity for the carrier signals, we measure the frequency response of microphones with 8 smartphones. We initially fix the baseband frequency at 2 kHz and then vary the carrier frequency incrementally to get the frequency-selectivity curve. Figure 7(b) reports that the magnitude of the demodulated signal fluctuates with the increase of carrier frequency. In summary, to guarantee the efficiency of communication and inaudibility, the carrier frequency should be carefully chosen. In our implementation, the carrier frequency is set to 40 kHz.

Differentiated Gain Control. Recall that in Fig. 7(a), the frequency response gets worse at higher baseband frequencies under the nonlinearity effect. In order to increase the bandwidth and obtain flat frequency response at the same time, we design a DGC mechanism to balance the frequency response by amplifying the original poor frequency responses. The basic idea is to assign different gain coefficients i.e., using different transmitting power across subcarriers. In this way, the frequency response can be improved.

Denote the finally transmitted signal as:

$$s(t) = \sum_{i=1}^{N_{sc}} A_i g_i(t) cos(2\pi f_i t) \tag{12}$$

where N_{sc} is the number of subchannels and $g_i(t) = 0$ or 1, "0" refers to symbol "0" on the subcarrier and vice versa. A_i is the gain coefficient for the ith subchannel when there is a symbol, i.e., $g_i(t) = 1$. f_i is the frequency for the ith subcarrier. The DGC mechanism assigns different A_i for each subchannel according to its fading coefficient and keeps all $A_i \cdot g_i(t)$ $(i \geq 1)$ roughly the same. The effect of DGC mechanism is shown in Fig. 9. The top figure shows the result with all $A_i = 1$, i.e., without using the DGC mechanism, and the bottom figure demonstrates the case when the DGC mechanism is applied. We can observe a significant difference in terms of frequency response from the two figures. To be specific, with the help of DGC, the frequency response improves across the selected frequency range. This proves the effectiveness of the proposed DGC mechanism in UltraComm.

Modulation Depth. Modulation depth is directly related to the efficiency of the nonlinearity effect of microphones. We investigate the influence of modulation depth upon frequency response with eight microphones. The result in Fig. 7(c) demonstrates that frequency response improves with the increase of modulation depth. In order to maximize the efficiency of the nonlinearity effect, the modulation depth should be set to 100%.

3.5   Receiver Design

Compared to the transmitter, the design of receiver is lightweight. First, Ultra-Comm receiver recovers the OFDM signal by leveraging nonlinearity. Ultra-Comm synchronize the transmitter and the receiver by using the preamble. Then subcarrier demodulation and decoding are performed.

AM Demodulation. As described in Sect. 2, a microphone acts as a demodulator when it receives an AM-modulated signal. Thus, the baseband signals are recovered in a natural way. With our aforementioned design, high-frequency harmonics can be filtered by the LPF and the low-frequency baseband signals can be well received.

Preamble Detection. After recovering the OFDM signal, cross-correlation algorithm is used to detect the preamble. Meanwhile, channel estimation can be performed according to the strength of the preamble.

Subcarrier Demodulation and Symbol Decoding. We use FFT algorithm to demodulate the OFDM signal. After demodulating all the subcarriers, the data on each subchannel can be obtained. The data frame transmitted from the transmitter, is therefore, decoded according to the corresponding encoding schemes.

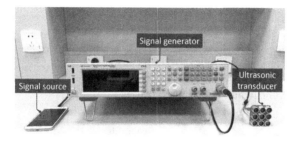

Fig. 10. Experimental setup. A smartphone is used as a signal source, and the signal generator does AM modulation. The modulated signal is transmitted via an array of 9 ultrasonic transducers [15].

4   Evaluation

In order to evaluate the performance of UltraComm, we conduct experiments in an office environment and analyze the influence of multiple factors. The received signal traces are processed and decoded in MATLAB. We summarize the main results as follows:

- A maximum of 16.24 kbps throughput is achieved on an iPhone 5S smartphone with 100 subcarriers ranging from 1.1 kHz to 19.9 kHz.
- The increase of guard interval and symbol duration can lower BER effectively yet undermine throughput.
- The increase of subcarrier number can improve throughput but increase BER.
- Communication distance and ambient noise have fundamental effect upon BER.

4.1   Experimental Setup

In our implementation, we choose different mobile devices as receivers and a set of benchtop equipment as transmitter respectively. Figure 10 is an overview of our experimental setup.

The transmitter is composed of three parts for benchtop-based implementation: (1) a signal source using a smartphone, (2) an AM modulator, which is actually a vector signal generator from Keysight [8], and (3) a narrow-band ultrasonic transducer array [15] or a high-quality full-band ultrasonic speaker Vifa [9]. To elaborate, the smartphone sends baseband signal to the signal generator, by which the baseband signal is modulated onto the high-frequency carrier and the modulated signal is transmitted via the ultrasonic transducer, the driving power is limited below 0.17 W in all the experiments except the user study of inaudibility.

System parameters are listed in Table 2. Some parameters are different among receivers. For example, the available bandwidth is different between iPhone X and iPhone 7, because the nonlinear frequency responses varied from devices.

Table 2. Parameters in UltraComm.

OFDM parameter	Value
Frequency Band	N/A *
Subcarriers	N/A *
Subchannel Bandwidth	200 Hz
Subcarrier Modulation	2ASK
Frame	Preamble + 100 symbols
Preamble	5.1 kHz, 15.1 kHz; 10 ms
Symbol Duration	5 ms, 10 ms
Guard Interval	≥ 0.5 ms
AM Parameter	**Value**
Carrier Frequency	40 kHz
AM Depth	100%

* The parameters vary among different receivers.

Table 3. Throughput with different smart devices.

Smart devices	OS	Microphone	Throughput (kbps)	BER (%)
iPhone X	iOS 11.4	Top mic	14.91	1.47
iPhone X *	iOS 11.4	Top mic	13.11	7.6
iPhone 7	iOS 12.1.4	Back mic	15.57	4.61
iPhone 6S	iOS 12.1.4	Back mic	15.24	4.86
iPhone 5S	iOS 10.3.3	Top mic	16.24	1.45
iPhone 5S †	iOS 12.1.4	Top mic	14.75	1.21
iPhone 4S	iOS 9.3.5	Bottom mic	13.11	1.59

* The communication distance is 1 m, the others are 20 cm.

† Another iPhone 5S with identical technical spec.

4.2 Macro-benchmark Evaluation

Throughput of UltraComm. To examine the throughput of UltraComm with different receivers, we choose 6 kinds of representative mobile devices. The receiver is placed in front of the transducer array at a distance of 20 cm, with ambient noise of about 45 dB sound pressure level (SPL) measured by a professional decibel meter. Table 3 reports the parameters and results of the 6 different receivers. We can conclude that the throughput, in a manner, depends on the devices and is proportional to the available subcarriers. The diversity is attributed to the difference among audio interfaces, especially the MEMS microphones' nonlinearity frequency response.

Different Microphones. As we know, most of smart devices have several microphones, for example, iPhone X has three microphones, one is placed at the

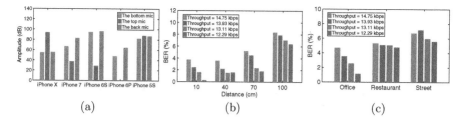

Fig. 11. (a) The nonlinear frequency responses of top, bottom and back microphone (mic) with different smart devices; (b) The impact of communication distance on BER; (c) The impact of ambient noise in three scenarios on BER, the range of SPLs are 45–55 dB, 55–65 dB, and 65–80 dB respectively.

bottom, and two in the top. To achieve a high throughput, we need to choose the microphone with the best nonlinear frequency response. Thus, we tested five different mobile devices, the results are shown in Fig. 11(a). The nonlinearity effect of the top microphone in iPhone 6Plus is almost negligible. For iPhone X and iPhone 5S, the top microphones are preferred, and the back microphones are preferred for iPhone 7 and iPhone 6S in UltraComm.

4.3 Micro-benchmark Evaluation

BER with Different Communication Distance. In this section, we quantify BER at various distances. In general, a shorter communication distance leads to a lower BER, because a shorter distance always means a larger signal-to-noise ratio (SNR) for a given SPL. To explore the impact of communication distance on BER, we use the iPhone X smartphone as a receiver, the ambient noise is measured to be about 45 dB, and the throughput is varied from 12.29 kbps to 14.75 kbps by choosing different number of subcarriers.

Figure 11(b) shows the impact of distance on BER. We can find that BER worsens with the increase of distance. The values of BER are 3.76%, 2.43%, 1.62%, and 0.28% at a distance of 10 cm. When the distance increases to 100 cm, the BER rose to 8.39%, 7.91%, 7.07%, and 6.42% as the SNR worsens. The fundamental influence of distance upon BER, on the other hand, hurts throughput. In order to further increase the distance of UltraComm and reduce BER, we wish to improve distance with more complicated design in the future work.

BER with Different Ambient Noise. In addition to the communication distance, the ambient noise is also a key attribute that influences the performance of UltraComm. Thus, we examine the BERs in three scenarios: office, restaurant, and street by simulating the three scenarios, the SPLs of the corresponding ambient noise are set to 45–55 dB, 55–65 dB, and 65–80 dB respectively. In all experiments, the ultrasonic transducer is positioned 20 cm away from the iPhone X, the transmitter power is set to 0.16 W, and the throughput is also varied from 12.29 kbps to 14.75 kbps by choosing different number of subcarriers. From

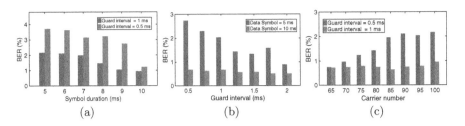

Fig. 12. (a) The impact of symbol duration on BER; (b) The impact of guard interval on BER; (c) The impact of subcarrier number on BER.

Fig. 11(c), we conclude that BER worsens with the increase of ambient noise, which is because the SNR decreases simultaneously for a given transmitter power. Therefore, it's necessary to increase transmitter power to suppress the BER in a noisy scenario.

The Impact of Symbol Duration on UltraComm. The throughput is affected by symbol duration, a short symbol duration may be difficult to decode and cause a high BER in case of poor communication channels that suffer from low SNR. Thus, we evaluate the performance of UltraComm with different symbol duration. We choose iPhone 5S as the receiver, the guard intervals are set to 1 ms and 0.5 ms respectively, the number of subcarriers is 100 with communication distance of 10 cm and ambient noise of about 55 dB in an office.

Figure 12(a) shows the impact of symbol duration on BER. We can find that BER drops significantly after symbol duration is larger than 7 ms, because if the symbol duration increases, the energy per symbol increases. BER drops from 2.17% to the lowest value of 0.95% when the guard interval is 1 ms. Therefore, there exists a tradeoff between BER and symbol duration.

Throughput is affected by symbol duration too, since a shorter symbol duration can transmit more symbols within a certain time, so throughput enhances when symbol duration decreases. And we also noticed that the average BER is lower when the guard interval is 1 ms, because a longer guard interval can improve the signal robustness, we will discuss it later.

The Impact of Guard Interval on UltraComm. Reducing the duration of guard interval can enhance coding rate directly. However, reducing guard interval will increase BER, because the inter-symbol interference (ISI) can't be effectively controlled when the value of guard interval is too short. Choosing a longer guard interval means decreased overhead due to unnecessary idle time. Thus, a proper guard interval is crucial to optimize the relationship between BER and throughput.

As Fig. 5 shows that the rise and ringing time of demodulated signal is about 0.5 ms, then it is possible to eliminate ISI when the value of guard interval is 0.5 ms. To explore the impact of guard interval on BER, we conduct the following experiment. We choose the iPhone 5S as a receiver, 10 cm as the communication distance and alter throughput between 13.38 kbps and 16.96 kbps when symbol duration is set to 5 ms. When symbol duration is 10 ms, throughput is varied from 7.85 kbps to 8.96 kbps. The ambient noise is about 55 dB consistently in this set of experiment.

From Fig. 12(b) shows the effect of guard interval on BER. As expected, BER is higher than the others when guard interval uses a smaller value, say 0.5 ms. With the increase of guard interval, BER remains within a certain range from 2.74% to 0.9% when the data symbol duration is 5 ms, BER keeps at a lower range from 0.68% to 0.51% when the data symbol duration is 10 ms, which means the ISI is effectively suppressed by increasing guard interval and data symbol duration.

Throughput will drop with increases of guard interval, so, Low BER is at the expense of the coding rate (Throughput declines by 12.39% and 21.1% respectively). To make a tradeoff, we choose 0.75 ms as the guard interval for Ultra-Comm.

The Impact of Subcarrier Number on UltraComm. The number of subcarriers is an important factor on the transmission performance. To evaluate the impact of the number of subcarriers on the performance of UltraComm, we conducted the experiment by changing number of subcarriers. The receiver is iPhone 5S, the data symbol durations are 5 ms and 10 ms with guard interval of 1 ms, 10 cm as the communication distance and ambient noise of about 55 dB in an office.

Figure 12(c) shows that reduction of subcarrier number leads to decrease of BER. When the number of subcarriers is 65, BER has the lowest value of 0.74%. Because reduction of subcarrier number can improve the tolerance of Ultra-Comm against the intermodulation distortion which is the reason of crosstalk between subcarriers, then this amount of crosstalk can increase BER. Reduction of subcarrier number also increase the transmission power of each subcarrier. Thus, the SNR increases accordingly. Reduction of the number of subcarriers is a simple method to improve communication performance, but at the expense of reducing throughput, the throughput will drop with the decrease of subcarrier number.

5 Related Work

Acoustic communication can be divided into the following categories, and details can be found in Table 1.

Audible Sound Communication. This is the most common acoustic communication approach and the entire audible frequency band can be utilized. In Dhwani [14], the authors implement a sound-based near field communication (NFC), by transmitting modulated signals in audible frequency band. Zhang et al. propose PriWhisper [16], an audible communication system for secure information exchange in very short range (≤ 0.5 cm). The drawback of this category is that sounds can be heard, resulting in usability and security issues.

Inaudible Sound Communication. To address the poor user-experience issue, several mechanisms have been proposed to achieve inaudible communication by exploiting the information-hiding technique. Lope et al. [30] and Matsuoka et al. [25] design and implement a data transmission system that superposes the transmitting signal in speech or music to avoid discomforting the human ear. To better "hide" sound, more complicated schemes [17,29] have been proposed. Among which, Dolphin [17] implements a dual-channel communication which multiplexes low frequency audible music with high frequency encoded data signals without affecting the existing sound. The limitation of inaudible sound communication is the low throughput, e.g., only 500 bps for the aforementioned Dolphin. The limitation comes from the nature of the information-hiding method.

Near-ultrasonic Sound Communication. Near-ultrasonic sound ranging from 18 kHz to 22 kHz can be inaudible to most people but can still be received by microphones. Utilizing this property, Lee et al. demonstrate a system called Chirp that deliver data in indoor environment using near-ultrasonic audio chirp signal [33]. Santagati et al. [34] design and implement the U-wear communication system with GMSK modulation scheme to acquire 2.76 kbps throughput. Ka et al. [31] enable inaudible acoustic communication with low volume near-ultrasound to ensure low error rate. Ed Novak al. [3] provide a mechanism for ultrasonic proximity networking, it achieves throughput of 4.9 kbps at an ideal distance of 5–20 cm. Although inaudible, the exploitation of near-ultrasonic sound faces the problem of low throughput due to the narrow bandwidth.

Ultrasonic Communication. Real ultrasonic communication has also been studied in depth. In a proposed multi-tone FSK (MFSK) modulation-based communication system [28], ultrasound is used to transmit signals through metal. However, those solutions cannot be transplanted to mobile devices. Roy et al. [27] present a method called BackDoor, a system exploiting two separate speakers operating in ultrasonic frequency band and nonlinearity in microphone to generate audible frequency signal which can be regulated to carray data and finally achieve 4 kbps communication rates. However, FM used in BackDoor has poorer spectral efficiency than some other modulation formats, such as phase modulation and AM. Thus, it's could not achieve higher communication rate with limited bandwidth.

DolphinAttack [7] present a completely inaudible attack on speech recognition system, that modulates voice commands on ultrasonic carriers (e.g., $f > 20$ kHz) to achieve inaudibility. By leveraging the nonlinearity of the microphone circuits, the modulated voice can be successfully demodulated and interpreted by the speech recognition system.

UltraComm stands out from the aforementioned literature, which falls short in either throughput or inaudibility. In essence, UltraComm is able to transmit signals using all available bandwidth of audible sound (e.g, 0–20 kHz), by modulating the OFDM signal onto a higher carrier frequency (>20 kHz) to achieve inaudibility rather than using two separate ultrasonic signals played by two speakers. In this way, UltraComm can simultaneously achieve the two goals.

6 Conclusion

In this paper, we propose UltraComm, a high-speed and inaudible sound communication scheme for mobile devices. UltraComm modulate the coded acoustic signals on ultrasonic carriers before emitting and then the modulated acoustic signal can be recovered by utilizing the nonlinearity effect of microphone circuits and then decoded by UltraComm. We successfully realize and evaluate UltraComm on different mobile devices and achieve the highest throughput of 16.24 kbps at the premise of inaudible as far as we know.

References

1. Dog Park Software Ltd.: iSpectrum - Macintosh Audio Spectrum Analyze. Accessed May 2017
2. MarketsandMarkets. https://www.marketsandmarkets.com/Market-Reports/digital-signage-market-513.html. Accessed May 2019
3. Novak, E., Tang, Z., Li, Q.: Ultrasound proximity networking on smart mobile devices for IoT applications. IEEE Internet Things J. 6(1), 399–409 (2018)
4. Tseng, W.-K.: A directional audible sound system using ultrasonic transducers. Int. J. Adv. Res. Artif. Intell. 4(9) (2015)
5. Yan, C., Zhang, G., Ji, X., et al.: The feasibility of injecting inaudible voice commands to voice assistants. IEEE Trans. Dependable Secure Comput. (2019)
6. Nonlinear Acoustics. Academic Press, San Diego (1998)
7. Zhang, G., Yan, C., Ji, X., et al.: DolphinAttack: inaudible voice commands. In: Proceedings of the 2017 ACM SIGSAC Conference on Computer and Communications Security, pp. 103–117. ACM (2017)
8. N5172B EXG X-Series RF Vector Signal Generator, 9 kHz to 6 GHz. http://www.keysight.com/en/pdx-x201910-pn-N5172B. Accessed May 2017
9. Ultrasonic Dynamic Speaker Vifa. http://www.avisoft.com/usg/vifa.htm. Accessed 5 May 2017
10. Lazik, P., Rowe, A.: Indoor pseudo-ranging of mobile devices using ultrasonic chirps. In: Proceedings of the 10th ACM Conference on Embedded Network Sensor Systems, pp. 99–112. ACM (2012)
11. Cobham: Intermodulation Distortion. http://aeroflex.com/. Accessed 3 Oct 2018
12. Liang, C.P., Jong, J., Stark, W.E., et al.: Nonlinear amplifier effects in communications systems. IEEE Trans. Microw. Theory Tech. 47(8), 1461–1466 (1999)
13. Ohno, S., Manasseh, E., Nakamoto, M.: Preamble and pilot symbol design for channel estimation in OFDM systems with null subcarriers. EURASIP J. Wirel. Commun. Netw. 2011(1), 2 (2011)
14. Nandakumar, R., Chintalapudi, K.K., Padmanabhan, V., et al.: Dhwani: secure peer-to-peer acoustic NFC. In: ACM SIGCOMM Computer Communication Review, vol. 43, no. 4, pp. 63–74. ACM (2013)
15. Jinci Technologies: Open structure product review. http://www.jinci.cn/en/goods/112.html. Accessed 5 May 2017

16. Zhang, B., Zhan, Q., Chen, S., et al.: PriWhisper: enabling keyless secure acoustic communication for smartphones. IEEE Internet Things J. **1**(1), 33–45 (2014)
17. Wang, Q., Ren, K., Zhou, M., et al.: Messages behind the sound: real-time hidden acoustic signal capture with smartphones. In: Proceedings of the 22nd Annual International Conference on Mobile Computing and Networking, pp. 29–41. ACM (2016)
18. Gerasimov, V., Bender, W.: Things that talk: using sound for device-to-device and device-to-human communication. IBM Syst. J. **39**(3.4), 530–546 (2000)
19. Hanspach, M., Goetz, M.: On covert acoustical mesh networks in air. arXiv preprint arXiv:1406.1213 (2014)
20. Wambacq, P., Sansen, W.M.C.: Distortion Analysis of Analog Integrated Circuits. Springer, Heidelberg (2013)
21. Chen, G.K.C., Whalen, J.J.: Macromodel predictions for EMI in bipolar operational amplifiers. IEEE Trans. Electromagn. Compat. **4**, 262–265 (1980)
22. Fiori, F., Crovetti, P.S.: Nonlinear effects of radio-frequency interference in operational amplifiers. IEEE Trans. Circuits Syst. I: Fundam. Theory Appl. **49**(3), 367–372 (2002)
23. Fiori, F.: A new nonlinear model of EMI-induced distortion phenomena in feedback CMOS operational amplifiers. IEEE Trans. Electromagn. Compat. **44**(4), 495–502 (2002)
24. Graffi, S., Masetti, G., Golzio, D.: New macromodels and measurements for the analysis of EMI effects in 741 op-amp circuits. IEEE Trans. Electromagn. Compat. **33**(1), 25–34 (1991)
25. Matsuoka, H., Nakashima, Y., Yoshimura, T.: Acoustic communication system using mobile terminal microphones. NTT DoCoMo Tech. J **8**(2), 2–12 (2006)
26. Kune, D.F., Backes, J., Clark, S.S., et al.: Ghost talk: mitigating EMI signal injection attacks against analog sensors. In: 2013 IEEE Symposium on Security and Privacy, pp. 145–159. IEEE (2013)
27. Roy, N., Hassanieh, H., Roy Choudhury, R.: Backdoor: making microphones hear inaudible sounds. In: Proceedings of the 15th Annual International Conference on Mobile Systems, Applications, and Services, pp. 2–14. ACM (2017)
28. Hosman, T., Yeary, M., Antonio, J.K., et al.: Multi-tone FSK for ultrasonic communication. In: 2010 IEEE Instrumentation & Measurement Technology Conference Proceedings, pp. 1424–1429. IEEE (2010)
29. Yun, H.S., Cho, K., Kim, N.S.: Acoustic data transmission based on modulated complex lapped transform. IEEE Signal Processing Lett. **17**(1), 67–70 (2009)
30. Lopes, C.V., Aguiar, P.M.Q.: Aerial acoustic communications. In: Proceedings of the 2001 IEEE Workshop on the Applications of Signal Processing to Audio and Acoustics (Cat. No. 01TH8575), pp. 219–222. IEEE (2001)
31. Ka, S., Kim, T.H., Ha, J.Y., et al.: Near-ultrasound communication for TV's 2nd screen services. In: Proceedings of the 22nd Annual International Conference on Mobile Computing and Networking, pp. 42–54. ACM (2016)
32. Peng, C., Shen, G., Zhang, Y., et al.: BeepBeep: a high accuracy acoustic ranging system using cots mobile devices. In: Proceedings of the 5th International Conference on Embedded Networked Sensor Systems, pp. 1–14. ACM (2007)
33. Lee, H., Kim, T.H., Choi, J.W., et al.: Chirp signal-based aerial acoustic communication for smart devices. In: 2015 IEEE Conference on Computer Communications (INFOCOM), pp. 2407–2415. IEEE (2015)
34. Santagati, G.E., Melodia, T.: A software-defined ultrasonic networking framework for wearable devices. IEEE/ACM Trans. Netw. (TON) **25**(2), 960–973 (2017)

A New Coordinated Multi-points Transmission Scheme for 5G Millimeter-Wave Cellular Network

Xiaoya Zuo[1(✉)], Rugui Yao[1], Xu Zhang[2], Jiahong Li[2], and Pan Liu[2]

[1] School of Electronics and Information, Northwestern Polytechnical University,
Xi'an 710072, Shaanxi, China
zuoxy@nwpu.edu.cn
[2] Xi'an Institute of Space Radio Technology, Xi'an 710100, Shaanxi, China

Abstract. Millimeter-wave network based on beamforming is an interference-limited network. In order to mitigate the interference for the 5G millimeter-wave cellular network, the concept of cooperative multi-beam transmission (Beam-CoMP) is proposed in this paper to improve cell capacity. For users in the beam overlapping zone, there is strong interference between beams, so for such users, overlapping beams provide services to users through cooperation. This method can solve the problems of poor edge coverage and serious interference of overlapping coverage of beams at the same time. The specific process of beam cooperation is given and the Beam-CoMP method proposed is simulated to verify its effectiveness in improving the UE performance. The results show that cell capacity increases with the increase of the number of users in the service beam.

Keywords: Millimeter-wave · 5G · CoMP · Capacity · Interference

1 Introduction

With the development of high-speed wireless communication technology, millimeter-wave technology has more and more important applications in future wireless networks. 5G puts forward higher requirements for link rate, link delay and system energy efficiency. Therefore, in a series of new technologies [1–3], millimeter wave technology (30–300 GHz) has become one of the most important technologies recognized by the industry. For the applications of millimeter wave technology, opportunities and challenges coexist [4]. On the one hand, millimeter-wave band provides a large bandwidth, which can provide higher system capacity. On the other hand, millimeter-wave communication usually needs beam forming to increase the coverage distance because of the large propagation loss of millimeter-wave. Although millimeter-wave network and traditional network have different channel characteristics, antenna structure and hardware constraints, millimeter-wave network based on beamforming is still interference-limited network, that is, system capacity is mainly affected by the mutual interference in the network [5]. The important means to improve system capacity and spectrum efficiency is to reduce the network interference. Different from traditional

X. Chu et al. (Eds.): QShine 2019, LNICST 300, pp. 205–216, 2020.
https://doi.org/10.1007/978-3-030-38819-5_13

interference, in millimeter-wave networks, due to the directional narrow-beam characteristics, millimeter-wave interference will increase significantly in the overlapping coverage area, which will directly affect the system performance and user service quality.

In traditional cellular networks, in order to reduce network interference and improve the quality of service for the users in overlapping areas of cells, a cooperative multi-point transmission (CoMP) technology [6–9] is proposed, which aims at reducing interference and enhancing transmission through coordination or cooperation among multiple base stations and sectors. CoMP is divided into interference coordination and joint transmission. The interference coordination mainly avoids the interference between beams by joint beamforming. Joint transmission achieves signal enhancement by transmitting the same information through multiple beams. At present, there are two main types of joint transmission CoMP, including inter-CoMP and intra-CoMP [10]. Inter-CoMP is a cooperative transmission between different sites; intra-CoMP is a cooperative transmission between multiple sectors of the same site. At present, there are many studies on inter-CoMP, including link capacity, link interrupt probability, asynchronous reception performance, and the impact of delay and return capability on link performance. But inter-CoMP needs a feedback network to exchange information between different sites, so the system complexity is high [11]. For intra-CoMP, the literature [12] compares its link performance with that of non-CoMP systems, and points out that intra-CoMP can bring link gain. The literature [13] compares the link performance gain of intra-CoMP with that of inter-CoMP, and points out that the performance of intra-CoMP is inferior to that of inter-CoMP. Meanwhile, a method to improve the link performance is given, that is, to increase the number of sectors in a cell. Intra-CoMP has advantages in information interaction complexity, time delay and system synchronization because all information exchanges are on the same site.

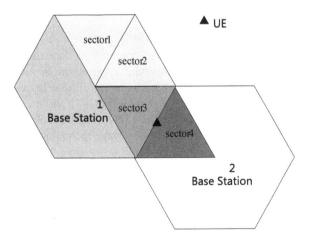

Fig. 1. CoMP system schematic diagram.

The above analysis shows that inter-CoMP is not practical because of its high system complexity, which is mainly due to the limitations of user grouping and scheduling, channel estimation and feedback, synchronization and information feedback when different sites cooperate. Although intra-CoMP does not have the problem of high complexity of inter-CoMP, the performance gain of intra-CoMP is not as good as that of inter-CoMP. As shown in Fig. 1, inter-CoMP is the CoMP of different sites, such as sector3 and sector4. Both sectors have larger signal strengths at the user. Intra-CoMP is the CoMP of different sectors of the same site, such as sector3 and sector2. Because of the traditional antenna deployment and sector division, the signal strengths of sector2 at the user is small, so the gain of cooperation with sector3 is not as obvious as that of inter-CoMP.

In order to solve the above problems, the concept of cooperative multi-beam transmission (Beam-CoMP) is proposed in this paper, and it is introduced into beamforming-based millimeter-wave network to improve cell capacity. This method can solve the problems of poor edge coverage and serious interference of overlapping coverage of beams at the same time. Each sector of the site is a large-scale array antenna, which forms multiple beams to serve users in the sector by beamforming. In order to maximize resource utilization, full bandwidth frequency multiplexing of each beam is implemented. According to the location of users, users can be divided into two categories: users in non-overlapping zone and users in overlapping zone. For users in non-overlapping zone, users' services are provided by a single beam, in which multiple users share the whole time-frequency resources, and such users are relatively less disturbed by other beams. For users in overlapping zone, there is strong interference between beams, so for such users, overlapping beams provide services to users through cooperation. Beam-CoMP can eliminate interference and enhance signal diversity. Different from traditional CoMP, inter-CoMP is the cooperation of different sites, intra-CoMP is the cooperation of different sectors of the same site, and Beam-CoMP is the cooperation of different beams of the same site in the same sector.

Introducing Beam-CoMP into the beamforming-based millimeter-wave network is expected to solve the existing CoMP problems and bring the following obvious advantages:

(1) Increase the signal intensity of the users covered by the beam edge.

The signal quality of beamforming-based users in the edge coverage area is worse than that in the center area, which makes the service quality of edge users poor. By means of Beam-CoMP, users at the edge of beams can transmit jointly through multi-beams, which enhances the signal strength and improves the quality of service.

(2) Reduce interference in millimeter-wave networks and increase cell capacity.

The main interference in millimeter-wave network comes from inter-beam interference. Beam-CoMP can eliminate inter-beam interference, which can greatly reduce interference and improve cell capacity.

(3) Make up for the shortcomings of traditional CoMP and reduce the complexity of the system.

Because Beam-CoMP collaborates in the same sector of the same site, data interaction, synchronization and delay processing are easy to implement, and the system complexity is low. At the same time, there is no lack of signal intensity caused by the problem of sector coverage when adjacent sectors cooperate in intra-CoMP, which will lead to significant capacity improvement.

2   System Model

Firstly, the cell structure of 5G millimeter wave cellular network is defined as shown in Fig. 2. In the cell, network units mainly include sites and users. Large-scale antenna arrays are used in the base station. Cells are divided into several sectors by different antennas. Through beam forming technology, each sector can form multiple beams at the same time and serve multiple users separately. Assuming that a service-providing beam is random beamforming, it randomly points to a location in the sector. If the beam covers a user to be served, the beam will point to this location unchanged. If there is no user to be served in the coverage area randomly pointed by the beam, the beam will randomly point to another location until it finds users to be served. For users, we use Poisson Point Process (PPP), which is commonly used in stochastic geometry theory, to describe its distribution, that is, the user obeys PPP process with density. Users are randomly distributed in the sector.

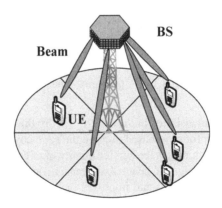

Fig. 2. Block structure diagram of 5G system.

Assuming that *BS* serves *N UEs* in the cell, there are *N* transmission links in the cell. In the link i of $Beam_i$ Service UE_i, the receiving power Pr_i is

$$Pr_i[dBm] = P_t[dBm] + G_t[dBi] + G_r[dBi] - PL[dB] \tag{1}$$

Where P_t is the transmission power of the base station, G_t is the gain of the transmitting antenna, G_r is the gain of the receiving antenna, and PL is the path loss between the sender and the receiver. Assuming that each beam is aligned with the user it serves during transmission, the maximum antenna gain G_t is obtained at this time. If the user uses omnidirectional antenna, the value G_r should be 0 dBi. The path loss of signal propagation is calculated by using the channel model in millimeter wave LOS environment.

$$PL[dB] = \alpha + 10\beta \lg d + X_\sigma \tag{2}$$

The parameters in the model are measured at 28 GHz in Manhattan LOS environment. And $\alpha = 45.3$, $\beta = 2.9$, d is the distance between users and the base station, $\sigma = 0.04$.

Assuming the received total interference power of UE_i is P_{Ii}, the single to noise ratio of UE_i can be described as

$$SIN R_i = \frac{P_{r_i}[mw]}{N[mw] + P_{I_i}[mw]} \tag{3}$$

According to Shannon's formula, the capacity of this link is

$$C_i = B \log_2(1 + SINR_i) \tag{4}$$

Where B is the bandwidth. Cell capacity is the sum of all link capacity, and

$$c = \sum_{i=1}^{N} c_i \tag{5}$$

The cell capacity of cooperation between beams is the sum of the capacity of two types of users. One is the capacity of users in the overlapping zone $C_{overlap}$, and the other is the capacity of users in the non-overlapping zone $C_{nonoverlap}$. For the capacity of users in the non-overlapping zone of the beam, the capacity can be calculated directly according to the above method. For the user in the overlap zone, K interference beams and service beams cooperate to provide services for the user, and the interference between beams PI is converted into useful signal P_r. And the $SINR$ is

$$SINR(i) = \frac{Pr + \sum_{k=0}^{K} PI_k}{N_0} \tag{6}$$

Where N_0 is the Gaussian white noise. Assuming that there are N users in the beam overlapping region and M users in the non-overlapping region, the capacity can be described as,

$$C = C_{overlap} + C_{nonoverlap}$$

$$= \sum_{i=1}^{N} C_{overlap}(i) + \sum_{j=1}^{M} C_{nonoverlap}(j)$$

$$= \sum_{i=1}^{N} B_i \log_2\left(1 + \frac{P_r + \sum_{k=0}^{K} PI_k}{N_0}\right) + \sum_{j=1}^{M} B_j \log_2\left(1 + \frac{P_r}{N_0}\right)$$

$$(7)$$

3 The Proposed Coordinated Multi-points Transmission Scheme

In the mode of single-beam service for multi-users, multi-beam cooperation provides services for users in the overlapping zone. This can not only avoid the inefficiency of single-beam service, but also solve the problem of the degradation of UE performance at the edge of the beam when single-beam provides service for multi-users. In the Beam-CoMP transmission technology proposed in this section, the base station has the ability of multi-beam cooperative communication, and each beam can serve multiple UEs with full frequency band reuse.

As shown in Fig. 3, when allocating the frequency resources for the UEs in the beam overlapping area and non-overlapping area, the station firstly allocates the frequency bandwidth resources required by UEs in the non-overlapping area using OFDM technology according to the transmission requirements. The remaining system frequency bandwidth resources are allocated to the overlapping UEs at the beam edge. By utilizing the advantages of multiple beams easy to cooperate in the same single base station, the performance of beam edge UEs can be enhanced by cooperation. The transmitter of the base station modulates the data to the pre-allocated frequency band, and the receiver demodulates the data in the corresponding frequency band to complete the data transmission.

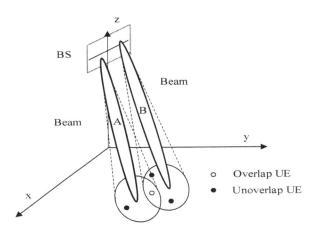

Fig. 3. The proposed Beam-CoMP scheme.

The specific process of beam cooperation is as follows:

(1) As shown in Fig. 3, assume that the total frequency resource bandwidth of the system is BW_o The beam $i(i = 1, 2, \ldots, n,\ n > 1)$ provides service for the users $UE_{ij}(j = 1, 2, \ldots, m_i,\ m_i > 1)$ in the non-overlapping region. Where n is the beam number, and m_i is the user number in the non-overlapping region of beam i. The users in the overlapping region are $UE_k(k = 1, 2, \ldots, l)$, and l is the user number.

When the system transmits data in the down link, the site sends information to UE with full frequency reuse. When the station and UE determine the connection, the station associates the beam i with the UE to establish the transmission link. Then go to step (2).

When UE transmits data up to the site, UE initiates a transmission request. After the site permits, the site connects the beam i to the UE to establish a transmission link. Then go to step (5).

(2) The cooperative beam i determines the minimum frequency resources required for all non-overlapping areas BW_i. As shown in Fig. 4, then go to step (3).

(3) Compare the minimum frequency resource bandwidth required BW_i for each beam serving UE_{ij} in the non-overlapping region. As shown in Fig. 5, the maximum bandwidth required is selected among all the individual beams participating in the collaboration max (BW_i). All UEs in the non-overlapping area of each beam are allocate with the same bandwidth max (BW_i). And the UEs in the overlapping region share the left bandwidth $BW R = BW - \max(BW_i)$, as shown in Fig. 6.

Through OFDM, the station modulates the data of UEs in the non-overlapping region to the corresponding frequency bandwidth BW_{ij} for transmission, and modulates the data of the users in the overlapping area to the corresponding bandwidth $BW R_k$ for data transmission. Then go to step (4).

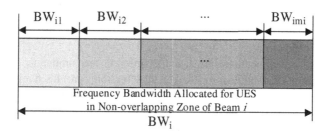

Fig. 4. Frequency bandwidth allocated for UES in non-overlapping zone of beam i.

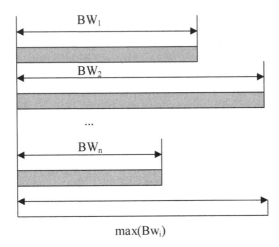

max(Bw$_i$)

Fig. 5. A schematic diagram of the minimum bandwidth required for UE in the non-overlapping region.

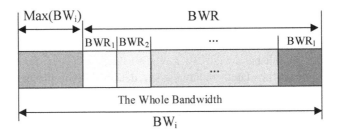

Fig. 6. Schematic diagram of total frequency resource bandwidth allocation.

(4) Each UE receives data individually and demodulates data on the corresponding frequency bandwidth.

Uplink resource allocation and data transmission are similar to downlink. The beam cooperation method proposed in this section can effectively enhance the transmission performance. In the case of single-beam serving multi-UEs, for users in the overlapping zone, multi-beam cooperation at the same site provides services for edge users. Multiple beam cooperation can improve the efficiency of resource utilization and service efficiency. At the same time, cooperative transmission among multi-beams can not only guarantee the normal communication of users in non-overlapping area, but also improve the performance of users in overlapping area. Moreover, because multi-beams in a single site cooperate, it is easy to collaborate among beams.

4   Simulation Results and Analysis

In this section, the Beam-CoMP method proposed in the previous section is simulated to verify its effectiveness in improving the UE performance. The simulation scenario assumes that there are overlapping beams in a sector of the cell. The specific simulation parameters are shown in Table 1. In the simulation, users are randomly distributed in the beam. Each beam in the sector is fully frequency reused, and the UE in each beam is served by the beam. For simplicity, the total frequency resources of the beam are divided equally. When there is no user in the beam, the beam will not work and will not interfere with the overlapping beams. The simulation takes 5000 times as the average.

Table 1. Simulation parameters of Beam-CoMP scenarios.

BS height	10 m	BS transmitter power	27 dBm
Cell radius	50 m	BS antenna gain	16 dBi
Antenna array	8 × 8	UE antenna gain	0 dBi
Carrier frequency	28 GHz	HPBW	$30°$
Bandwidth	500 MHz	Temperature	298 K

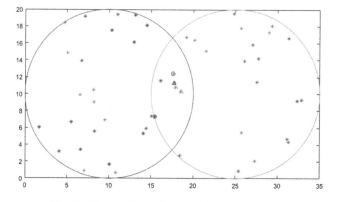

Fig. 7. Users with random positions in the beam.

In the beam overlapping model shown in Fig. 3, two beam overlapping (beam A and B) are taken as examples to illustrate the method of beam cooperation. Suppose there are four users in two beam ranges. The total frequency bandwidth of the system is BW. There are two users in beam A, three users in beam B and one user in the overlapping area of two beams. Users in non-overlapping area of beam A get BW/2 bandwidth, while users in non-overlapping area of beam B get BW/3 bandwidth. According to the beam cooperation method in the previous section, both beams allocate BW/3 frequency bandwidth to users in the overlap zone. Although the bandwidth resource of BW/6 is wasted in Beam A, the overlapping users can avoid the inter-beam interference and improve the performance because they get the same frequency resource of two beams.

For cells that do not use beam cooperation, the beam overlap model shown in Fig. 3 is also used for analysis. Assuming that the frequency resource of the system is BW, there are two users in beam A, three users in beam B and one user in the overlapping area between the two beams. In beam A, the frequency bandwidth allocated by each user is BW/2; in beam B, the frequency resource bandwidth allocated by each user is BW/3. Because there is no inter-beam cooperation, when the user in the overlapping zone receives the signal of beam A, he will be disturbed by beam B, and when the user in the overlapping zone receives the signal of beam B, beam A will interfere with it. Therefore, in this scenario, no matter which beam the user tries to receive in the overlapping region, the signal will be interfered by other beams, which will degrade the user's performance.

In the simulation, a random number of users are generated in the cell beam (beam A and beam B), and the frequency resources are allocated to each user in the beam. In the overlap zone, if two users share the same frequency, the user will be affected by the same frequency interference if they do not cooperate with each other. If the method of beam cooperation is adopted, user will not be affected by the same frequency interference. On the contrary, because of the same service frequency, both beams can cooperate to provide services for the user in the overlap zone and effectively improve the performance of users in the overlap zone. For users with different frequencies in the overlap area, they will not be subject to the same frequency interference.

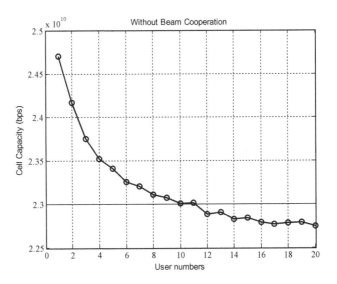

Fig. 8. User number versus capacity without beam cooperation.

Figure 8 shows the relationship between capacity and number of users in a non-beam cooperative cell. As can be seen from the simulation diagram, with the increase of the number of users, the cell capacity is gradually decreasing. This is because with the increase of the number of users, the probability of users existing in the overlapping zone is also increasing. So users in the overlapping zone are also increased by the interference between beams, and cell capacity tends to decrease.

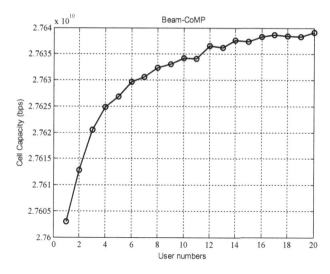

Fig. 9. User number versus capacity with beam cooperation.

Figure 9 shows the change of cell capacity with the increase of the number of users when there is beam cooperation. It can be seen from the graph that cell capacity increases with the increase of the number of users. This is because with the increase of the number of users, the number of users distributed in the overlapping area of the beam increases correspondingly. When there is co-frequency interference between users, because of the use of beam cooperation, users in the overlapping zone are provided by beam cooperation. And users are not disturbed, so they have better performance.

5 Conclusions

This paper proposed a simple and effective method to solve the beam interference problem in the 5G millimeter-wave cellular network. The specific process of beam cooperation is given and the proposed Beam-CoMP method is simulated to verify its effectiveness in improving the cell capacity. The results show that cell capacity increases with the increase of the number of users in the service beam. While without beam cooperation, with the increase of the number of users, the cell capacity is gradually decreasing because of the mutual interference. This method can solve the problems of poor edge coverage and serious interference of overlapping coverage of beams at the same time.

Acknowledgments. This work was supported in part by the National Natural Science Foundation of China (No. 61701407 and 61871327), the Natural Science Basic Research Plan in Shaanxi Province of China (No. 2018JM6037) and the Aerospace Science and Technology Fund.

References

1. Gupta, A., Jha, R.K.: A survey of 5G network: architecture and emerging technologies. IEEE Access **3**, 1206–1232 (2015)
2. Heath, R.W., Gonzalez-Prelcic, N., Rangan, S., et al.: An Overview of signal processing techniques for millimeter wave MIMO systems. IEEE J. Sel. Top. Sign. Process. **10**(3), 436–453 (2015)
3. Andrews, J.G., Buzzi, S., Choi, W., et al.: What will 5G be? IEEE J. Sel. Areas Commun. **32**(6), 1065–1082 (2014)
4. Karjalainen, J., Nekovee, M., Benn, H., et al.: Challenges and opportunities of mm-wave communication in 5G networks. In: 2014 9th International Conference on Cognitive Radio Oriented Wireless Networks and Communications, pp. 372–376. IEEE (2014)
5. Bai, T., Alkhateeb, A., Heath, R.W.: Coverage and capacity of millimeter-wave cellular networks. IEEE Commun. Mag. **52**(9), 70–77 (2014)
6. Lee, D., Seo, H., Clerckx, B., et al.: Coordinated multipoint transmission and reception in LTE-advanced: deployment scenarios and operational challenges. IEEE Commun. Mag. **50**(2), 148–155 (2012)
7. Shami, T.M., Grace, D., Burr, A., Zakaria, M.D.: User-centric JT-CoMP clustering in a 5G cell-less architecture. In: 2018 IEEE 29th Annual International Symposium on Personal, Indoor and Mobile Radio Communications (PIMRC), Bologna, pp. 177–181 (2018)
8. Schwarz, S., Rupp, M.: Exploring coordinated multipoint beamforming strategies for 5G cellular. IEEE Access **2**, 930–946 (2014)
9. MacCartney, G.R., Rappaport, T.S.: Millimeter-wave base station diversity for 5G coordinated multipoint (CoMP) applications. IEEE Trans. Wirel. Commun. **18**(7), 3395–3410 (2019)
10. Shang, P., Zhang, L., You, M.: Performance of uplink joint reception CoMP with antenna selection for reducing complexity in LTE-A systems. In: WCNC, pp. 977–982 (2015)
11. Martinez, A.B., Grieger, M., Festag, A., et al.: Sectorization and intra-site CoMP: comparison of Field-trials and system-level simulations. In: 2015 IEEE Global Communications Conference, pp. 1–7. IEEE (2015)
12. Khlass, A., Bonald, T., Elayoubi, S.E.: Analytical modeling of downlink CoMP in LTE-advanced. In: 2015 IEEE 81st Vehicular Technology Conference, pp. 1–5. IEEE (2015)
13. Riedel, I., Rost, P., Marsch, P., et al.: Creating desirable interference by optimized sectorization in cellular systems. In: 2010 IEEE Global Telecommunications Conference, pp. 1–5. IEEE (2010)

Network Management

Divide and Conquer: Efficient Multi-path Validation with ProMPV

Anxiao He$^{(\boxtimes)}$, Yubai Xie, Wensen Mao, and Tienpei Yeh

Zhejiang University, Hangzhou 310007, ZJ, China
{zjuhax,xiaoxiaobai,wsmao,3130001051}@zju.edu.cn

Abstract. Path validation has long be explored toward forwarding reliability of Internet traffic. Adding cryptographic primitives in packet headers, path validation enables routers to enforce which path a packet should
follow and to verify whether the packet has followed the path. How to
implement path validation for multi-path routing is yet to be investigated. We find that it leads to an impractically low efficiency when simply applying existing single-path validation to multi-path routing.

In this paper, we present ProMPV as an initiative to explore efficient
multi-path validation for multi-path routing. We segment the forwarding path into segments of three routers following a sliding window with
size one. Based on this observation, we design ProMPV as a proactive
multi-path validation protocol in that it requires a router to proactively
leave to its second next hop with proofs that cannot be tampered by its
next hop. In multi-path routing, this greatly optimizes the computation
and packet size. A packet no longer needs to carry all proofs of routers
along all paths. Instead, it iteratively updates its carried proofs that correspond to only three hops. We validate the security and performance of
ProMPV through security analysis and experiment results, respectively.

Keywords: Path validation · Multi-path routing · Source
authentication · Routing strategy

1 Introduction

Path validation has long been explored to secure the forwarding process of Internet traffic [2]. In the current Internet, both the source and the destination have
no control over the forwarding of their communication traffic. This leaves various
forwarding anomalies unnoticeble. For example, the source and the destination
may have signed up for a premium service (e.g., high bandwidth) for their communication. However, the service provider may direct their traffic along a path
with inferior performance. Such mis-forwarding can also be exploited to breach
security. Consider, for example, when the destination requires that all traffic
toward it be examined via a security middlebox. If an attack packet toward it
circumvents the security middlebox yet cannot be detected, the destination may
be attacked. To address these concerns, path validation enables routers to perform additional cryptographic primitives on packets. Specifically, it introduces

© ICST Institute for Computer Sciences, Social Informatics and Telecommunications Engineering 2020
Published by Springer Nature Switzerland AG 2020. All Rights Reserved
X. Chu et al. (Eds.): QShine 2019, LNICST 300, pp. 219–234, 2020.
https://doi.org/10.1007/978-3-030-38819-5_14

both enforcement and verification over the packet forwarding process. Forwarding enforcement aims to regulate routers of how to forward a specific packet. Forwarding verification aims to enable routers to check whether a packet has been forwarded as required. Both operations are implemented through packet-carried cryptographic proofs. The key idea is that routers add their proofs in packet headers toward an unforgeable forwarding history of packets. Current path validation solutions focus mainly on the single-path routing scenario and has an $O(n)$ overhead given an n-hop path.

As network develops rapidly, single-path routing cannot satisfy the demands of speed and security, thus multipath technology appeals. Multipath routing combines efficiency and robustness, allowing packets travel through multiple paths with same source to the same destination [3]. The balance between efficiency and security is critical for the deployment of Internet protocols [10]. However, simply use single-path validation scheme in multipath situation would cost an unacceptable overhead. First, in multipath situation, every node has a group of downstream node to choose, and with the path length increases, the number of nodes would grow in exponential form, making the validation cost too big to store. According to the measurement study in [11], for 300 million AS pairs, more than 50% of them can find at least tens of alternate paths while 25% of them have more than 100 alternate paths. Second, single-path schemes request the whole path's information to build a verification chain, but it is impossible in multipath situation since source may not know the entire path followed by a packet. With specific routing strategy, routers can only decide its next hop according to real-time network status [12]. Therefore, it is meaningless to pre-build a path as packet would change directions in the middle way unless we pre-compute all the possible ways, however, the cost is too large.

In this paper, we present ProMPV that achieves efficient multi-path validation [7,9] in a divide-and-conquer way. To investigate useful efficiency techniques, we start with analyzing the characteristics of existing single-path validation solutions. We find that a packet may not have to carry a router's proof to all the router's downstream routers for verification. The enforcement and verification of a forwarding path can be divided and each division conquers a segment of the forwarding path. Specifically, we segment the forwarding path into segments of three routers following a sliding window with size one. Consider, for example, an n-hop forwarding path $(r_1, r_2, ..., r_n)$. The segments ProMPV handles are (r_1, r_2, r_3), (r_2, r_3, r_4), (r_3, r_4, r_5), and so on. The key idea is that we can require r_1 to leave a proof to its next hop's next hop, that is, r_3. If r_3 can successfully verify the expected proof from r_1, it demonstrates that the intermediary r_2 forwards packets correctly without any misbehavior. Based on this observation, we design ProMPV as a proactive multi-path validation protocol in that it requires a router to proactively leave to its second next hop with proofs that cannot be tampered by its next hop. In multi-path routing, this greatly optimizes the computation and packet size. A packet no longer needs to carry all proofs of routers along all paths. Instead, it iteratively updates its carried proofs that correspond to only three hops.

In summary, we make the following major contributions to efficient multi-path validation.

- Identify the challenges of path validation in multi-path routing. We analyze the infeasibility of directly applying single-path validation solutions to multi-path validation.
- Propose a proactive multi-path validation technique that achieves efficient multi-path validation in a divide-and-conquer fashion.
- Design ProMPV based on the proactive divide-and-conquer technique.
- Prove the security properties of ProMPV.
- Implement ProMPV using OpenSSL and evaluate its performance. The time and space overhead of ProMPV is insensitive to the path length. Different key lengths can be selected under different security requirements to balance time cost and security level.

The rest of the paper is organized as follows. Section 2 reviews existing path validation solutions and underline their infeasibility to multi-path routing. Section 3 proposes ProMPV toward efficient multi-path validation using a divide-and-conquer technique. Section 4 details the ProMPV design. Section 5 proves the security of ProMPV. Sects. 6 and 7 prototype ProMPV and evaluate its performance. Finally, Sect. 8 concludes the paper.

2   Problem

In this section, we review existing single-path validation solutions and identify their infeasibility in multi-path routing. Nowadays, the number of Internet users and their requirement on bandwidth and quality are increasing more rapidly than ever. Single-path routing can no longer keep up with this pace. In comparison with single-path routing, multi-path routing can effectively avoid the situations like router failures and link congestion as more than one forwarding paths are available. Besides, idle network bandwidth can be fully utilized; the end-to-end delay can be reduced. From the security point of view, packets transmitted by multi-path routing are more difficult to be attacked because it is more challenging for the attacker to simultaneously control several alternate forwarding paths. Albeit multi-path routing is more advantageous than single-path routing in terms of fault tolerance, routing reliability, bandwidth utilization, and security, various challenges lie in multi-path validation.

2.1   Single-Path Validation

The initiative work on singe-path validaiton is ICING [5]. ICING introduces two types of proofs, Proof of Consent (PoC) and Proof of Provenance (PoP). PoCs are used for each router to demonstrate that is has the permission to forward certain packets. PoPs are used to prove that a router has processed certain packets. Both of these proofs are added to the corresponding verification fields in packet headers. When the packet propagates through the network, each node verifies whether the packet has followed its approved path. ICING performs path validation as follows. First, it check whether the single routing path is approved. The path can be confirmed by checking whether the PoC is consistent. Then each node confirms the previous routers by verifying its verification domain. Finally, the PoP is used to update its verification domain for all subsequent verification nodes. The PoP takes the first 8 bytes of the AES-CBC-MAC hash value. So every node can perform source authentication and path verification. In OPT, a PoP alike field called PVF is used. The source authentication and path verification are verified by PVF. PVF is a set of nested MAC values, and the source generates all PVFs in advance. The value of each path node is calculated using PVF. Source authentication and path verification only need to compare the calculation results given by the source. OPT lets the source to take over a large portion of computation that otherwise is performed by intermediate routers as in ICING. OPT is therefore much faster than ICING.

2.2 Infeasiblity to Multi-path Validation

As mentioned before, ICING and OPT are both single-path validation solutions. They need to determine the entire path before the session begins, including the path length and routers that the packet passes through. However, in multi-path routing, there are many paths connecting the source and the destination. These paths may pass through different routers and their path lengths are not fixed. The choice is depending on the routing strategy. So if we simply use single-path validation scheme in multi-path situation without modifying, multi-path would be considered as a set of many single paths. In this way, the overhead of time and space might be explosive with the number of possible forwarding paths.

Waste of Packet Size and Bandwidth. Traditional schemes need to build the complete path at first to help verify the packet. It is feasible in single path since there may be at most no more than 30 hops in a path [6] and every router knows exactly who is the next hop. But in multi-path situation, things are different. Routers do not know their next hops at the beginning, they need to choose them in real time according to network status such as link availability. This way, each router may have several choices for forwarding a packet to the next hop. If the source uses the normal way, the size complexity would be an exponential function related to the number of hops. It is a huge pressure on packet size. Also, it would cost much of the bandwidth used for transferring package data.

Low Efficiency. Path validation needs to compute many validation fields before the packet transfer to fast the validation process. The source can pre-compute some of these fields to accelerate the processing speed. However, in the multi-path situation, to verify each other, every two routers have to share a pair of symmetric keys and this would cost many calculation resources. Moreover, the source has to pre-compute many fields used for verification. All these computation lead to a low validation efficiency when many possible forwarding paths enforce a large amount of computation.

3   Overview

In this section, we construct a symmetric-key encryption scheme to address the aforementioned validation inefficiencies. It motivates out efficient multi-path validation ProMPV to be presented in Sect. 4.

3.1   Motivation

To address the limitations of the former schemes, we propose a new scheme with the following properties: symmetry and divide-and-conquer. First, we use symmetric encryption to minimize the key size at the same security level compared with when asymmetric encryption is used. This decreases the cost of key storage and increases the speed of computation. Second, since storing and validating an entire path lead to a high overhead, our scheme divides the path into several segments.

Symmetry. Our scheme uses symmetric-key encryption to minimize the amount of calculation and accelerate the processing speed. Asymmetric-key encryption can decrease the number of key pairs between every pair of routers. Although this can save some cost, its large key size and group size would cost more space. For example, given a 128-bit security level, symmetric-key encryption like AES only needs 128 bits to store a key while asymmetric-key encryption like DH needs 256 bits for key size and another $3,072$ bits for group size, and even ECC will needs other 256 more bits to store. Therefore, using symmetric-key encryption can save a lot of space and we can use it to store more validation parts. Besides, symmetric-key encryption is faster than asymmetric-key encryption. Since path validation is a part of packet, even a little delay per packet would cumulatively cause a large end-to-end delay. Using symmetric-key can simplify lots of computation like modulo or power, which both need a large amount of computation ability.

A major design challenge raised by symmetric-key encryption is the number of key pairs. Unlike asymmetric-key encryption using public key, to identify each other, every two routers have to share a pair of secret key. A number n of routers require a number $O(n^2)$ of keys. In multi-path validation, there might be more routers and now calculating and deriving keys would be much more complex. Our solution is to pre-compute as much proof related information as possible. Before packets start to transmit, routers have already identified each other and there is no need to derive the keys twice. Routers can thus store them locally rather than put them in the header.

Segmentation. As aforementioned, if we directly use a single-path validation algorithm in multi-path situation, we would face a challenge that the source does not know the entire path to the destination before hand. Since there exists lots of possibility, calculating all of them is impossible. Thus, we use a method of segmentation. Specifically, we segment the forwarding path into segments of three routers following a sliding window with size one. Consider, for example, an n-hop forwarding path $(r_1, r_2, ..., r_n)$. The segments ProvMPV handles are (r_1, r_2, r_3), (r_2, r_3, r_4), (r_3, r_4, r_5), and so on. The key idea is that we can require r_1 to leave a proof to its next hop's next hop, that is, r_3. If r_3 can successfully verify the expected proof from r_1, it demonstrates that the intermediary r_2 forwards packets correctly without any misbehavior. In multi-path routing, this greatly optimizes the computation and packet size. A packet no longer needs to carry all proofs of routers along all paths. Instead, it iteratively updates its carried proofs that correspond to only three hops.

How to choose the length of each segment is the key. It is obvious that the more routers a segment contains, the higher security level we get. The space complexity and difficulty of calculation, however, grow with the length. So what we should consider is its lower bound. Suppose that each segment only has two routers, then a collusion attack is easy to launch as adjacent malicious routers can fake the verification and transfer it to the next. If there are three nodes in a segment, even if a collusion attack occurs, the next segment would easily spot the attack and discard the packet. Our scheme would therefore use three as a balance of efficiency and security.

3.2   Encryption Construction

We now present our encryption scheme. Using AES-256, routers encrypt and decrypt the proofs to accomplish the verification with high security-level guaranteed. Using specific strategy, which we would introduce in Sect. 4.4, routers can determine its next hop, but it cannot control the second hop. Our solution is simple but effective: we use aggregate MAC to all the possibilities together so that the next hop can compute its next hop's signature and search it in the set to verify whether it can match.

We propose a new symmetric-key encryption scheme. It has three parts. The first part is used to record the sequence of identifier. The second part stores the information of the previous node, the current node and the next node. The third part stores the information of the node before last, the last node and the current node. Once decrypting the first part, router can use the sequence to verify the path order. And the portion of it would be used to decrypt the third part to accomplish path validation. If verification is passed, the second part would be updated to contain the downstream node's information. In this way, we guarantee the upstream nodes' verification and make sure the next hop is in the right path.

4   Design

In this section, we detail the design of ProMPV.

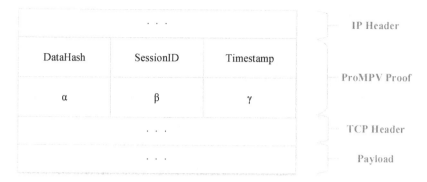

Fig. 1. ProMPV header architecture. DataHash, SessionID and Timestamp are traditional fields while ProMPV proof is designed uniquely. All the four parts are initialized by the source and only the fourth part need to be updated by the downstream routers.

4.1   Header Architecture

As shown in Fig. 1, ProMPV introduces its proof fields between the IP header and the TCP header. It contains four parts: DataHash, SessionID, Timestamp and ProMPV proof. The first three parts are regular parts of a verification scheme and the last one is unique as it is the core of our scheme. All these four fields are initialized by the source. The following routers only need to update the ProMPV proof.

DataHash. DataHash is the hash value of a given package's payload, written as $H(P)$. It is used to guarantee the integrity of packet. Hash function is shared with all the nodes. If attackers do not get the right function, they cannot forge a fake $H(P)$ which can pass the verification. However, if attacker is a malicious router in the path, then it can compute a valid $H(P)$ with changed payload, so simply put $H(P)$ in the packet header is not enough, DataHash must take part in the verification computation. When path validation begins to work, nodes calculate $H(P)$ independently and compare the result with DataHash stored in the header. If the result fits, packet's integrity is confirmed, otherwise, the packet is altered and router refuse and drop the packet.

SessionID. For every session, the source and the destination choose a SessionID to identify. It contains the hash value of nodes' ID and session initialization time. Routers generate symmetric keys according to it. And SessionID should be put into the computation. Otherwise we may suffer from path deviation attack. Suppose there are two node sequences: (r_1, r_2, r_3) and (r_1, r_2, r_4). r_2 is a malicious router and it transfer packet to r_4 rather than r_3. If we do not contain SessionID in the computation, r_4 can forge the proof and deceive others. With calculating SessionID, we guarantee only specific routers can take part in the process.

Timestamp. Timestamp records the time when the packet is created. As a part of computation, it is used to defend against replay attack. Without it, malicious router can copy an out-of-style message and send it to other routers to bypass the validation.

Table 1. Symbols and notations used in the section

P	The packet's payload
t_σ	The session initialization time
DataHash	The hash value of payload
SessionID	The hash value of nodes' ID and session initialization time
Timestamp	The time when packet is created
R_i	The ith router
ID_i	The ith router's ID
$K_{i,j}(=K_{j,i})$	The symmetric key shared between router R_i and R_i
Queue	Used to store the id of three routers
$Enc_{K_{i,j}}$	Encrypt the content d using symmetric key $K_{i,j}$
$Dec_{K_{i,j}}$	Decrypt the content d using symmetric key $K_{i,j}$
$H(d)$	Compute the hash value of content d using SHA-256

ProMPV Proof. As shown in Fig. 1, ProMPV proof consists of three parts: proof α, proof β and proof γ. We compute them according to the method proposed in Sect. 3.2. The computation needs the information of packet itself like DataHash, SessionID and router itself like router's ID and symmetric keys. Algorithm 1 describes the main working process of our scheme. And details are put in Sects. 4.2 and 4.3. Table 1 recaps the preceding fields and defines symbols to be used in later design details.

4.2   Proof Construction

Initialization. In this phase, routers generate and exchange symmetric keys with each other. Nodes store corresponding keys in a local table. And every router records its adjacent routers to form a routing table. In this way, they can confirm who is their next hop. Meanwhile, source generates DataHash, SessionID and Timestamp and enclose it into the header.

Construction on the Source. When a packet is created, the ProMPV proof field is empty, and source need to fill all three parts: proof α, proof β and proof γ.

Proof α: It is designed to store the information of a group of three continuous nodes: the one before last R_{i-2}, the previous one R_{i-1} and the current one R_i. Routers encrypt their ID using shared symmetric key between current router and its next router. Since source doesn't have a previous router, this field only contains the source itself.

Proof β: It is a set of all the possible path's information. The interval of it is the previous node R_{i-1}, current node R_i and next node R_{i+1}. When the previous node decide the current node according to the specific strategy, then it would traverse all possible next nodes, calculate their signature according to

Algorithm 1 and store them together. Since source do not have a previous node, the key used for encryption is shared between source and its next node.

Proof γ: Its content is similar with proof β, the only difference is that the interval of it is the node before last R_{i-2}, the last node R_{i-1} and the current node R_i. What's more, it is not computed but inherits Proof β before it updates. Thus, when source creates a packet, the content of proof γ is empty.

Algorithm 1: ProMPV Path Validation

---

1 **Function Source Initialization**
2   DataHash $\leftarrow$ H(P)
3   SessionID $\leftarrow H(t_\sigma \| ID)$
4   Timestamp $\leftarrow$ current time
5 **Function Update for General** R_i **in Path**
6   HASH_Values $\leftarrow$ empty **if** $ID_i == ID_{Destination}$ **then**
7   **End function**
8   Queue.dequeue()
9   Queue.enqueue(ID_i)
10   Proof $\alpha \leftarrow Enc_{K_{i,i+1}}(Queue)$
11   Proof $\beta \leftarrow$ proof γ
12   **if** $ID_i == ID_{Second-to-LastRouter}$ **then**
13   Forward the packet to Destination
14   **End function**
15   **for** *each next Router* $j=i+2$ ***from*** R_i ***to*** $R_{Destination}$ **do**
16   HASH_Value $=H(DataHash \| SessionID \| Timestamp \| ID_j)$
17   Proof γ += cipher_Set($Enc_{K_{i,j}}$(HASH_Values))
18   Forward the packet to next Router
19   Accept the packet and update Proofs
20 **Function Verification for General** R_i **in Path**
21   **if** $ID_i == ID_{Source}$ **then**
22   **End function**
23   Queue $\leftarrow Dec_{K_{i-1,i}}$(Proof α) **if** $Queue[R_{i-1}] \neq ID_{i-1}$ **then**
24   Drop the packet
25   **if** $ID_i \neq ID_{SecondRouter}$ **then**
26   Accept the packet and update Proofs
27   **End function**
28   **if** $HASH\_Values \neq Dec_{K_{i-2,i}}(Proof\ \beta)$ **then**
29   Drop the packet
30   **if** $H(DataHash \| SessionID \| Timestamp \| ID_i)\ NOT\ in$
         $HASH\_Values$ **then**
31   Drop the packet.
32   Accept the packet and update Proofs

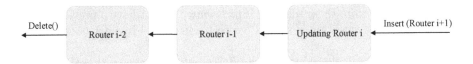

Fig. 2. Update process of proof α

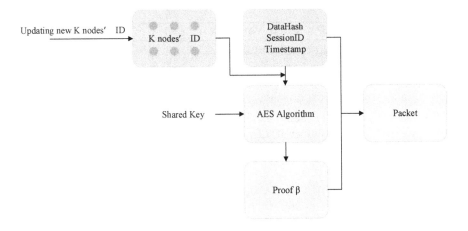

Fig. 3. Update process of proof β

Construction on Intermediate Routers. Intermediate routers only need to update ProMPV proof field. The other three field as DataHash, SessionID and Timestamp are remained, they are used to verify packet's confidentiality, integrity, authentication and non-repudiation.

Proof α: We use a queue to maintain the update of routers' id as Fig. 2 shows. The characteristic of queue is "first in first out", just like the traveling order. Current node push its next router into the queue and pop the node before last. Then current router encrypts the message with key shared with the next router. In this way, the update is guaranteed.

Proof β: The current router first clears the field. Then it travels the routing table and gets the possible nodes after next. Suppose its number is k, hash function would be used to compute k groups of hash values, after that they would be encrypted with corresponding keys each by each. Figure 3 shows the entire process.

Proof γ: When the current router R_i determines its next router R_{i+1}, proof γ inherits proof β before it updates.

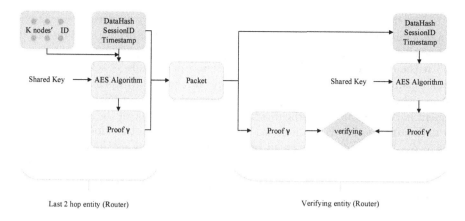

Fig. 4. Verification process of proof γ

4.3 Proof Verification

As aforementioned, DataHash, SessionID and Timestamp are used to defend attack, not directly take part in the validation. So the main task is to verify the ProMPV proof field. If all things can match, then router accepts the packet and transfers it to the next hop, otherwise, it drops the packet.

Proof α: As all the symmetric keys are stored in the local area, router R_i can decrypt the message using the key $K_{i-1,i}$. The decrypted message is a sequence of three nodes: R_{i-2}, R_{i-1} and R_i. Routers can judge whether the packet passes through the right path by this way. And the router id R_{i-2} would take part in the verification of proof γ.

Proof β: Because proof β is a kind of message authentication code provided to the next hop from the previous hop, it doesn't need to be checked when the current hop is being verified.

Proof γ: As Fig. 4 shows, after verifying the proof α, router R_i has already known the router before last R_{i-2}, so that it can find the corresponding symmetric key $K_{i-2,i}$ from local search. Router would link DataHash, SessionID, Timestamp and router id, calculate its hash value using the shared hash function and encrypt it to get a signal. Since proof γ is set of such signals, the only thing router needs to do is search from it to see whether there exists a signal fits each other. If there exists one, the verification is done, or it fails.

4.4 Routing Strategy

From preamble, we can find that the another core design skill of our scheme is the choose of routing strategy, since proof α and proof γ both depend on selecting a next hop first. Besides, a good strategy can greatly improve the efficiency.

According to our ProMPV algorithm, the routing strategy we need to use should be a dynamic, distributed router selection algorithm. Multi-path routing can be controlled by a specific algorithm to ensure that multi-path routing is generated without closed loop [8], and the next hop path node is selected through various parameters, such as multi-path acyclic algorithm. Each network node distinguishes other network nodes into a forward set and a backward set. The element in the forward set indicates that the element is one of the potential routing nodes. If one node B is a forward set's element of the other node A, the node A is also a backward set's element of the node B. As long as the correctness of the forward set and backward set elements is maintained, it is ensured that each time the data packet is forwarded to the elements in the forward set, the routing path is guaranteed to be loop-free. In addition, through specific parameters such as delay, bandwidth utilization, throughput, etc., or a certain policy given by the Internet service provider, such as bypassing certain regions or countries, forcing routing through specific nodes, etc., it can select specific output node in the forward set to meet the advantages of reliability and throughput.

5   Security

It is proved here that when both the source and the receiver are trusted, this multi-path route has the attributes of source authenticity and path verification. This attribute applies to any network configuration, including the configurations where networks contain malicious entity nodes.

Packet Alteration. When the malicious node R_i changes the content of data packet, such as modifying the data packet payload and DataHash, the malicious node does not know the shared key between the previous node R_{i-1} and the next node R_{i+1}. So the forgery of Proof β is not achievable and attacker can only forge Proof γ. When the packet is forwarded to the next entity node R_{i+1}, R_{i+1} uses the forged DataHash to verify the Proof β which cannot be forged. Then it can detect the packet exception, thus resisting Packet Alteration attack.

Packet Injection. Data injection attacks for general positions are easily to be detected due to the presence of hash operation and shared key encryption. So it is difficult to forge or attack. A valid packet injection operation can be replaying a previously packet header and injecting it into the current data packet. However, this replay attack can be protected by determining if the current Timestamp is correct [4].

Packet Deviation. In multi-path segmentation routing, the path deviation attack is actually equivalent to attacking the segment route. Since the next hop(R_{i+1}) is determined, the current router(R_i) will calculate a set of routers for the one after the next hop(R_{i+2}) based on the information of the next hop router(R_{i+1}). After a path offset attack, the next router that arrives at the packet will tell if the updated next hop router is in the pre-computed router set. Therefore, under the condition that each segment route is correct, the validation of validator Proof α, Proof β of each packet can effectively resist path offset attacks.

DoS Attack. In this segmented multi-path routing, each node only needs to keep a fixed number of keys, and it has strong defense against memory attacks. However, the defense capability in computing is weak. Due to the use of a large quantity of encryption and decryption operations, DoS attacks can exhaust the computation power of the victim node by sending a large number of packets.

Collusion. In this segmented multi-path routing, the source authentication and path verification depend on whether the router works as it is, that is, the data packet is normally forwarded according to the protocol. When there are no two consecutive malicious routers in the path, the segmented multi-path route can detect attack and thus resists collusion attacks. However, when there are two consecutive malicious routers on the path, they can forge at the same time, so that the data such as DataHash, SessionID, Timestamp, Proof β, and Proof γ are malicious but consistent. At this time, the downstream routers cannot know that the data packet has been modified, then continue to forward the packets. This situation can be improved by increasing the length of the segment path, but at the meantime it increases the time and space overhead.

6   Implementation

We use OpenSSL [1], which can be concluded by three main functions: SSL protocol library, application, and cryptographic algorithm library. In this experiment, we call correlated function in the cryptographic algorithm library, including the symmetric encryption algorithm AES with 128-bits, 192-bits, 256-bits key and the information digest hash algorithm SHA.

The key sequence and network topology are randomly generated at initialization phase and the relevant hash values are initialized using EVP_Digest with EVP_sha256 being the parameter. Operations for each node (including the source and destination) are divided into two functions: Verification and Update. In the Verification, the decryption function EVP_DecryptInit_ex, EVP_DecryptUpdate, EVP_DecryptFinal_ex in the OpenSSL library are used to decrypt the AES keys of different digits. Similarly, in the Update, the symmetric encryption function EVP_EncryptInit_ex, EVP_EncryptUpdate and EVP_EncryptFinal_ex are able to handle AES encryption operations under different security level.

7   Evaluation

In this section, we compare ProMPV with ICING. Due to the calculation requirement, the experiment run on a 4 core cloud server with Intel Xeon Skylake 6146 (3.2 Hz) and 8 GB memory provided by Tencent. In order to obtain reliable data, all reported statics are average over 10000 runs.

The two main parameters that influence the experiment are total length of the path and security level. According to Figs. 5 and 6, the choice of path length does

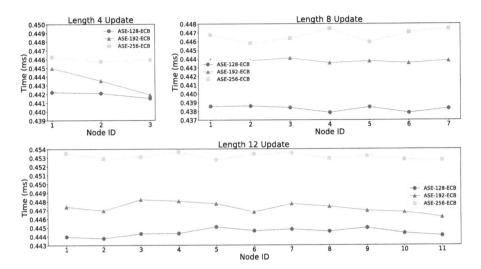

Fig. 5. Proof update time with different security level and path length.

not have much effect on time overhead, because ProMPV cares mainly about segment length. On the other hand, the higher the security level of the encryption algorithm is, the more the method costs. Therefore, ProMPV is flexible for users to determine segment length and security level basing on their own needs. To balance safeness and cost, users can use higher security level or enhance segment length to improve security, or use lower security level or reduce segment length to cut down cost.

As is shown, the time required for the update is much greater than the verification, since the verification only needs to verify Proof α, Proof γ, and the update requires Proof α, Proof β and Proof γ. In addition, Fig. 5 has only $n - 1$ nodes, because the last node's updating time, which only needs to update the Proof α and Proof γ, is much smaller than others and doesn't have a representative meaning.

7.1   Time Overhead

As expected, the time overhead is not related to total length of the path. Also, time cost and node ID are not positively correlated. The controllable factor that influence time overhead is the security level of encryption algorithm, higher security level means more calculation in the process which costs more time.

In the segmented multi-path environment, the update of proof is only related to the number of connected nodes of each node so lines are smooth, while ICING's processing time is proportional to the path length. Since ICING uses cache, the processing time improves dramatically, for creating is $2.6x + 40.1$ μs, and for verifying is $2.6x + 24.4$ μs, where x is the path length. Given a 12 nodes path, the creation time and verification time are 71.3 μs and 55.6 μs respectively. Our

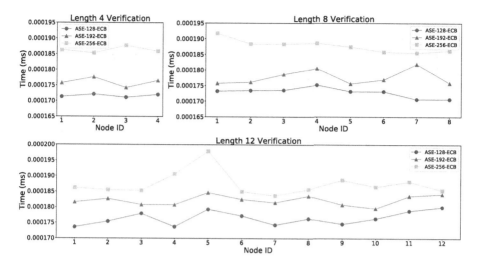

Fig. 6. Proof verify time with different security level and path length.

Table 2. Proof β (or γ) size in 80-bit security level.

Node number	1	2	3	4	5	6	7	8	9	10
Proof β(or γ) size (byte)	10	20	30	40	50	60	70	80	90	100

solution uses the AES algorithm with 256-bit key. It is tested in fully-connected case that each node is connected to 15 other nodes. The time of creating and verifying are about 4.3×10^{-5} s and 5.12×10^{-3} s. And ProMPV can also use cache to accelerate speed and improve performance.

7.2 Space Overhead

As shown in Table 2, the size of proof β (or γ) is positively correlated to the number of connected nodes of each segment's next node, because ProMPV requires information out of the segment to verify the path. Therefore, total length of the path is hardly a factor of space overhead. Also, the security level decides space that each node takes.

Under same security level, the ProMPV header space increases slowly by a much smaller constant compared with ICING as the path grows. For instance, under an 80-bit security level, 10 bytes would add to the proof size of ProMPV for each node while the proof size of ICING increases by 42 bytes [5]. Therefore, our scheme saves header space and makes multi-path validation more feasible.

8   Conclusion

We design and achieve a new multi-path routing scheme, satisfying path validation and source authentication. By cutting entire path to small segments, we overcome the weakness of single-path routing. If we can guarantee every segment's safety, the reliability of path validation scheme can be guaranteed. Besides, the working time doesn't relate to path length as segment method is used but relates to the number of nodes its next node connects with. With specific routing strategy, we can limit the proof size and accelerate speed. And by changing the security level or the segment length, we can sacrifice security to get speed or sacrifice speed to get security. Both theory and experiment tell our scheme's superiority. For future work, we plan to achieve hardware acceleration on it to improve the computation speed without using more computation power.

Acknowledgement. This work is supported by The Natural Science Foundation of Zhejiang Province under Grant No. LY19F020050. We would also like to thank Professor Kai Bu for mentoring us on the project.

References

1. OpenSSL: Cryptography and SSL/TLS Toolkit. https://www.openssl.org/
2. Bu, K., Yang, Y., Laird, A., Luo, J., Li, Y., Ren, K.: What's (not) validating network paths: a survey. arXiv:1804.03385 (2018)
3. He, J., Rexford, J.: Toward internet-wide multipath routing. IEEE Netw. **22**(2), 16–21 (2008)
4. Lee, T., Pappas, C., Perrig, A., Gligor, V., Hu, Y.C.: The case for in-network replay suppression. In: ACM AsiaCCS, pp. 862–873 (2017)
5. Naous, J., Walfish, M., Nicolosi, A., Mazières, D., Miller, M., Seehra, A.: Verifying and enforcing network paths with ICING. In: CoNEXT (2011)
6. Paxson, V.: End-to-end routing behavior in the internet. In: ACM SIGCOMM, pp. 25–38 (1996)
7. Segall, A.: Optimal distributed routing for virtual line-switched data networks. IEEE Trans. Commun. **27**, 201–209 (1979)
8. Singh, R., Singh, Y., Yadav, A.: Loop free multipath routing algorithm, January 2016
9. Villamizar, C.: OSPF optimized multipath (OSPF-OMP), September 2019
10. Wu, B., et al.: Enabling efficient source and path verification via probabilistic packet marking. In: IWQoS (2018)
11. Xu, W., Rexford, J.: Miro: multi-path interdomain routing. In: ACM SIGCOMM (2006)
12. Yang, X., Wetherall, D.: Source selectable path diversity via routing deflections. ACM SIGCOMM **36**, 159–170 (2006)

AHV-RPL: Jamming-Resilient Backup Nodes Selection for RPL-Based Routing in Smart Grid AMI Networks

Taimin Zhang, Xiaoyu Ji, and Wenyuan Xu$^{(\boxtimes)}$

Zhejiang University, Hangzhou, China
{zhangtaimin,xji,wyxu}@zju.edu.cn

Abstract. Advanced metering infrastructure (AMI) is the core component of the smart grid. As the wireless connection between smart meters in AMI is featured with high packet loss and low transmission rate, AMI is considered as a representative of the low power and lossy networks (LLNs). In such communication environment, the routing protocol in AMI network is essential to ensure the reliability and real-time of data transmission. The IPv6 routing protocol for low-power and lossy networks (RPL), proposed by IETF ROLL working group, is considered to be the best routing solution for the AMI communication environment. However, the performance of RPL can be seriously degraded due to jamming attack. In this paper, we analyze the performance degradation problem of RPL protocol under jamming attack. We propose a backup node selection mechanism based on the standard RPL protocol. The proposed mechanism chooses a predefined number of backup nodes that maximize the probability of successful transmission. We evaluation the proposed mechanism through MATLAB simulations, results show the proposed mechanism improves the performance of RPL under jamming attack prominently.

Keywords: Smart grid · Advanced metering infrastructure (AMI) · Jamming · RPL

1 Introduction

Advanced metering infrastructure uses tremendous smart meters as sensing devices to collect user's power usage information, and also as auxiliary devices for power grid monitoring. Smart meters usually adopt wireless technologies for data transmission. Due to the complex and varying electromagnetic environment of the smart meters' installation location, the wireless connection between smart meters are featured with of high packet loss and low transmission rate. Therefore, AMI is considered as a representative of the low power and lossy networks

Supported by National Key R&D Program of China (2018YFB0904900, 2018YFB09 04904).

X. Chu et al. (Eds.): QShine 2019, LNICST 300, pp. 235–251, 2020.
https://doi.org/10.1007/978-3-030-38819-5_15

(LLNs) [1]. In the AMI network communication environment, ensuring reliable and real-time transmission of data is a challenging task, and the key factor to achieve this goal is efficient and robust routing algorithms.

A large amount of research on routing protocols in AMI networks have been counducted, among which IPv6 routing protocol for low-power and lossy networks (RPL) [2] proposed by the IETF ROLL working group is considered to be the best candidate. The aim of the RPL protocol was to overcome routing problems in resource-constrained devices, and security has not been paid enough attention to. Jamming attack is a common attack in wireless networks, it is easy to conduct while can degrade the network's transmission performance severely. In RPL networks, the network topology update frequency is low, and each node transmits data to the data center using a single default node (named preferred parent) as the next hop. When jamming attack causes the preferred parent node's failure, the packet loss rate will increase rapidly. On the other hand, the transmission frequency of RPL networks' control packets is low, so the network topology repair process after the jamming attack is slow. Renofio et al. [3] simulated the performance of an 80-node AMI network implementing RPL protocol under jamming attack. The results show that the repair time of the network topology significantly exceeds the duration of the jamming attack. Considering the low cost and easy-to-implement features of jamming attacks, it poses a significant security threat to RPL networks.

For the above-mentioned jamming attacks, the most easy while efficient defense method is to select backup nodes for each node in the RPL network. When the preferred parent node is no longer available, the RPL node can continue the data transmission by switching to the backup nodes when jamming attack happens, thereby improving the overall transmission performance of the network. Backup nodes selection mechanisms have been studied in existing work to improve RPL networks' transmission performance in congestion scenarios [4–6]. However, backup nodes selection in jamming attack scenarios is essentially different to that in congestion scenarios. The congestion problem is caused by the excessive communication load. The probability of being congested is independent on different nodes. Therefore, increasing backup nodes can increase the probability of successful transmission. In jamming attack scenarios, the probability of transmission failure on different nodes is not independent. If both the preferred parent node and the backup node are within the jamming range, it is very likely that transmission failure will occur on the two nodes at the same time when jamming attack happens. In the rest of this paper, we refer to this phenomenon as the fault correlation between different RPL nodes. Therefore, simply increasing number of backup nodes does not necessarily increase the probability of successful transmission under jamming attack. It is necessary to consider the fault correlation while selecting backup nodes in order to maximize the possibility of successful transmission.

In this paper, we propose AHV-RPL, a backup nodes selection mechanism that can improve the performance of standard RPL protocol under jamming attack. To solve the above-mentioned fault correlation problem, we propose a fault correlation calculation method based on the availability history vector (AHV) metric proposed by Mustafa et al. [7]. The proposed mechanism construct a backup nodes set with the least fault correlation, thus the routing performance of the RPL network under jamming attack can be improved. The main contributions of this paper are as follows:

- We propose a novel backup nodes selection mechanism based on the standard RPL protocol. Compared to other backup nodes selection methods, the proposed mechanism can choose backup nodes that have minimum fault correlation to the preferred parent node, thus increases the probability of successful transmission under jamming attack.
- We propose an efficient AHV delivery mechanism for the RPL's DODAG (Destination Oriented Direct-ed Acyclic Graph) construction process. In this mechanism, each node can calculate its own AHV based on the AHV information it received from the parent nodes.
- The proposed mechanism is evaluated through MATLAB simulations. Results show that our backup nodes selection mechanism can improve the RPL's transmission performance under jamming attack evidently.

We organize the remainder of the paper as follows. In Sect. 2, we discuss the related work. We introduce jamming attack models and formulate the problem in Sect. 3. In Sect. 4, we present our framework for backup nodes selection and give implementation of our algorithms. In Sect. 5, we validate the proposed mechanism through MATLAB simulations. Finally, we conclude in Sect. 6.

2   Related Work

2.1   RPL Background

The RPL protocol is a distance vector routing protocol for low-power lossy networks. Its design follows the topology concept of directed acyclic graphs. Objective function (OF) is used to map the network into multiple non-coincident destination oriented directed acyclic graphs (DODAGs). DODAG has a tree topology and each DODAG corresponds to one root node (DODAG root). All paths point to the root node, which is generally used as a data aggregation node or as a gateway node to connect to an external network (such as Internet).

In order to form a DODAG, each node that has joined the RPL network (referred to as RPL node in the rest of the paper) is assigned with a rank value. Nodes with high rank values selects nodes with lower rank values as their parent node, and the root node has the lowest rank value in the DODAG. The rank value of the node is calculated according to the Objective Function (OF). The commonly used objective function is MRFOF developed by the IETF ROLL Working Group [8]. Assume that the node N_j is the parent node of node N_i, then the rank value of node N_i can be calculates according to MRFOF function:

$$R(N_i) = R(N_j) + ETX(N_i, N_j) \qquad (1)$$

where $R(x)$ represents the rank value of node x in DODAG, and ETX (Expected Transmission Count) is a route metric defined as:

$$ETX = \frac{1}{D_f \times D_r} \tag{2}$$

where D_f refers to the probability that node N_i successfully transmits a packet to node N_j, and D_r refers to the probability that node N_i successfully receives the packet from node N_j. The smaller the ETX, the better the link quality between the node N_i and node N_j, and the higher the packet transmission rate. Conversely, the larger the ETX, the more unstable the link.

A node that has not joined the RPL network needs to select one of the neighboring RPL nodes as the preferred parent node. Then the node can join the network through the preferred parent node. In order to select a preferred parent node, the node first needs to receive the DODAG Information Object (DIO) messages broadcasted by other RPL nodes. Then it extracts the rank value of the source node and the objective function (OF) from the DIO message. The node can calculate its own rank value based on the source node's rank and the OF. Assume that node N_i receives multiple DIO messages from m RPL nodes, and let $\mathcal{N}_r = \{N_{r_1}, N_{r_2}, \ldots, N_{r_m}\}$ represents the set of m RPL nodes. For $N_{r_m} \in \mathcal{N}_r$, the node N_i calculates its own rank value according to Eq. 1, and obtains a set $\mathcal{R} = \{R_1, R_2, \ldots, R_m\}$. In this set, node N_i selects the minimum value as its own rank value and selects the corresponding node as the preferred parent node.

After all nodes have selected the preferred parent node, the construction of the RPL network topology is completed. And all RPL nodes transmit data to the root node through their preferred parent nodes, this process is called uplink data transmission. When the preferred parent node is unavailable, each RPL node needs to reselect the preferred parent node through the repair mechanism.

2.2   RPL Security

The RPL protocol is considered to be the most suitable routing protocol for smart grid communication scenarios. At present, there are a lot of work to study the application of RPL protocol in smart grid environment [9–13]. Although the RPL protocol has broad application prospects in the smart grid, some research also pointed out the security problems of the RPL protocol. Zaidi et al. [14] studied the RPL black hole attack. The attacker uses malicious nodes to attract normal traffic in the network and discard all received packets, which has a great impact on network transmission performance. Mayzaud et al. [15] studied the version number attack against RPL. By using malicious nodes to broadcast malicious messages with manipulated version numbers to the RPL network, the network topology is reorganized and formed. This attack can cause a large number of routing loops, which can reduce the network's life. Wallgren et al. [16] pointed out the harm of identity theft attacks against RPL. The attacker uses malicious nodes to simultaneously clone the identity information of multiple legitimate nodes in the network, thereby achieving the purpose of controlling a large number of nodes on the network. To defense this attack, the RPL nodes needs to be authenticated in combination with the identity information of the node and the registered location information. In addition, wormhole attacks, sybil attacks, and sinkhole attacks in normal wireless sensor networks are also applicable to networks based on RPL routing protocols [17].

2.3 Availability History Vector (AHV)

Mustafa et al. proposed the available history vector (AHV) metric to evaluate the network performance under jamming attack [7]. AHV uses a sequence of bit 0 and bit 1 to represent the availability of a link (or a path) in a past period of time. Specifically, bit 0 means the link (or path) is jammed and can not be used for data transmission, and bit 1 means the link (or path) is available for data transmission.

An efficient way to obtain the AHV of a link is to map the packet delivery rate (PDR) into bit 0 and bit 1 by comparing the PDR with a predefined threshold. Packet delivery rate (PDR) refers to the ratio of successfully transmitted data packets to the total number of transmitted data packets. If node N_i transmits data packets to node N_j, the link PDR between node N_i and node N_j can be defined as:

$$PDR = \frac{C_r}{C_s} \tag{3}$$

where C_s is the total number of packets sent by the N_i node, and C_r is the total number of packets received by the N_j node.

The path AHV can be calculated based on the link AHV. The details of calculating AHVs are given as follows.

- **Link AHV calculation.** As mentioned above, link AHV can be obtained by mapping the link PDR into bit 1s and bit 0s. Specifically, let $A_{i,j}$ be the link between node N_i and node N_j. The AHV of link $A_{i,j}$ can be denoted as $\mathbf{a}_{i,j} = [a_{i,j}^1, a_{i,j}^2, ..., a_{i,j}^t]$. $a_{i,j}^t$ represents the availability of link $A_{i,j}$ at time t and it can be calculated by comparing it to a threshold θ:

$$a_{i,j}^t = \begin{cases} 1, & PDR_i \geq \theta \\ 0, & PDR_i < \theta \end{cases} \tag{4}$$

- **Path AHV calculation.** The path AHV is derived from the link AHVs. Assume path H_j is composed of i links denoted as $A_1, A_2, \ldots, A_i$. Let $\mathbf{a}_i = [a_{i,j}^1, a_{i,j}^2, ..., a_{i,j}^t]$ be the AHV of link A_i, and $\mathbf{h}_j = [h_j^1, h_j^2, ..., h_j^t]$ be the AHV of path H_j. Let $\wedge$ be the bit "and" operation, then the path AHV can be derived from the link AHV:

$$\begin{aligned} \mathbf{h}_j &= [h_i^1, h_i^2, \ldots, h_i^t] = \mathbf{a}_1 \wedge \mathbf{a}_2 \wedge \ldots \mathbf{a}_i \\ h_j^t &= a_1^t \wedge a_2^t \wedge \ldots a_i^t \end{aligned} \tag{5}$$

- **Combination AHV calculation.** In practice, there are usually more than one path between the source node and the destination node. Let V be the combination of several path between the source node and the destination node, AHV is also capable of representing the availability history of the path combination V. Assume the path combination V is composed of path $H_1, H_2, \ldots, H_j$. Let $\mathbf{h}_j = [h_j^1, h_j^2, \ldots, h_j^t]$ be the AHV of path H_j, and $\mathbf{v} = [v^1, v^2, \ldots, v^t]$ be the AHV of combination V. Let $\vee$ be the bit "or" operation, then the combination AHV can be derived from the path AHV:

$$
\begin{aligned}
\mathbf{v} = [v^1, v^2, \ldots, v^t] &= \mathbf{h}_1 \vee \mathbf{h}_2 \vee \ldots \mathbf{h}_j \\
v^t &= h_1^t \vee h_2^t \vee \ldots h_j^t
\end{aligned}
\tag{6}
$$

3   Problem Formulation

3.1   Jamming Attack

The jamming attack utilizes the open nature of the wireless channel and transmit jamming signal at the same frequency as the RPL nodes. This will lead to error bits in the transmitted packets. Thus the data packets cannot pass the verification on the receiver side and will be discarded.

According to the jamming behavior, jammer can be classified into active jammer and reactive jammer [18]. Active jammers do not consider network channel conditions, and use persistent jamming signals to block communication between network nodes. Such attacks can be easily detected. Reactive jammers keep silent when the channel is idle, and transmit jamming signals when there is data transmission on the channel. Due to the stealthy characteristic of reactive jammers, they are more difficult to be detected. The mechanisms designed in this paper are primarily designed to defend RPL networks from reactive jammers.

The signal noise ratio (SNR) indicator is generally used to measure the intensity of the jamming attack. SNR refers to the ratio of the normal signal strength to the jamming signal strength, which is defined as:

$$
SNR = \frac{P_S}{P_N}
\tag{7}
$$

where P_S is the strength of the normal signal and P_N is the strength of the jamming signal.

If presented in decibels (dB), Eq. 7 is converted to:

$$
SNR(dB) = 10 \log_{10} \frac{P_S}{P_N} = P_{d_S} - P_{d_N}
\tag{8}
$$

where $P_{d_S} = 10 \log_{10} P_S$ and $P_{d_N} = 10 \log_{10} P_N$.

In general, there is a positive correlation between PDR and SNR. That is, as SNR increases, the value of PDR rises. The mapping between SNR and PDR can be obtained by mathematical derivation. At a given SNR, the probability of a transmission error for each bit of the transmitted data is $Q\sqrt{2kE_b/N_0}$ [19], where $k \approx 0.85$. E_b/N_0 is the ratio of the average signal strength to the noise signal strength when transmitting each bit of data, and its value is the same as the signal to noise ratio SNR. The function $Q(\cdot)$ represents the probability that the random variable X in the Gaussian distribution $X \sim N(0,1)$ is greater than the threshold z, namely:

$$Q(z) \triangleq p(X > z) = \int_z^\infty \frac{1}{\sqrt{2\pi}} e^{-y^2/2} dy \tag{9}$$

Since the process of erroneous transmission of each bit is independent of each other, assuming that the data packet transmitted between node N_i and node N_j is M bits, the above mapping relationship can be used to derive the link PDR between the node N_i and the node N_j as:

$$PDR = \prod_{i=1}^{M} (1 - Q(\sqrt{2kSNR^i})) \tag{10}$$

where SNR^i corresponds to the signal-to-noise ratio when transmitting the ith bit.

3.2 Failure Correlation

Since the jammer has a certain transmission range, the communication of all nodes located within the jamming range will be affected when jamming attack occurs. Not only the nodes located in the jamming range are affected, nodes that transmit data through the affected nodes will not be able to transmit data. We name this phenomena as fault correlation. As shown in Fig. 1, nodes 4 and 5 lose communication with their preferred parents when jamming attack occurs, so nodes 4 and 5 are fault correlated.

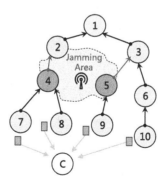

Fig. 1. An example of the fault correlation between node 4 and node 5.

As each node in RPL network selects only a single preferred parent node to transmit data to the root node, if two RPL nodes are fault correlated, their child nodes also have the same fault correlation characteristics. As shown in Fig. 1, node 4 and node 5 are subject to reactive jamming attacks. When the jammer is not active, assume that node C selects node 8 as its preferred parent node, and it selects a backup node from node 7, 9 and 10. If node C selects node 7 or node 9 as the backup node, it will not be able to send data to the root node when jamming attack happens. That is because node 7, node 8 and node 9 are fault correlated since their parent nodes (node 4 and node 5) are fault correlated. If node C selects node 10 as the backup node, it can quickly switch to node 10 and maintain communication with the root node when jamming occurs.

In order to facilitate the quantitative analysis of fault correlation, we adopted the availability history vector (AHV) metric proposed by Mustafa et al. [7]. By continuously recording the link availability according to Eq. 4, a time-varying sequence $a = [a^1, a^2, \ldots, a^t]$ can be obtained, which is the AHV. More generally, assuming that there is a communication path H between node N_i and node N_j, the path can be either a single-hop link or a path composed of multiple links. Then the AHV of the path H can be defined as $h = [h^1, h^2, \ldots, h^t]$, where $h^t \in 0, 1$ represents the availability of path H at time t.

Based on the AHVs defined above, fault correlation can be calculated quantitatively. Notice that there are multiple different paths between node N_i and node N_j. For example, in Fig. 1 there are different paths between node C and node 1, such as C-7-4-2-1, C-8-4-2-1 and C-9-5-3-1 etc. Assume that the AHVs of two paths H_k and H_n are $\mathbf{h}_k = [h_k^1, h_k^2, \ldots, h_k^t]$, and $\mathbf{h}_n = [h_n^1, h_n^2, \ldots, h_n^t]$. Let $\wedge$ denote the bitwise *and* operator, and $\neg$ denote the bitwise *not* operator. Then the fault correlation between paths H_k and H_n can be defined $\phi(H_k, H_n)$:

$$\phi(H_k, H_n) = \sum_{i=1}^{t} \neg h_k^i \wedge \neg h_n^i \tag{11}$$

As the fault correlation between paths H_k and H_n become higher, more bit 0 will occur on the same positions in $\mathbf{h}_k$ and $\mathbf{h}_k$, thus the value of the metric $\phi(H_k, H_n)$ becomes larger. And the lower the fault correlation, the lower the value of the metric $\phi(H_k, H_n)$. Further, the metric can be extended to calculate the fault correlation of a set of paths $\mathcal{H} = \{H_1, H_2, \ldots, H_k\}$. Let $\phi(\mathcal{H})$ denote the fault correlation of the path set $\mathcal{H}$, then:

$$\phi(\mathcal{H}) = \sum_{i=1}^{t} \left(\bigwedge_{j=1}^{k} \neg h_j^i \right) \tag{12}$$

4   Design

The existing backup node selection mechanisms for the RPL protocol are not applicable to the jamming attack situation. The main reason is that the fault correlation between the RPL nodes is not considered in these mechanisms. Based on the AHV definitions and fault correlation metric, we propose AHV-RPL, a backup nodes selection mechanism for the RPL protocol's resistance against jamming attacks.

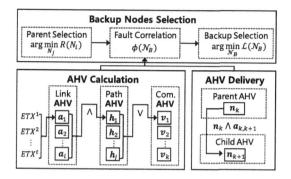

Fig. 2. The framework of AHV-RPL.

4.1 Overview of AHV-RPL

The framework of AHV-RPL is shown in Fig. 2. The proposed AHV-RPL mainly contains three process, i.e. the AHV calculation process, the AHV delivery process, and the backup nodes selection process.

In the AHV calculation process, each node calculate link AHV, path AHV and combination AHV according to Eqs. 4 to 6. The standard RPL protocol uses the metric EXT instead of PDR to indicate the link quality. However, we can map the metric EXT in to link AHV in a similar way to Eq. 4. Let $a = [a^1, a^2, \ldots, a^t]$ denote the AHV of a link, then it can be calculated based on the link's EXT at different times:

$$a^t = \begin{cases} 1, & ETX \leq \theta \\ 0, & ETX > \theta \end{cases} \tag{13}$$

where EXT is defined in Eq. 2 and θ is a predefined threshold. Based on the link AHV, path AHV and combination combination AHV can be efficiently calculated.

Each RPL node can easily calculate the link AHV based on the metric EXT. To calculate path AHV and combination AHV, each node have to obtain path AHV from its parent nodes and deliver the path AHV to its children node. During the DODAG construction process, each RPL node obtains a path AHV from its preferred parent, and calculates the AHV of the link between itself and the parent node. Then it updates the path AHV and deliver it to its children node. By doing so, each RPL node in the network can maintain a link AHV and a path AHV.

The backup nodes selection process is used in the DODAG construction process of the standard RPL protocol. After selecting the preferred parent node, the fault correlation calculation is performed on each RPL node to select a set of backup nodes that has the least fault correlation with the preferred parent.

The improved AHV-RPL protocol enables the RPL node to quickly switch to the backup nodes for uplink data transmission when the RPL network is subjected to jamming attack, thereby improving the overall anti-jamming ability of the network.

Algorithm 1. Node AHV Delivery

1: **Input** : Node AHV n_{i-1} of the preferred parent N_{i-1},
2: **Output** : Node AHV n_i of the preferred parent N_i,
3: **Procedures** :
4: **if** Node N_i is the root node **then**
5:     Initializing $n_0 = [n_0^1, n_0^2, \ldots, n_0^t]$.
6:     For $n_0^i \in n_0$, set $n_0^i \leftarrow 1$.
7:     Broadcasts DIO message that contains n_0.
8: **else**
9:     Receive DIO message from node N_{i-1}.
10:     Extract n_i from DIO message.
11:     Calculate link AHV a_i.
12:     Update node AHV $n_i = n_{i-1} \wedge a_i$.
13:     Broadcasts DIO message that contains n_i.
14: **end if**

4.2 AHV Delivery

The proposed backup nodes selection mechanism requires RPL nodes to obtain calculate the AHV of its default path to the root node. However, each RPL node can only obtain the link AHV information from the surrounding nodes within its receiving range. Therefore, in the process of constructing DODAG, a delivery mechanism of the path AHV is needed. So that each RPL node can calculates the AHV of its own default path to the root node from its parent node's DIO message.

For each RPL node, its default path to the root node is composed of a sequels of preferred parent nodes and is settled once the DODAG is constructed. Thus, we can define node AHV as the AHV of a node's default path to the root node. For node N_i, assume its default path to the root node is composed of the node set $\mathcal{N} = \{N_1, N_2, \ldots, N_i\}$, where N_{i-1} is the preferred parent of N_i. Let $a_{i-1,i}$ denote the AHV of link $A_{i-1,i}$, and $a = [a_{i-1,i}^1, a_{i-1,i}^2, \ldots, a_{i-1,i}^t]$. Then the node AHV of node N_i is defined as:

$$
\begin{aligned}
n_i &= [n_i^1, n_i^2, \ldots, n_i^t] = a_{0,1} \wedge a_{1,2} \wedge \cdots a_{i-1,i} \\
n_i^t &= a_{0,1}^t \wedge a_{1,2}^t \wedge \cdots \wedge a_{i,i-1}^t
\end{aligned}
\tag{14}
$$

where $a_{0,1}$ represents the link AHV between the root node (denoted as N_0) and node N_1.

For a concise representation, we represents $a_{i-1,i}$ as $a_i = [a_i^1, a_i^2, \ldots, a_i^t]$. From the definition of node AHV, we can see that the AHV of each RPL node can be recursively derived from the node AHV of its preferred parent:

$$
\begin{aligned}
n_i &= [n_i^1, n_i^2, \ldots, n_i^t] = n_{i-1} \wedge a_i \\
n_i^t &= n_{i-1}^t \wedge a_i^t
\end{aligned}
\tag{15}
$$

In the above method for calculating the node AHV, RPL nodes receive DIO messages broadcast by their parent node during the DODAG construction process. Each RPL node updates and maintains its own node AHV information according to their parent nodes' AHV. Then, they transmit their node AHV information downward through DIO messages. The process is shown in Algorithm 1. First, the root node initializes its own node availability vector n_0, where $n_0 = [1^1, 1^2, \ldots, 1^t]$. That is, the availability of the root node at each moment is always of value 1. From Eq. 15, we can see that along the path number of bit 1 in the node AHV of the child node is reduced compared to the parent node's AHV, which means the overall usability is degraded.

4.3   Backup Nodes Choosing

To defend against jamming attacks, each RPL node have to select several backup nodes after selecting the preferred parent during the DODAG construction process of the standard RPL protocol. When a RPL node loses communication with its preferred parent due to jamming attack, it can quickly switch to a backup node and maintain data transmission towards the root node. This section presents the details of the proposed backup nodes selection mechanism. When the DODAG construction process is completed, each RPL node will be able to maintain several fault-independent backup nodes along with the preferred parent node.

The backup nodes selection process can be divided into two steps. First, assuming that the node N_i has selected the preferred parent node N_{p_0} and calculated its own Rank. Node N_i can choose nodes with lower rank value among the neighbor nodes as the candidate backup nodes, thereby obtaining a candidate backup node set $\mathcal{N}_P = \{N_{p_1}, N_{p_2}, \ldots, N_{p_k}\}$. Then node N_i selects q nodes from the candidate backup node set $\mathcal{N}_P$ to form a back node set $\mathcal{N}_B = \{N_{b_1}, N_{b_2}, \ldots, N_{b_q}\}$, $\mathcal{N}_B \subseteq \mathcal{N}_P$. The AHV of the backup node set is denoted as m_B.

The requirement for the backup node set $\mathcal{N}_B$ is that the fault correlation metric $\phi(\mathcal{N}_B)$ is as small as possible. In order to calculate the fault correlation metric $\phi(\mathcal{N}_B)$, node N_i is first required to calculate its node AHV n_{b_q+1} according to each parent node $N_{b_q} \in \mathcal{N}_B$. Then node N_i calculates the AHV m_B of the parent node set $\mathcal{N}_B$ based on the AHVs $\{n_{b_1+1}, n_{b_2+1}, \ldots, n_{b_q+1}\}$ obtained in the last step. Let $A_{b+q,i}$ denote the link between node N_{b_q} and node N_i, and its link availability is $a_{b_j,i}$. According to Eq. 15, when node N_i selects node N_{b_q} as the parent node, its own node AHV is:

$$
\begin{aligned}
n_{b_q+1} &= [n^1_{b_q+1}, n^2_{b_q+1}, \ldots, n^t_{b_q+1}] = n_{b_q} \wedge a_{b_q,i} \\
n^t_{b_q+1} &= n^t_{b_q} \wedge a^t_{b_q,i}
\end{aligned}
\tag{16}
$$

Referring to the calculation method of the combination AHV, the AHV of the alternate parent node set $\mathcal{N}_B$ can be derived from Eq. 16. m_B can be expressed as:

$$
m_B = [m^1, m^2, \ldots, m^t] = \bigvee_{j=1}^{q} n_{b_j} \wedge a_{b_j,i}
\tag{17}
$$

Based on the AHV of the above-mentioned backup node set, the fault correlation metric $\phi(\mathcal{N}_B)$ of the backup node set $\mathcal{N}_B$ can be defined as:

$$\phi(\mathcal{N}_B) = \sum_{i=1}^{t} \left(\bigwedge_{j=1}^{q} \neg n_{b_j+1}^i \right) \tag{18}$$

At the same time, we want the overall availability of the backup node set $\mathcal{N}_B$ to be as large as possible. Thus, we denote the overall availability metric as $\psi_{\mathcal{N}_B}(\boldsymbol{m}_B)$, which is defined as:

$$\psi_{\mathcal{N}_B}(\boldsymbol{m}_B) = \sum_{i=1}^{t} m^i \tag{19}$$

The proposed mechanism for the backup node set $\mathcal{N}_B$ requires the fault correlation metric $\phi(\mathcal{N}_B)$ to be as small as possible, the overall availability index $\psi_{\mathcal{N}_B}(\boldsymbol{m}_B)$ to be as large as possible. Therefore, we can define an optimization function $\mathcal{L}(\mathcal{N}_B)$ as:

$$\mathcal{L}(\mathcal{N}_B) = \frac{\phi(\mathcal{N}_B)}{\psi_{\mathcal{N}_B}(\boldsymbol{m}_B)} \tag{20}$$

The process of forming the above-mentioned back node set $\mathcal{N}_B$) can be described as an optimization problem that minimizes the optimization function $\mathcal{L}(\mathcal{N}_B)$:

$$\begin{aligned} &\underset{\mathcal{N}_B}{\arg\min} \ \mathcal{L}(\mathcal{N}_B) \\ &s.t. \ \mathcal{N}_B \subseteq \mathcal{N}_P \end{aligned} \tag{21}$$

The mechanism proposed in this section solves the above optimization problem and selects a back parent node set for each node in the DODAG construction process. To solve this optimization problem, a greedy algorithm is used. At each step, the RPL node selects a candidate backup node that minimizes the optimization function $\mathcal{L}(\mathcal{N}_B)$ and adds it to the backup node set. The details are shown in Algorithm 2.

5   Evaluation

The performance of the proposed AHV-RPL protocol is evaluated through MATLAB simulations. In order to demonstrate the effectiveness of the proposed mechanism under jamming attacks, the performance of AHV-RPL is compared with the standard RPL protocol. At the same time, in order to reflect the superiority of the proposed mechanism compared to the existing backup nodes selection mechanism, we set up a greedy backup node selection mechanism as reference. In the greedy backup node selection mechanism, each RPL node selects nodes with highest node availability as the back nodes after choosing the preferred parent node. The simulation results show that the proposed mechanism preforms better than the greedy backup nodes selection mechanism under jamming attack.

Algorithm 2. Backup Nodes Selection

1: **Input :** Candidate Node Set $\mathcal{N}_P$,
2: **Output :** Backup Node Set $\mathcal{N}_B$,
3: **Procedures :**
4: Initialize $\mathcal{N}_P = \emptyset, \mathcal{L}(\mathcal{N}_B) = 0, k = 1$.
5: **while** $k \leq q$ **do**
6:     Choose node $N_{p_k} \in \mathcal{N}_P$ that minimize $\mathcal{L}(\mathcal{N}_B \cup N_{p_k})$.
7:     Add node N_{p_k} to $\mathcal{N}_B$.
8:     Update $\mathcal{L}(\mathcal{N}_B) = \mathcal{L}(\mathcal{N}_B \cup N_{p_k})$.
9:     Delete node N_{p_k} from $\mathcal{N}_P$.
10:    $k \leftarrow k + 1$
11: **end while**

Table 1. Definition of the parameters in simulation

Parameter	Meaning	Value
L	Size of AMI network	500 m
P_J	Transmit power of jammer	25 mW
P_T	Transmit power of smart meter	10 mW
G	Gain of the antenna	1
P_N	Power of ambient noise	−80 dBm
f_T	Signal frequency	2.4 GHz
η	Path loss exponent	2.40

5.1 Simulation Setup

The simulation simulates a 60-node RPL network with node locations randomly distributed in the range $[0, 500] \times [0, 500]$, as is shown in Fig. 3. The entire network constitutes a directed acyclic graph where node 1 is the root node. The arrows between the nodes represent the communication links. Table 1 shows the parameter values set during the simulation.

In order to evaluate the performance of the proposed mechanism, we define the end-to-end PDR of RPL node N_i as:

$$PDR_i = \frac{C_{r_i}}{C_{s_i}} \tag{22}$$

where C_{s_i} represents the total number of packets sent by the node N_i to the root node, and C_{r_i} represents the total amount of packets received by the root node from the node N_i. Based on Eq. 22, assume that there are n RPL nodes in the network, then the average end-to-end PDR of the RPL network can be defined as:

$$PDR_A = \frac{1}{n} \sum_{i=1}^{n} PDR_i \tag{23}$$

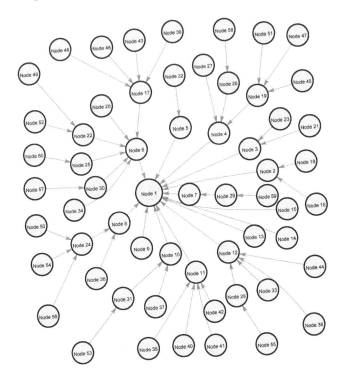

Fig. 3. Topology of the simulated RPL network.

5.2   Results

Using the defined average end-to-end packet delivery rate evaluation metrics, we compares the improved AHV-RPL protocol with the standard RPL protocol under jamming attacks. In order to reflect the superiority of the proposed mechanism over existing backup nodes selection mechanism, we setup a greedy backup node selection mechanism. In the greedy backup node selection mechanism, each node selects nodes with the lowest ETX value as the backup nodes.

Figure 4 shows the average end-to-end packet delivery rate of the network when the number of candidate nodes N is different under the jamming attack. The standard RPL (named 'Original' in the figure) is used as a reference. As the number of candidate nodes N increases, the performance of the greedy backup node selection (named 'Greedy' in the figure) and the proposed AHV-RPL (named 'AHV' in the figure) are improved. The performance of the proposed AHV-RPL is better than that of the greedy backup node selection. When the number of backup nodes reaches three, the performance of the proposed AHV-RPL is 39.7% higher than that of the greedy backup node selection algorithm, and the average packet delivery rate is 14.6 times that of the standard RPL algorithm.

Figure 5 shows the effect of the jammer's transmit power on the performance of the proposed algorithm. Assuming that the number of backup parent nodes for each node is 3, the jammer's transmit power is set to a different value between

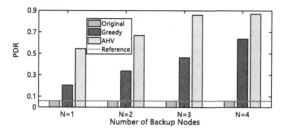

Fig. 4. Impact of number of backup nodes.

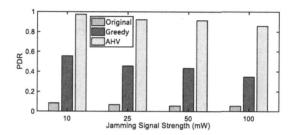

Fig. 5. Impact of jamming signal strength.

10 mW and 100 mW, and the power of the normal node is 10 mW. It can be found that the performance of the greedy backup node selection algorithm and the proposed AHV-RPL algorithm are attenuated as the signal strength of the jammer increases. When the interference source transmission power is 100mW, the average end-to-end packet delivery rate of the proposed AHV-RPL algorithm is still above 85%, and the greedy alternate node selection algorithm is reduced to less than 35%. When the jammer's transmit power is increased from 10mW to 100mW, the packet delivery rate of the greedy backup node selection algorithm is reduced by 21%, and the AHV-RPL algorithm is reduced by 11%. It can be seen that the robustness of the AHV-RPL algorithm is better than that of the greedy backup node selection algorithm.

Figure 6 shows the impact of jammer's location on the average end-to-end packet delivery rate of the whole network. Assume that the number of whole parent nodes of each node is 3, the jammer's transmit power is 10mW, and the normal node power is 10mW. The root node of the network is at (235, 254), and the x and y coordinates of the interferer are set to different values between 100 and 400, respectively. It can be found that the closer the location of the jammer is to the root node, the lower the average end-to-end packet delivery rate of the standard RPL and the greedy backup node selection algorithm. This is because RPL nodes close to the root node have a large number of child nodes. When these RPL nodes are interfered, the sub-nodes have strong fault correlation, so the performance of standard RPL and the greedy backup is degraded. The proposed AHV-RPL mechanism takes into account the characteristics of fault correlation, so its performance is less affected by the location of the jammer.

The experimental results show that the average end-to-end packet delivery rate of the AHV-RPL algorithm is higher than 85% no matter where the jammer is, and its performance is better than the standard RPL and greedy backup node selection algorithm.

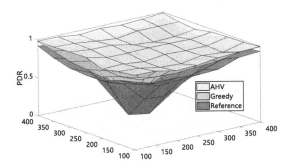

Fig. 6. Impact of jammer's position.

6   Conclusion

The RPL routing protocol in the smart grid is vulnerable to jamming attack, and the data transmission performance of the network will be greatly affected under jamming attack. An easy while efficient defense method to defend RPL network against jamming attacks is to select backup nodes for each node in the RPL network. Existing backup node selection mechanisms for the RPL protocol are mainly to solve the load balancing problem and it not applicable to the jamming attack scenario. In view of the above problems, this paper proposed an improvement mechanism for the RPL protocol. We analyzed and modeled the performance degradation problem of RPL network under jamming attack. Based on the AHV metric, the fault correlation between nodes can be quantitatively analyzed using our the fault correlation metric we developed. Based on this, a backup nodes selection mechanism is proposed to construct a backup node set with the least fault correlation for each RPL node. When the preferred parent node of a RPL node fails due to the jamming attack, it can quickly switch to the backup node and continue data transfer towards the root node. Finally, the performance of the proposed AHV-RPL are evaluated through MATLAB simulations. The results show that the proposed mechanism can greatly improve the performance of the standard RPL protocol under jamming attack.

References

1. Ancillotti, E., Bruno, R., Conti, M.: RPL routing protocol in advanced metering infrastructures: an analysis of the unreliability problems. In: Proceedings of the Sustainable Internet and ICT for Sustainability, SustainIT, Pisa, Italy, pp. 1–10 (2012)
2. Winter, T., et al.: RPL: IPv6 routing protocol for low-power and lossy networks. IETF RFC 6550 (2012)

3. Renofio, J.R.R., Pellenz, M.E., Jamhour, E., Santin, A.O., Penna, M.C., Souza, R.D.: On the dynamics of the RPL protocol in AMI networks under jamming attacks. In: Proceedings of the IEEE International Conference on Communications, Kuala Lumpur, Malaysia, pp. 1–6. ICC (2016)
4. Pavkovic, B., Theoleyre, F., Duda, A.: Multipath opportunistic RPL routing over IEEE 802.15.4. In: Proceedings of the International Symposium on Modeling Analysis and Simulation of Wireless and Mobile Systems, MSWiM, Miami, Florida, USA, pp. 179–186 (2011)
5. Duquennoy, S., Landsiedel, O., Voigt, T.: Let the tree bloom: scalable opportunistic routing with ORPL. In: Proceedings of the ACM Conference on Embedded Network Sensor Systems, SenSys, Roma, Italy, pp. 2:1–2:14 (2013)
6. Tahir, Y., Yang, S., McCann, J.A.: BRPL: backpressure RPL for high-throughput and mobile iots. IEEE Trans. Mob. Comput. **17**(1), 29–43 (2018)
7. Mustafa, H.A., Zhang, X., Liu, Z., Xu, W., Perrig, A.: Jamming-resilient multipath routing. IEEE Trans. Depend. Secur. Comput. **9**(6), 852–864 (2012)
8. Gnawali, O., Levis, P.: The minimum rank with hysteresis objective function. IETF RFC 6719 (2012)
9. Ancillotti, E., Bruno, R., Conti, M.: The role of the RPL routing protocol for smart grid communications. IEEE Commun. Mag. **51**(1), 75–83 (2013)
10. Ropitault, T., Lampropulos, A., Pelov, A., Toutain, L., Vedantham, R., Chiummiento, P.: Doing it right - Recommendations for RPL in PLC-based networks for the Smart Grid. In: Proceedings of the IEEE International Conference on Smart Grid Communications, pp. 452–457. SmartGridComm, Venice, Italy (2014)
11. Ho, Q., Gao, Y., Rajalingham, G., Le-Ngoc, T.: Robustness of the routing protocol for low-power and lossy networks (RPL) in smart grid's neighbor-area networks. In: Proceedings of the IEEE International Conference on Communications, pp. 826–831. ICC, London, United Kingdom (2015)
12. Yang, Z., Ping, S., Sun, H., Aghvami, A.: CRB-RPL: A Receiver-Based Routing Protocol for Communications in Cognitive Radio Enabled Smart Grid. IEEE Trans. Veh. Technol. **66**(7), 5985–5994 (2017)
13. Lemercier, F., Montavont, N.: Performance Evaluation of a RPL Hybrid Objective Function for the Smart Grid Network. In: Proceedings of the International Conference on Ad Hoc Networks and Wireless, ADHOC-NOW, pp. 27–38. Saint-Malo, France (2018)
14. Zaidi, S.A.R., Ghogho, M.: Stochastic geometric analysis of black hole attack on smart grid communication networks. In: Proceedings of the IEEE International Conference on Smart Grid Communications, SmartGridComm, Tainan, Taiwan, pp. 716–721 (2012)
15. Mayzaud, A., Badonnel, R., Chrisment, I.: A distributed monitoring strategy for detecting version number attacks in RPL-based networks. IEEE Trans. Netw. Serv. Manag. **14**(2), 472–486 (2017)
16. Wallgren, L., Raza, S., Voigt, T.: Routing attacks and countermeasures in the RPL-based Internet of Things. IJDSN **9**(8) (2013)
17. Kamgueu, P.O., Nataf, E., Djotio, T.N.: Survey on RPL enhancements: a focus on topology, security and mobility. Comput. Commun. **120**, 10–21 (2018)
18. Wei, X., Wang, Q., Wang, T., Fan, J.: Jammer localization in multi-hop wireless network: a comprehensive survey. IEEE Commun. Surv. Tutorials **19**(2), 765–799 (2017)
19. Rappaport, T.S.: Wireless Communications - Principles and Practice. Prentice Hall, Upper Saddle River (1996)

Privacy Protection Routing and a Self-organized Key Management Scheme in Opportunistic Networks

Yang Qin[✉], Tiantian Zhang, and Mengya Li

School of Computer Science and Technology, Harbin Institute of Technology (Shenzhen), Shenzhen, China
csyqin@hit.edu.cn, 3344316263@qq.com, 1532732482@qq.com

Abstract. The opportunistic network adopts the disconnected store-and-forward architecture to provide communication support for the nodes without an infrastructure. As there is no stable communication link between the nodes, so that forwarding messages is via any encountered nodes. Social networks based on such opportunistic networks will have privacy challenges. In this paper, we propose a privacy protection scheme routing based on the utility value. We exploit the Bloom filter to obfuscate the friends lists and the corresponding utility values of nodes in order to make the routing decisions. This is easy to implement with high performance. Considering no infrastructure and stable link in opportunistic networks, this paper presents a self-organized key management system consisting of an identity authentication scheme based on the zero-knowledge proof of the elliptic curve and a key agreement scheme based on the threshold cryptography. The nodes prove their identities by themselves, and each node carries a certificate library to improve the authentication efficiency and success rate. In order to ensure the forward security and improve the session key agreement rate and the success rate, we exploit threshold cryptography to divide the session key, which could reduce the communication consumption of the traditional Diffie-Hellman (DH) algorithm. The experimental simulation results show that the proposed schemes are much better than the existing schemes for opportunistic networks.

Keywords: Opportunistic network · Routing · Privacy protection · Key management system

1 Introduction

In recent years, the rapid popularization and development of mobile devices have promoted many new technologies with taking advantages of their growing processing power and storage space. One of the most rapidly developing technologies is the opportunistic network, which organizes these mobile devices in a disconnected ad hoc manner. Such opportunistic networks can be used to create new applications, such social networks, et.al. However, because of no infrastructure and stable communication

© ICST Institute for Computer Sciences, Social Informatics and Telecommunications Engineering 2020
Published by Springer Nature Switzerland AG 2020. All Rights Reserved
X. Chu et al. (Eds.): QShine 2019, LNICST 300, pp. 252–268, 2020.
https://doi.org/10.1007/978-3-030-38819-5_16

link, traditional security schemes, such as the public key infrastructure (PKI), are not suitable for opportunistic networks. Shikfa [1] pointed out the security problems in opportunistic networks, such as node selfishness [2, 3], routing security, and privacy protection. To ensure the practicability of the network, security issues, such as identity authentication and message transmission, must be considered. Since the opportunistic network needs to rely on intermediary devices to forward messages, there may be different privacy issues for different routing protocols. For example, the routing protocol that forwards messages based on the similarity of user attributes [4–6] needs to protect the attribute information. The routing protocol that forwards messages based on the utility values [7–10] needs to protect the friends list and the corresponding utility values. The routing protocol that forwards messages based on location information [11] needs to protect the location of the node. In addition, the social network routing forwards messages via nodes in the sender or recipient's social networks, which may disclose the friends lists of nodes. So the privacy disclosure is an important problem with social networks. How to choose the appropriate next-hop node while protecting the user's privacy is a hot topic in current research.

In order to ensure opportunistic networks security and availability, the key management system must be considered. The traditional PKI key management system based on certificate authority (CA) is not applied to opportunistic networks because there is no infrastructure and all nodes are equally self-organized in opportunistic networks. There is no CA that can always stay online to obtain the node's public key certificate.

In addition, during message transmission, in order to implement the PGP, forward security usually needs to be maintained. The existing solution generally adopts the DH key agreement protocol [9] or its variants, such as ECC-based key agreement protocol [10]. However, the communication overhead is relatively large, and thus is not applicable in the opportunistic network due to the high delay. Therefore, new algorithms are needed to solve these problems.

Therefore, we propose a privacy protection routing scheme and a self-organized key management scheme, which makes the following contributions:

- We introduce the Bloom filter to protect nodes privacy in the opportunistic network. We use the Bloom filter to store the friends list and the corresponding utility values of nodes, which obfuscates node privacy and introduces uncertainty to ensure network security.
- We present a self-organizing key management system based on the zero-knowledge proof of the elliptic curve and the threshold cryptography, which consists of identity authentication and key agreement. The system generates certificates, including identity information, public and private keys, and TTL relying on nodes themselves. In addition, the nodes also prove their identity on their own.
- We exploit threshold cryptography to divide the shared session key, and separate key agreement from message transmission to ensure forward security and speed up the session key agreement procedure.

The rest of the paper is organized as follows. Section 2 shows the related works. Section 3 is the detailed design of the privacy protection scheme. Section 4 is the design of the self-organized key management scheme, including identity authentication based on the zero-knowledge proof and the key agreement algorithm based on the threshold cryptography. We evaluate the performance of all schemes proposed in the paper in Sect. 5. And Sect. 6 concludes the paper.

2   Related Works

In order to prevent malicious nodes from stealing the privacy of the node, Cadger and Curran [11] separated the privacy of the node from the real ID of the node to protect the node's privacy by geographic routing. Zhi [12] proposed an anonymous geographic routing algorithm. An anonymous table was used to store the node's fake ID and the corresponding geographic locations in order to avoid the leakage of identity and location information by geographic routing in communication. Zhou [13] proposed a novel threshold credit incentive strategy (TCBI) for a vehicle delay tolerant network and a TCBI-based privacy-preserving packet forwarding protocol, which can resist harmful attacks on vehicles and protect vehicle privacy well. Pidgin [14] is a privacy-preserving interest and content sharing scheme for opportunistic networks that does not disclose privacy to the untrusted party. Its main idea is to use CP-ABE to regulate content access, and Pidgin uses public key encryption and keyword search (PRKS) scheme to encrypt plaintext CP-ABE policy to protect privacy. TRSS [15] is a trust routing scheme based on social similarity, which establishes the social trust of nodes according to the trust-worthiness of nodes and their encounter history. On the basis of social trust, the untrusted nodes are detected and deleted from the trusted list. When forwarding messages, only the data packets of trusted nodes are forwarded to ensure system security. Boldrini [16] proposes a context-aware framework for routing and forwarding in opportunistic networks, which uses user behavior and social relationships to drive the forwarding process. The framework divides network users into groups by using key management, and protects the privacy of nodes through strict contact control. However, introducing key management is too complex for opportunistic networks. Parris et al. [17] proposed the Obfuscated Social Network Routing embedding each node in the nodes' social networks into a Bloom filter, and making a routing decision according to the Bloom filter. However, the Obfuscated Social Network Routing - only obfuscating the node's identifier – cannot compare the utility values to make the correct decision.

In order to be able to obtain the user's public key without a CA, Shamir [18] proposed an identity-based cryptosystem (IBC), which allowed users to verify other users' signatures without exchanging public keys. However, the scheme assumed the existence of a trusted key generation center. Boneh [19] first proposed a practical algorithm for identity encryption. The system was based on the Weil pairing and has chosen ciphertext security. Seth [20] proposed a hierarchical identity-based cryptograph (HIBC), which was the first proposed identity cryptography for DTN networks. This scheme proposed a solution that used opportunistic connections to initiate secure channels by disconnected users, authenticate each other through opportunistic links, and protect disconnected users from identity leakage attacks. Kumar [21] proposed a secure and effective threshold key distribution protocol. The protocol does not require any secure channel to issue the private key, and is secure until the threshold number of KPAs is compromised. Another solution is the certificateless encryption proposed by Al-Riyami and Paterson [22], which needs a trusted third-party key generation center (KGC) that contains the system's master key. Liu [23] proposed IKM, an identity based key management scheme, which is a new combination of identity based and threshold cryptography. IKM is a certificateless solution, because the public key of mobile node can be directly derived from its known IDs plus some public information, which eliminates the need of certificate-based authentication public key distribution in traditional public key management scheme. Capkun [24] proposed an ad-hoc key management system in which each node acts as a CA to authenticate other nodes, eventually forming a chain of certificates that authenticate the node by looking up the chain of certificates. However, the certificate chain needs to form a complete trusted link, which is less efficient and has a lower success rate of authentication.

3   Privacy Protection Routing Scheme

In this paper, a scheme based on the Bloom filter is proposed to obfuscate the friends list and the corresponding utility values. It can protect the privacy of nodes.

3.1   Bloom Filter

The Bloom filter is a probabilistic data structure that maps elements to vectors by multiple hashes, which supports the probabilistic querying. Here, it is assumed that the *ID* information ID_l of a node's friend is embedded within the Bloom filter. First use *10* different random number generators $(F_1, F_2, ..., F_{10})$ to generate *10* fingerprints information $(f_1, f_2, ..., f_{10})$. Then using a random number generator G maps $(f_1, f_2, ..., f_{10})$ to *10* integers $g_1, g_2, ..., g_{10}$ in the range of *1* to *100,000*, and set the value of the *10* positions to *1* (see Fig. 1).

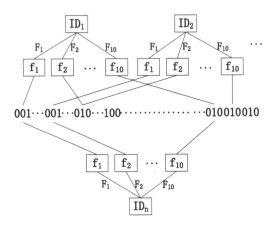

Fig. 1. The principle of the Bloom filter.

Suppose that we want to determine whether the node ID_n is in the Bloom filter. We use the same mapping function to execute the same processing, and observe whether all the *10* positions are *1*. If the nodes are in the Bloom filter, they must be all *1*. However, at this time, a "false positive" may occur, that is, the actual node is not in the, but all its positions are found to be *1*. This is because these *10* positions may be cross-mapped by other nodes, so that misjudgment may occur. We evaluate the misjudgment probability further in Sect. 3.3. Because of the misjudgment, the Bloom filter is used to protect the privacy.

3.2 Privacy Protection Routing Scheme

Parris et al. [17] adopted the Bloom filter to obfuscate the friends list to protect privacy, which can only verify whether node a satisfies the Bloom filter. Assuming that node a forwards a message to node d through intermediate node b or intermediate node c, the next-hop node needs to be correctly chosen without knowing the accurate utility values of node b and c reaching to node d. However, the scheme Parris proposed cannot compare the utility values and make correct decisions. Therefore, this paper makes improvements to this scheme by adding more information about the utility values in the Bloom filter. As shown in Table 1, we add a binary vector (Vector 2) in which each element corresponds to each element of the previous binary vector (Vector 1).

Table 1. The information is stored by nodes.

Vector	Description	Example
1	Storage of the friend information of the node	1010110010101...10010...010000
2	Storage of the utility value of the node	0010010010100...10010...010000

It is used to store utility values of the node reaching to other nodes. For example, the utility value of a node reaching to another node is *0.7*. Then *7* positions among *10* positions chosen randomly, where the friend node *ID* is hashed in Vector *1*, in Vector *2* to *1* (assuming that *10* hash functions are chosen).

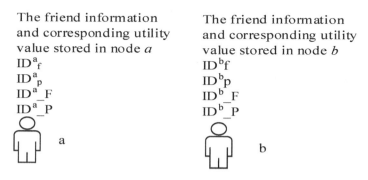

The friend information and corresponding utility value stored in node *a*

ID^a_f
ID^a_p
ID^a_F
ID^a_P

a

The friend information and corresponding utility value stored in node *b*

ID^b_f
ID^b_p
ID^b_F
ID^b_P

b

Fig. 2. The information is stored in nodes.

Algorithm 1 : Initialize Network

1: Procedure initNetwork()
2: *m* presents the size of vectors in the Bloom filter, and the initial value of m is set to *500*.
3: *k* refers to the number of hash functions in the Bloom filter, and its initial value is *10*.
4: *n* refers to the size of the network.
5: for ID^i in network:
6:    init(ID^i_f) //Initialize the friends list of ID^i.
7:    init(ID^i_p) //Initialize the utility values list of ID^i.
8: The initial value of *P_INIT* is set to *0.75*.
9: The initial value of *BETA* is set to *0.25*.
10: The initial value of *GAMMA* is set to *0.98*.
11: end procedure

After initialization by Algorithm *1*, supposing that node *a* encounter node *b*, Fig. 2 shows information stored in the nodes. If node *a* needs to send a message to node *d*, node *b* transmits ID^b_f and ID^b_p to node *a*. Node *a* decides whether to send the message to node *b* by comparing P_{f_bd} which is the probability that node *b* reaches the destination node *d* with P_{t_ad} which is the probability that node *a* itself reaches the destination node *d*. Then ID^a_F, ID^a_P, ID^a_f and ID^a_p are updated, which includes an aging update and direct encounter nodes and transfer node update. At this time, updating and forwarding operations are carried out on node a via executing Algorithm 2, and the same operations are carried out on node b.

Algorithm 2: Aging Updating and The Utility Value Update of Directly Encountered Nodes and Transferring Nodes

1. Procedure updatePrediction (ID^a, ID^b)
2. Node b transmits $ID^b{}_f$ and $ID^b{}_p$ to node a.
3. for c in ID^a_F:
4. $P_{t\_ac} = P_{t\_ac\_old} * (GAMMA^\wedge\ timeDiff)$
5.   // Predict aging probability of P_{t_ac}.
6. $P_{t\_ab} = P_{t\_ab\_old} + (1 - P_{t\_ab\_old}) * P\_INIT)$
7. //Predict initial probability of P_{t_ab}.
8. if $ID^b{}_f[H^1{}_{ID}{}^d]$, $ID^b{}_f[H^2{}_{ID}{}^d]$, ..., $ID^b{}_f[H^k{}_{ID}{}^d] = 1$ then
9. $P_{f\_bd} = (ID^b{}_p[H^1{}_{ID}{}^d] + ID^b{}_p[H^2{}_{ID}{}^d] + ... + ID^b{}_p[H^k{}_{ID}{}^d])/k$
10.   //Calculate the utility value of node b related to node d
11.   if $P_{f\_bd} > P_{t\_ad}$ then
12.   Transfer to node b
13. Reset $ID^a{}_f$, $ID^a{}_p$ to 0 and update them according to ID^a_F and ID^a_P
14. for c in ID^a_F:
15.   if c in $ID^b{}_f$ then
16. $P_{t\_ac} = P_{t\_ac\_old} + (1 - P_{t\_ac\_old}) * P_{t\_ab} * P_{f\_bc} * BETA$
17.   Calculate $H^1{}_{ID}{}^c$, $H^2{}_{ID}{}^c$ ... $H^k{}_{ID}{}^c$
18. $ID^a{}_f[H^1{}_{ID}{}^d]$, $ID^a{}_f[H^2{}_{ID}{}^d]$, ..., $ID^a{}_f[H^k{}_{ID}{}^d] = 1$
19.   Select Pt_ac*k random positions in the
20.   corresponding $ID^a{}_p$ positions, and set the
21.   value of these positions to 1. Assuming that there is
22.   already s positions, then set the value of the other
23. Pt_ac*k-s random positions to 1 in addition
24. End procedure

Important notations for Algorithm 1 and 2 are summarized in Table 2.

Table 2. Notation

Symbol	Description
friends	Vector 1, mapping the friend ID to k different positions by k hash functions
predictions	Vector 2, storing the utility value
m	The length of friends and predictions
friends[i]	The value of the ith position in friends
predictions[i]	The value of the ith position in predictions
n	The size of the network
k	The number of hash functions in the Bloom filter
H^i	The ith hash function

(continued)

Table 2. (*continued*)

Symbol	Description
$H_{ID}^{i\ a}$	The positions that ID^a is hashed to by hash functions
ID_f^a	The friend array of ID^a
ID_p^a	The predictions array of ID^a
ID^a_F	The friends set of ID^a $\{ID^a\_{F1}, ID^a\_{F2}, ..., ID^a\_{Fn}\}$. Each node stores their friend list and utility value to generate the friends and predictions, which is the node privacy
ID^a_P	The friends' utility value set of ID^a $\{P_{t\_ab}, P_{t\_ac}, ...,\}$. This is the node privacy
P_{t_ab}	The utility value of ID^a about ID^b
P_{f_ab}	The utility value of ID^a related to ID^b is calculated according to ID_f^a and ID_p^a
network	All nodes of the network
P_INIT	Predict probability initialization constant, $P_{t\_ab} = P_{t\_ab\_old} + (1 - P_{t\_ab\_old}) * P\_INIT)$
BETA	Predict probability transfer value scaling constant, and calculate the transferring probability from a to c through intermediate node b, $P_{t\_ac} = P_{t\_ac\_old} + (1 - P_{t\_ac\_old}) * P_{t\_ab} * P_{f\_bc} * BETA$
timeDiff	The time from the last update used to calculate the aging probability
GAMMA	Predict probabilistic aging constants, $P_{t\_ac} = P_{t\_ac\_old} * (GAMMA^{timeDiff})$

3.3 Misjudgment Probability Analysis

Assuming that there are m bits in each vector, the encountered node has n friends, and there are k random hash functions that are independent of each other. The friend node's ID is mapped to k positions which are set to 1 after hashing once, then the probability that a position is not set to 1 is $1 - 1/m$. The probability that this position is not set to 1 after hashing for k times is $(1 - 1/m)^k$. Then the probability that the position has not been set to 1 yet is $(1 - 1/m)^{kn}$ after n friends are hashed. So the probability of a position being set to 1 in an array is $1 - (1 - 1/m)^{kn}$. In order to determine whether a node is its friend, k hash functions are required to hash the node to k positions, so the probability of all these positions being 1 is $(1 - (1 - 1/m)^{kn})^k \approx (1 - e^{-kn/m})^k$. If the bloom filter is used for storage, the probability of misjudgment is generally very low for $k * n < m$, such as about 0.01 for $k * n = m$. However, when it is used for privacy protection as here, it can make $k * n > m$. Table 3 lists the comparison of misjudgment probability when $k = 10$ and m/($k * n$) under different circumstances, where the greater the misjudgment probability, the greater the privacy protection degree.

Table 3. Comparison of misjudgment probability under different m/($k * n$).

m/($k * n$)	0.4	0.45	0.5	0.55	0.6	0.65	0.7	0.75	1
$(1 - e^{-kn/m})^k$	0.424	0.317	0.233	0.170	0.123	0.089	0.064	0.046	0.01

4 Self-organized Key Management System

Considering that there is no infrastructure in the opportunistic network such as the certificate authority (CA) and there is no stable link causing the communication overhead being relatively large, the traditional identity authentication scheme and key agreement scheme are not suitable. Therefore, according to the characteristics of opportunistic networks mentioned above, we design a self-organized key management system, including an identity authentication scheme based on the zero-knowledge proof and a key agreement scheme based on the threshold cryptography.

4.1 Identity Authentication Scheme

The identity authentication scheme is applied for opportunistic networks that automatically allocate IP addresses, such as the allocation scheme proposed by Weniger [25]. The detailed process of the scheme based on elliptic curve based the zero-knowledge proof protocol is shown below.

System Initialization. Firstly, broadcasting the generator P and hash function H over the whole network. Then each node i generates public and private key pairs (P_i, S_i), and private identity $X_i = [x_1, x_2, \ldots\ldots, x_k]$ and public identity $Q_i = [Q_1, Q_2, \ldots\ldots, Q_k]$ on its own. Then the node's certificate is $(Q_i, TTL, P_i, H(Q_i), S_i(TTL))$, where $H(Q_i)$ is the IP address of the node that is unique in the network. TTL is the life time of the public-private key pair (P_i, S_i). Finally, sending its certificate to the encountered node to store and verify.

Certificate Verification Phase. At the phase, if node A requests to verify the identity of node B, then node B transmits the certificate $(Q_i, TTL, P_i, H(Q_i), S_i(TTL))$ and $V = r * P$ (r is randomly generated by B) to A.

Firstly, node A checks whether the certificate is timeout. If not, $H(Q_i)$ is calculated and verifies whether the certificate is correct. If not, it indicates that the identity is wrong, otherwise it randomly generates k random numbers $(m_1, m_2, \ldots\ldots, m_k)$, and transmits them to node B. Then node B calculates $r + \sum_{i=1}^{k} m_i * x_i$ and returns to node A. Because $Q_i = x_i * P$, $V = r * P$, node A can verify whether $(r + \sum_{i=1}^{k} m_i * x_i) * P$ is equal to $V + \sum_{i=1}^{k} m_i * Q_i$. If so, B's public identity can be trusted.

Certificate Exchange Phase. Since there is no stable communication link between the source node and the destination node in an opportunistic network, if we use the above zero-knowledge proof authentication scheme to verify node's identity, the verification between the nodes needs to be verified through multiple communications. Therefore, if the destination node is not in the communication range of source node, the delay may be large and the efficiency is low.

Therefore, each node need store the certificates of other nodes locally. The number of certificates stored can be adjusted according to the node's own storage resources.

Messaging Phrase. Suppose node A wants to transmit a message to node B, then node A first checks whether there is the certificate of node B in the local trusted certificate library, and if so, it transmits, otherwise, node A performs the above authentication procedure.

Certificate Update Phase. Each node regularly updates the local certificate library. If P_i time out, the certificate will be removed from the certificate library, which is a passive update. In addition, if the node thinks that their public key is insecure, it can re-generate a new public-private key pair to form a new certificate and sends it to their neighbors.

4.2   Key Agreement Scheme

The key agreement protocol using the asymmetric key and DH key exchange algorithm can effectively resist man-in-the-middle attack and solve forward security. However, the DH key agreement protocol requires one-trip communication, whereas the zero-knowledge proof scheme requires two trips for identity authentication. Therefore, the DH key agreement protocol can be used to generate the session key during authentication. However, if the session key needs to be updated with the DH algorithm, the delay in the opportunistic network will be large.

Considering the characteristics of opportunistic networks, this paper presents a solution using threshold cryptography to encrypt the session key. The transmission process is divided into two parts. One part of the transmission for messages that is longer, and the other part of the transmission for session key, which is shorter.

We use the classical Lagrange interpolation polynomial threshold cryptography algorithm, proposed by Shamir [18], to divide the session key using (t, n) threshold scheme $(t \leq n)$, which divides it into n sub-session keys transmitted via the intermediate nodes to the destination node. If the number of sub-session keys transmitted successfully is greater than or equal to t sub-session keys, the destination node can restore the session key. Otherwise, the session key cannot be restored.

First, we need to select a finite field F_q, which satisfies the condition of $q \geq n$. Let t be the threshold, and encrypt the session key $SKey$. The source node sends $SKey's$ fragments to other intermediate nodes, and the intermediate nodes are represented by $p = \{p_1, p_2, \ldots \ldots, p_n\}$.

At the phase of key distribution, the source node randomly generates a $t - 1$ degree polynomial G in a finite field F_q, denoted as

$$g(x) = a_0 + a_1 x + a_2 x^2 + \ldots + a_{k-1} x^{t-1} \tag{1}$$

Then n sub-session keys $s_i = g(x_i)$, $i = 1, 2, \ldots \ldots, n$, are generated [18], which are transmitted to n encountered nodes.

Suppose that there are t nodes involved in the reconstruction, in which the master sub-session key is set as (i_r, s_{i_r}), $r = 1, 2 \ldots, t$. Then according to the Lagrange interpolation polynomial formula (2), we can calculate the $t - 1$ degree polynomial G [18].

$$\sum_{r=1}^{t} s_{i_r} \prod_{\substack{j=1 \\ j \neq r}}^{t} \frac{x - i_j}{s_{i_r} - s_{i_j}} \tag{2}$$

Then substitute $x = 0$ for the final calculation of the session key $SKey = g(0)$ [18]. It can be seen that only when at least t nodes collaborate, the forward security will be broken. The security of this scheme is high enough in some cases with low requirements.

4.3 Safety Analysis

Due to the puzzle of the elliptic curve encryption in zero-knowledge proof, an adversary cannot obtain r randomly generated by nodes. Then $S_A(\sum_{I=1}^{K} m_i * x_i)$ cannot be obtained, so the authentication protocol proposed in this paper is theoretically safe.

For key agreement scheme proposed in this paper, even if one party leaks fragments of the key, nodes in the network must have at least four fragments (for example, using the (4, 10) threshold) to restore a shared key, which greatly increases the difficulty for the malicious nodes to recover the session key. Moreover, since the shared key is generated by source node, the shared key can be transmitted at the same time with the message. Though the safety factor is smaller than using the DH algorithm, it is more suitable for the opportunistic network.

4.4 Performance Analysis

Figure 3 shows the interaction of the zero-knowledge proof authentication protocol.

Small Communication Overhead. Compared with other schemes using the certificate chain [26–28], authentication between nodes does not need to form a certificate chain. Even if the nodes are not in contact with each other, validation can be done via a certificate store or by actively sending authentication requests. Figure 3 shows that certificate verification requires two rounds of communication, with relatively low traffic.

This paper is based on ECC encryption authentication scheme, so the performance is relatively high.

High Reliability. Compared with authentication schemes based on identity cryptography, certificateless authentication and threshold cryptography, the proposed scheme in this paper are more suitable for the opportunistic network without an infrastructure, because all the schemes existing assume that there are trusted nodes in the network.

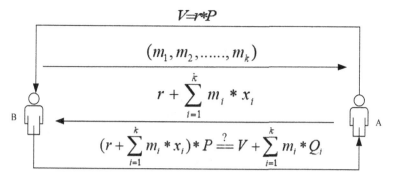

Fig. 3. Zero-knowledge Identity Authentication

Schemes based on threshold cryptography only solve the problem of private key hosting, but authentication requires the node to connect to a certain number of server nodes. The scheme proposed in this paper can be verified without trusted server nodes, so its reliability is higher than other schemes.

High Robustness. In this paper, the session key generated by one party is used to improve the success rate of communication, which is a completely self-organized authentication scheme.

For the session key encrypted with threshold cryptography, we consider that n nodes in the network carry session key fragments and the probability of reaching the destination node within the network lifetime (TTL) is p, then the probability of at least t nodes reaching the destination node within the TTL can be calculated according to binomial distribution

$$\sum_{i=t}^{n} p^i (1-p)^{n-i} \tag{3}$$

For DH key agreement algorithm, it is enough to have a single successful transmission, so the probability can be calculated as:

$$(1 - (1-p)^n)^3 \tag{4}$$

In the ideal case where each node has the same probability of reaching the destination node, considering that $t = 4$, $n = 10$, and the p is relatively large, the probabilities are both basically closed. But for the expected time, the scheme proposed in this paper is a one-way transmission, while the DH algorithm is a round-trip transmission. In the specific environment, the success rate of the scheme proposed here is higher with smaller transmission delay.

5 Evaluation

5.1 Privacy Protection Experiment Design and Result Analysis

Simulation. According to Sect. 3.3, the ratio of $m/(k*n)$ can directly influence the misjudgment probability. The greater $m/(k*n)$, the smaller the misjudgment probability. And the greater the misjudgment probability, the greater the privacy protection level will be. So we used $m/(k*n)$ to measure the privacy protection level. We conducted simulation experiments to observe the effects of different privacy protection levels on message delivery probability, overhead and average latency in the opportunistic network.

The simulation experiment was carried out with *ONE* (Opportunitistic Network Environment simulator). Assuming that the size of the network n is 120, and the number of hash functions k is 10. The values of the vector's size m in the Bloom filter are $[504; 567; 630; 693; 756; 819; 882; 945]$. So $m/(k*n) = [0.4, 0.45, 0.5, 0.55, 0.6, 0.65, 0.7, 0.75]$. Considering that according to Algorithm 2, when mapping the utility values of the node to the Bloom filter, we need randomly choose $P_{f\_bd}*k$ positions from the k positions that the corresponding friend node *ID* is mapped to, and the $P_{f\_bd}*k$ positions are set to 1. So the values of P_{f_bd} may be different for each experiment under the same experiment environment. Then the repetitive experiment results may be different under the same experiment environment. Therefore, in order to ensure the accuracy of the experiment results, we performed two groups of experiments under the same experiment environment, denoted as *BF1* and *BF2*, respectively. The results show the comparisons of our scheme and ProphetRouter routing protocol without privacy protection, denoted as *Origin*, in terms of message delivery probability, overhead, and average latency.

Result Analysis. Figure 4 shows that with the increase of the $m/(k*n)$, the message delivery probability decreases within an acceptable range, and the average transmission delay is significantly reduced, which may be associated with the decrease of message delivery probability. In addition, because the intermediate node needs to transmit ID_f^b and ID_p^b to the source node, the increase of overhead is relatively obvious. Though introducing the privacy protection scheme has decreased the message delivery probability, the privacy protection level of the network has been increased.

5.2 Key Agreement Experiment Design and Result Analysis

Simulation. The comparative experiment between DH algorithm and threshold cryptographic key agreement (TE) algorithm was also carried out with *ONE* using SprayAndWaitRouter routing protocol. We verify the performance of the TE algorithm according to three indicators: message delivery probability, overhead, and average latency in opportunistic networks. The number of hosts in the network is varied among $[120, 150, 180, 210, 240, 270, 300]$. We performed four experiments with DH (5), DH (10), TE (4, 5), and TE (4, 10) in order to observe the effects of DH algorithm and TE algorithm on message delivery probability, overhead and average latency in the

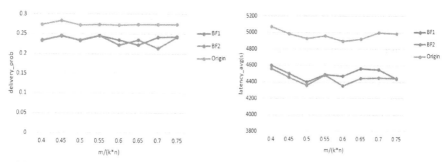

(a) Comparison of delivery probability.   (b) Comparison of average latency.

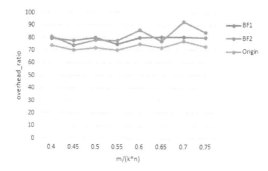

(c) Comparison of overhead.

Fig. 4. Performance comparison before and after adding the privacy protection routing scheme.

opportunistic network. For the simulation of the key agreement algorithm based on threshold cryptography (TE algorithm), TE (4, 5) indicates that at least 4 of 5 packets transmitted successfully can recover the key, and so does TE (4, 10). DH (5) represents that 1 of 5 packets transmitted successfully can restore the key, and so does DH (10). Considering that message *M1* need to be transmitted, firstly it is determined whether *M1* is a shared key or not. If so, *M1* is divided into 10 fragments according to TE algorithm, which is presented as *M1* = {*M1S0*, *M1S1*, *M1S2*, *M1S3*, *M1S4*, *M1S5*, *M1S6*, *M1S7*, *M1S8*, *M1S9*}. During transmission, if the encounter node is the destination node, *M1* will be directly transmitted to the destination node. Otherwise, it determines whether the message fragment has been sent to the encounter. If not, the fragment will be sent to the encounter.

Result Analysis. Figure 5(a) shows that as the number of nodes increases, the success rate of transmission shows the upward trend. And it can be seen that in the cases of TE (4, 5) and TE (4, 10), the TE algorithm is significantly better than the DH algorithm.

Figure 5(b) shows that with the increase of the number of nodes, for DH (5) and TE (4, 5), the transmission delay shows an overall increasing trend. Because if the number of nodes in the network increases with a small number of sprays, the probability of forwarding to the effective node is reduced, resulting in the increase of transmission delay. And if increasing the number of sprays, such as DH (10) and TE (4, 10), the transmission delay shows an overall decreasing trend. In addition, we can get that the average latency of TE algorithm is lower than the traditional DH scheme due to the smaller communication overhead.

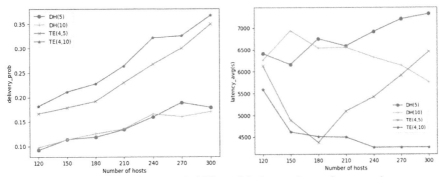

(a) Comparison of delivery probability. (b) Comparison of average latency.

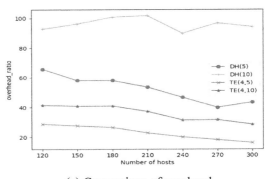

(c) Comparison of overhead.

Fig. 5. Performance comparison of the TE algorithm and the DH algorithm.

Figure 5(c) shows that as the number of nodes increases, the overhead of the system changes. It can be seen that the greater the number of the sprays, the bigger the system overhead. And because the DH scheme needs to response, the overhead of DH scheme is bigger than the DH scheme. In the case that the TE algorithm transmits 5 session key messages, the DH algorithm needs to transmits 10 session key messages for a round-trip. Therefore, the TE algorithm is obviously better than the DH algorithm.

According to the experiments, using privacy protection routing scheme improves the security of node privacy without significantly reducing the success rate of transmission. The average delay is not significantly changed, but the overhead of the system has increased. From the simulation experiment performed for the key agreement scheme, it can be seen that this scheme has obvious advantages in performance except for the loss of forward security.

6   Conclusion

The routing in opportunistic networks needs to compare the utility values of the source node and the intermediate nodes reaching to the destination node, which will reveal the privacy of the nodes. Therefore, this paper designs a lightweight privacy protection routing scheme based on the Bloom filter to obfuscate the node friends list and utility values introducing uncertainty to protect node privacy.

In addition, the lack of infrastructure and stable link in the opportunistic network leads to that there is no trusted third party to verify node's identity and increases the communication cost when performing key agreement using the DH algorithm. Therefore, we propose the identity authentication scheme based on zero-knowledge proof to verify certificates without a third party. What is more, we present a key agreement algorithm based on threshold cryptography, which only needs one-way communication to negotiate the session key. In general, the schemes proposed in this paper are more suitable for opportunistic network than other traditional schemes, and they can significantly improve the performance of the networks.

Acknowledgements. The work is supported by the Science and Technology Fundament Research Fund of Shenzhen under grant JCYJ20170307151807788, JCYJ20160318095218091.

References

1. Shikfa, A.: Security issues in opportunistic networks. In: International Workshop on Mobile Opportunistic Networking, pp. 215–216 (2010)
2. Ciobanu, R.I., et al.: Sprint-self: social-based routing and selfish node detection in opportunistic networks. Mob. Inf. Syst. **15**(6), 1–12 (2015)
3. Li, L., Qin, Y., Zhong, X., et al.: An incentive aware routing for selfish opportunistic networks: a game theoretic approach. In: International Conference on Wireless Communications & Signal Processing, pp. 1–5 (2016)
4. Nguyen, H.A., Giordano, S., Puiatti, A.: Probabilistic routing protocol for intermittently connected mobile ad hoc network (propicman). In: World of Wireless, Mobile and Multimedia Networks, pp. 1–6 (2007)
5. Daly, E.M., et al.: Social network analysis for information flow in disconnected delay-tolerant manets. IEEE Trans. Mob. Comput. **8**(5), 606–621 (2009)
6. Hui, P., Crowcroft, J., Yoneki, E.: Bubble rap: social-based forwarding in delay-tolerant networks. IEEE Trans. Mob. Comput. **10**, 1576–1589 (2008)
7. Juang, P., Oki, H., Yong, W., et al.: Energy-efficient computing for wildlife tracking: design tradeoffs and early experiences with zebranet. In: International Conference on Architectural Support for Programming Languages and Operating Systems, pp. 96–107 (2002)
8. Lindgren, A., et al.: Probabilistic routing in intermittently connected networks. ACM Sigmobile Mob. Comput. Commun. Rev. **7**(3), 19–20 (2004)
9. Boldrini, C., Conti, M., Jacopini, J., et al.: Hibop: a history based routing protocol for opportunistic networks. In: World of Wireless, Mobile and Multimedia Networks, pp. 1–12 (2007)
10. Pan, H., et al.: Bubble rap: social-based forwarding in delay-tolerant networks. In: IEEE Educational Activities Department, pp. 1576–1589 (2011)

11. Cadger, F., et al.: A survey of geographical routing in wireless ad-hoc networks. IEEE Commun. Surv. Tutorials **15**(2), 621–653 (2013)
12. Zhi, Z., Choong, Y.K.: Anonymizing geographic ad hoc routing for preserving location privacy. In: IEEE International Conference on Distributed Computing systems Workshops, pp. 646–651 (2005)
13. Zhou, J., et al.: Secure and privacy preserving protocol for cloud-based vehicular DTNs. IEEE Trans. Inf. Forensics Secur. **10**(6), 1299–1314 (2017)
14. Asghar, M.R., Gehani, A., Crispo, B., et al.: Pidgin: privacy-preserving interest and content sharing in opportunistic networks. In: ACM Symposium on Information, Computer and Communications Security, pp. 135–146 (2014)
15. Yao, L., et al.: Secure routing based on social similarity in opportunistic networks. IEEE Trans. Wirel. Commun. **15**(1), 594–605 (2016)
16. Boldrini, C., et al.: Exploiting users' social relations to forward data in opportunistic networks: the hibop solution. Pervasive Mob. Comput. **4**(5), 633–657 (2008)
17. Parris, I., Henderson, T.: Privacy-enhanced social-network routing. Comput. Commun. **35** (1), 62–74 (2012)
18. Shamir, A.: Identity-based cryptosystems and signature schemes. Lect. Notes Comput. Sci. **21**(2), 47–53 (1984)
19. Dan, B., Franklin, M.: Identity-based encryption from the weil pairing. SIAM J. Comput. **32** (3), 213–229 (2001)
20. Seth, A., Keshav, S.: Practical security for disconnected nodes. In: Secure Network Protocols (2005)
21. Kumar, K.P., Shailaja, G., et al.: Secure and efficient threshold key issuing protocol for ID-based cryptosystems. IACR Cryptology ePrint Archive 2006/245 (2006)
22. Al-Riyami, S.S., Paterson, K.G.: Certificateless public key cryptography. In: Laih, C.-S. (ed.) ASIACRYPT 2003. LNCS, vol. 2894, pp. 452–473. Springer, Heidelberg (2003). https://doi.org/10.1007/978-3-540-40061-5_29
23. Liu, W., et al.: Securing mobile ad hoc networks with certificateless public keys. IEEE Trans. Dependable Secur. Comput. **3**(4), 386–399 (2006)
24. Capkun, S., et al.: Self-organized public-key management for mobile ad hoc networks. IEEE Trans. Mob. Comput. **2**(1), 52–64 (2003)
25. Weniger, K., Zitterbart, M.: IPv6 autoconfiguration in large scale mobile ad-hoc networks. In: Proceedings of European Wireless (2002)
26. Yi, S., Kravets, R.: Composite key management for ad hoc networks. In: International Conference on Mobile and Ubiquitous Systems: Networking and Services, pp. 52–61 (2004)
27. Ngai, E.C.H., Lyu, M.R.: Trust and clustering-based authentication services in mobile ad hoc networks. In: International Conference on Distributed Computing Systems Workshops, pp. 582–587 (2004)
28. Chang, C.P., Lin, J.C., Lai, F.: Trust-group-based authentication services for mobile ad hoc networks. In: International Symposium on Wireless Pervasive Computing, pp. 16–18 (2006)

Author Index

Printed in the United States
By Bookmasters